Corporate Lives

A Journey into the Corporate World

Corporate Lives

A Journey into the Corporate World

George de Mare

with Joanne Summerfield

 **Van Nostrand Reinhold Company**

New York   Cincinnati   Atlanta   Dallas   San Francisco

Van Nostrand Reinhold Company Regional Offices:
New York Cincinnati Atlanta Dallas San Francisco

Van Nostrand Reinhold Company International Offices:
London Toronto Melbourne

Library of Congress Catalog Card Number: 76-945
ISBN: 0-442-22079-0

Manufactured in the United States of America

Published by Van Nostrand Reinhold Company
450 West 33rd Street, New York, N.Y. 10001

Published simultaneously in Canada by Van Nostrand Reinhold Ltd.

15 14 13 12 11 10 9 8 7 6 5 4 3 2 1

Library of Congress Cataloging in Publication Data

Main entry under title:

Corporate lives : a journey into the corporate world.

    1. Executives—United States—Correspondence,
reminiscences, etc. 2. Corporations—United States.
I. De Mare, George. II. Summerfield, Joanne.
HF5500.3.U54C67   658.4   76-945
ISBN 0-442-22079-0

My marks and scars I carry with me to be a
witness for me. . . .
                              Pilgrim's Progress

I listen to the voices and when I put down
what they say, it's right. Sometimes I don't
like what they say but I don't change it. . . .
                              William Faulkner

Preface

Time has speeded up.

A culture with its multitude of life styles, its ways of looking at the world passes or changes within a lifetime.

The America of the 20s and 30s is gone with only its medley of fugitive voices to hint at how it was. What these studies attempt to do is to capture the life styles of representative people of the America of the latter part of the twentieth century.

I have tried to capture and transcribe the voices themselves telling how it was, the voices within seven of the major areas of our culture: the worlds of the corporation, of education, of politics, of the professions, of science, of the arts and of the underworld. *Corporate Lives* is the first of these studies.

My own life style has been shaped in two worlds—as a novelist and as a corporation executive, and with the aid of a number of experts and authorities who live in each of these worlds I have tried to select and hold for posterity the "lives" these worlds have shaped.

Again, this is intended as raw material. I have tried to avoid any viewpoint. The "lives" transcribed here are for the use of historians and sociologists when we who have lived them have long passed into eternity.

GEORGE DE MARE

Acknowledgment

This work is a collaboration of many people. Although the concept, investigation, selection and final shaping of the material are mine, the quality of these "lives" belongs to the subjects themselves, and their names should ordinarily be on the book. Also acknowledged should be many friends, mentors, colleagues and others who led me to my subjects and assisted in many essential ways but who cannot be named because they might provide clues that would break the disguises, revealing the actual persons whose lives we have recorded. Thus the only name with mine on this work is that of my colleague, Joanne Summerfield, whose warmth, perception and gift of understanding made possible the depth and sensitivity of these interviews. The concept of this and the total study was inspired by the technique of taping used by the late Oscar Lewis in his great works *The Children of Sanchez* and *La Vida*, in which he taped the lives of members of families in the subculture of poverty.

Contents

Corporate Lives

A Journey into the Corporate World

PROLOGUE

The Voices You Hear in this Book are the Voices of Real Executives in Real Corporations . . .

What is it like to be a "corporation man" in the America of today? What kind of life does such a man live? What are his motivations, his hopes, his experience? What kind of man is he really? Does he fit his stereotypes, the popular image projected by social thinkers, novelists and the public imagination?

The voices you hear in this book are the voices of real executives in real corporations telling how it really is. Because of their frankness and straightforwardness and to protect them, their names and the names of their companies have been changed and their characteristics somewhat disguised. But what they had to say about their lives in the corporation was recorded on tape and, except for editing to eliminate repetition and achieve coherence, this is what they said and how they said it.

This book, then, is a journey into the world of corporate life, an odyssey that took three years and brought me with my associate, Joanne Summerfield, and our tape recorders and notebooks deep into a world I had known twenty years ago and had left under unusual circumstances, drummed out, it might be said, because of a novelistic interpretation that, while it achieved some popularity, was not palatable to the tastes of that time.

We live in a period when the corporation has reached its lowest ebb in the esteem of the public, where what has been called the most powerful single economic form in human history, the instrument through which most of the world's major work is accomplished, is under constant and severe attack. Many of those who manage corporations and who have committed their lives to them are considered to have shared some of the dehumanization and corruption that the public ascribes to the corporate life style.

Some of this animus we encountered in preparing this work. I spoke with editors who felt that while this work would be of interest, much of it would be

1

dry and stereotyped because corporate life is a wasteland. Others wanted no part of a project which they believed would simply glorify or puff the corporation even more than it had been glorified in the palmier days of business. There was one who felt that no one would really tell the truth about this kind of life.

These were not feelings I shared then nor do I share them now nor did I share them when my first novel destroyed my career as a minor executive. Yet corporate life is one of the major life styles of our culture and it seemed to me in any major attempt to explore American life styles, the world of the corporation was the place to begin.

In all except the last of these beliefs the editors expressed, however, I suspect there is some element of validity. A few of our corporate executives did have life styles that seem to fit stereotypes and that would bore those who do not like executives. A few might be said to have viewed the corporate life style perhaps unrealistically because of the pleasure they found in their work and some, of course, we found did consider the corporate world a wasteland. But I am convinced that in these tapings in this work the truth was told insofar as the subjects could tell it, that nothing was glossed over or held back. We learned things about our subjects' lives that they had never told anyone else before, even their wives or closest friends.

Many works have outlined the functions of the executive and a number of sociologists and novelists have commented on and analyzed the corporate world. The fashions of the last hundred years during the rise of the corporation have depicted corporate life in the press alternately as a stifling and unrewarding grind, a proving ground for ruthless and ambitious men, a materialistic, ritual-bound bureaucracy, the place for the American boy to go, and again today, a spiritual dead end for men who can find no better way to spend a life. What, then, is it really like?

Oddly enough, except for so-called "success stories," nobody has seriously thought to ask those who actually have spent their lives in it. However, several kinds of books touch on this world, some of them very perceptively. The first group consists of serious works on management, a relatively new art with old roots, works associated with such names as Henri Fayol of France, Frederick W. Taylor and Chester I. Barnard, whose *Functions of the Executive* is one of the classics in this area.

A second group of books consists of those on business and businessmen themselves, such as Marian Beard's *A History of Business*, Daniel J. Boorstin's *The Americans: The Democratic Experience* and works presenting case studies on business, such as *Corporations in Crisis* by the editors of *Fortune* and case studies such as those used at the Harvard Graduate School of Business.

A third group of works consists of those by sociologists, economists and economic philosophers and thinkers such as Peter Drucker, Robert L. Heilbroner, Adolph Berle and John Galbraith. A fourth group consists of the lives of well-known, successful or significant persons, past and present, in the business world, such as Matthew Josephson's *The Robber Barons*, Ernest Dale's *The Great Organizers*, Alfred Sloan's *My Years with General Motors* and similar works.

Finally, there are works of fiction, such as *The Rise of Silas Lapham*, and more modern novels, such as *Executive Suite*, *The Durable Fire*, *The Man Who Broke Things* and *The Empire*, which touch on life in the business world and attempt to catch its atmosphere and ambiance.

While many of these works are very perceptive and throw much light on corporate life, past and present, they have in total helped build up the darker myth and conventional picture of the corporate world. No single study, then, has collected what representative persons who have lived their lives in the corporate world have to say about it. It is this we have undertaken to do in these taped "lives" as an important part of a study of life styles in our culture today.

To set a framework for this study, then, I suppose we should begin by trying to describe what the corporation actually is as it exists today, apart from its legal definition and its emotional aura or "personality."

Legally, of course, the corporation is defined as "an association of individuals created by law or under authority of law into a body having a continuous existence irrespective of that of its members and with powers and liabilities distinct from those of its members." Such an instrument, it was found, seems to take on a life of its own and can be used to do the major work of the world. However, useful as the corporation has become as the modern world's major economic instrument, the emotional overtones remain ominous, as they have almost from the beginning. They can be glimpsed in the famous phrases of Sir Edward Coke in a famous case: "The corporation cannot commit treason nor can it be outlawed nor excommunicated, for it hath no soul." And later William Hazlitt commented: "Corporations feel neither shame, remorse, gratitude nor goodwill," but perhaps the best picture of the rise of the corporation and its background comes from Adolf A. Berle, Jr.'s noted work *The Corporation in Modern Society:*

"As a legal institution, the corporation has its roots in medieval history. It was used by Angevin, Tudor, and Stuart kings in England partly as a means of getting things done, partly as an extended arm of royal power. Speculation, dishonesty, and financial excesses caused the South Sea Bubble crash in 1720, and so discredited the corporation as an institution that for nearly one hundred years thereafter it was virtually outlawed in the English-speaking world. Grudgingly its use was resumed as the nineteenth century opened, both in Britain and in the nascent United States, though under severe limitations. It won its way to wide use in the mid-nineteenth century. As the century drew to its close, it had become a commercial instrument of formidable effectiveness, feared because of its power, hated because of the excesses with which that power was used, suspect because of the extent of its political manipulations within the political state, admired because of its capacity to get things done. From the turn of the twentieth century to the present, nevertheless, its position as a major method of business organization has been assured. Although it was abused, no substitute form of organization was found. The problem was to make it a restrained, mature, and socially useful instrument." ". . . feared because of its power, hated because of the excesses with which that power was used, suspect because of the extent of its political manipulations within the political state, admired because of its capacity to get things done . . ."—this description written almost 40 years ago still well sums up the general feeling about the corporation. But what is the corporation? What kind of an organization are we talking about when we hear these voices telling of their lives "in the corporate world?"

Let me first note that we are speaking here of the giant corporation, the Fortune 500 or Fortune 1,000 corporation, the corporation with hundreds of millions, with billions in assets, thousands and tens of thousands of employees and shareholders. We are speaking not of the thousands of little companies but of the great corporate giants with offices, plants and distributing centers throughout the country and in most cases throughout the world. In this work more than half of the corporations dealt with are multinationals and four of them dominate their industries and represent the major influence in their markets.

But even here those who have never been a corporate minion will have difficulty visualizing what is involved. They will have trouble knowing really what exactly a corporation is. They hear of assembly lines like those so brilliantly depicted in Charlie Chaplin's *Modern Times* (particularly as remembered from the immortal lunch-hour scene where the assembly line worker has his corn on the cob served him on a machine at mouth level on the assembly line and tries to keep up with the accelerating cob so that he seems to be having his teeth brushed by it). They hear of the faceless office workers in vast areas seated at a sea of desks like those in the insurance company scenes in the film *The Apartment*, everyone under the spell of the clock from nine to five. They equate the corporation with vast bureaucracies of automatons, mindlessly working under procedures spelled out for them in painstaking detail, as someone once remarked about the Navy, "a system devised by geniuses to be run by morons." And, of course, there is some truth in all of these exaggerations. But this does not get to the essence of the corporation.

Nor does the other side of the coin—a description of what the corporation does. To say that corporations are there to provide electricity, to run trains and fly planes, to provide telephone service, to supply copying machines, toothpaste or any number of other goods or services seems somehow to miss the point of the corporate world, as seen by those who live in it.

These people—supervisors, managers, executives—know all that. They also know that somewhere in the upper reaches of their world there is a board of directors with the power to set policies and the ultimate responsibility for the direction of the corporation in which they live and breathe and have their being. They know that this board has the power even to fire the president or chief executive, should they decide it necessary for the survival or well-being of the company. They know that high in the stratosphere, there is a chief executive officer, sometimes known as the chairman, sometimes as the president and often called the Old Man or Old Iron Pants or the Gray Eminence, or some other even less flattering name.

They know that there are a couple of hundred thousand shareholders out there, people who have bought the company's stock (and these executives may be among them also) and they know how unimportant these people are—a bunch of fairweather friends, here today, gone tomorrow, in for the ride and out when the going gets tough. But they know everybody has to pay lip service to these "owners" of the business. They know also about the structure of the company, which of the major corporate functions dominate, whether this is a production company, where engineers are king or a marketing company where salesmen are king or a financially dominated company where accountants and financial officers are king. They know how the company has been set up, whether by functions or by areas or by product lines or by markets. They know and appreciate what the company considers its main concern—its customers, whether they are other organizations buying big machines or raw materials or the government ordering supplies or people buying toothpaste or people buying subway tokens or people paying the gas and electric bill.

They know all these things about the corporation but more than that, deeper than that, they know what the corporation truly is.

For to these men, who have given their lives or at least their allegiance to the company, the corporation exists as a solid entity, a building where they work, faces they see every day, people they know across the country and across the world, who have metaphorically pledged their allegiance also, a network of power positions that they occupy or aspire to, a function that calls not so much for their skills and experience as for their care and concern, for the fact is the executive's job of planning, organizing, administering and reviewing is a matter of caring more than anything else. It reaches beyond the most artful skill and the most usable experience into the realm of anxiety and concern for the lives of others involved in the enterprise, for the success of their own assignments and for the prestige, the prosperity and the honor of the organization as a whole and its work in the world.

So we see cases—and some in this work—where men and women have done stupid and terrible things for their corporations, where executives have lied and cheated not for themselves but for what they conceived of as the welfare of their enterprise. We see cases where exceptionally able or gifted men have failed in the corporate world, not because they were not skilled or experienced enough, but because they didn't care enough. And we see cases of men who have perhaps given too much of their lives for what we as outsiders consider trivial or less than earth-shaking ends.

Can you, then, as an executive, sit in your office and visualize the plants out in Ohio and in Milan and in Stuttgart with their machinery whirring, workers on fabricating lines and assembly lines and in laboratories? Can you see the gathering of the raw materials for this production? Can you see salesmen fanning out from offices all over the land to take orders and make presentations? Can you see orders being processed in offices and moving in a sea of paperwork to computer centers and accounting divisions? Can you see warehouses and distributing centers filling with product to be delivered? Can you move to the headquarters office and see the plans for new business, for new product, for eliminating dying products, for financing, for costing, for marketing? Can you see the constant reviewing of what has happened? Are we meeting our targets? Are we winning? Are we losing? Can you see all this each day, each week, each month?

But for you, the rising executive, this is only one part of what you see, what you know and it is not your main concern. Your main concern is what you yourself do. Are you the service manager in charge of getting the big machines serviced on time and at the least cost? Are you the assistant vice president in charge of customer loans? Are you the plant manager who must see that production schedules are met? Are you the vice president of marketing with a new product to be tested in one of your territories? Whoever you are, it is your job and your people—those you depend on to get the assignment done—that you worry about.

And you know something else. You know that nothing works without you— without you and the thousand faceless people like you. You may say, as you often do, that it wouldn't make one iota of difference if you dropped dead tomorrow, that it would all go on, will all go on just as well without you—there're a thousand others like you to take your place—but the truth is you know you are there for the duration and it doesn't matter how great the objective, how brilliant the president, how powerful the board of directors, if you—not you alone but you and the others like you who care—don't do what has to be done, the company will no longer exist as this company at this moment. It will become just a useless collection of buildings and raw materials, half-finished products and unproductive bank accounts, and aimless people. It would no longer be the Company. It would be nothing. So you know and the others like you know that those who care are the Company.

These, then, are the people we went into the corporate world to tape. The questions may be asked: How have these subjects been selected and in what way can they be said to be representative?

We can, of course, make no claim that the method we have used in selecting the "lives" we have recorded is in any way statistically determined. There have been a number of polls of executives conducted by the American Management Association and others on questions and issues of the day, on how they feel about success ("the failure of success") or about their careers. But except in a very superficial way statistics seem to us to be meaningless in a study of this sort. We were looking for people who had pledged their allegiance, who could give us some of the ambiance, the quality of life of the corporate world.

The quality of life, of course, depends in large degree on the quality of the individual involved. There are men and women of thought, cultivation and brilliance in the corporate subculture and there are ruthless, stupid and dishonest denizens of this world also, just as would be found in the worlds of politics, academia, science or the arts. Nevertheless, the corporate world is one of the largest and most powerful in our society, does have a distinct ambiance, and as an environment is selective of certain characteristics. What these are may be glimpsed in these "lives," and what we think we found we shall try to show.

To achieve this, we have selected a set of corporate lives from each level, from the young executive through middle and top management to the chairman of the board. We selected a woman and a Black to indicate their experiences in this world. We also selected from among four situations: those who were considered successful, those who enjoyed their lives in this world, those who considered themselves failures, and those who found corporate life uncongenial to them. Finally, we arranged what we found in the form through which our journey seemed to take us in the corporate hierarchy, from those who are entering this world and taking uncertain steps into its ambiance to those who are getting there with their deepening pleasure and authority, one peaking at the middle management level, to those who, as they rose into higher management, begin to feel the increasing pressures and dangers, one slipping and plunging from the heights, finally to the one who reached the top and who tells us how he did it, the chairman of the board. . . .

What sort of questions, then, it may be asked, did we put to our subjects and what kind of dialog did we have with them under what circumstances? Were they hesitant or reluctant to undertake what in many ways was a profound and searching self-exploration? Finally, why did they agree to this plumbing of their life experiences?

First, as to the kinds of questions, we wanted basically not only opinions and feelings about this world but a collection of experiences, and so our questions covered the whole gamut of our subjects' lives. We asked five kinds of questions. A sampling follows of each category:

First, background:

Could you relate initially something about your background? What kind of childhood did you have? Happy? Unhappy? What did your parents do? What were your circumstances? Your relationship with your parents? Your brothers and sisters? Who was the main influence of your early life? What experiences do you remember best about growing up?

Then we asked something about education:

Now could you turn to your education and schooling? Where did you go to school? Can you remember how it was? What experiences did you have there that seemed significant to you? How about college? What subjects did you take? What friends did you have? What can you say about your university education and beyond which now seems to you significant?

Third, we moved into the early experiences with the job and work:

What were your early jobs and how did you get into the field you find yourself in? What do you remember about the world when you were first starting your career? Was it hard to get a job? Had you always wanted this kind of work? What does your job involve? Can you give me a typical day in your working life? I'll leave this recorder and tape and perhaps you'll record in detail a representative working day for you in the company. Give me some experiences on the job that show what it is like to do this kind of work for this company.

Fourth, we asked for some opinions, feelings and experiences about the quality of life the subject lived within the corporation:

What kind of life is the corporate life as you know it? What kind of company and how like or unlike most corporations it it? Have you found this life style congenial or uncongenial to you or some of each and in what ways? What would you say to your son if he asked you what kind of world this corporate world is? What experiences have you had—specific experiences—that illustrate what this kind of life is like? Have you found this kind of life stultifying or broadening to you? Or some of each and in what ways? How would you say the corporate world compares in terms of freedom, variety and interest with other life styles in academia, the government, political life, the arts and science? Give examples of your experiences to illustrate what is particularly good and bad about living the corporate life.

And finally:

How would you say you have done in your career? Do you feel you've succeeded generally? That you've failed? Or have succeeded or failed to some degree? Please explain and give examples. If you had it to do over again, would you go into the corporate world? Live the life you've lived? What changes would you have made?

These were the types of questions we asked. For reasons which had to do largely with the sort of subject we were seeking, with two exceptions, none of those we selected for publication had the slightest hesitancy, once they committed themselves, to probing their deepest feelings and the darkest corners of their lives. These were people who had pledged allegiance to a company. Every life has its moment of darkness and moment of truth and to understand any life style these must be probed. Our subjects, as the reader will see, probed and revealed their own with an honesty and forthrightness that make their self-examinations deeply significant.   A few lacked the insight to understand what was happening to them.   In the first taping we see a young man stumbling around who was not aware of what he was revealing about himself in all his relationships.   In the second taping, we follow a young woman fighting her way into the corporate jungle.

Let me turn now to the two exceptions to our general approach of taping and disguising with their permission and cooperation, representative individuals. They are our third and ninth lives.   The third "life" is a conglomerate.   For excellent reasons, our subjects here would not or could not consent, except in one case, to be taped as individuals.   Yet the life styles, the attitudes they represent, though rare, seem to me so true to the corporate world that I could not leave them out.   By using characteristics of three of these subjects, however, each is disguised.   The ninth "life" however, is our version of the character of one of our subjects, a complete reconstruction, based on the shattering experience which is the major reason for this reconstruction.   The attitudes, feelings and experiences are all genuine and, I believe, authentically represent the life styles of the man who feels his career a failure and the corporation a wasteland and the man who broke under pressure and temptation.

When Joanne Summerfield and I started on our odyssey, we had no idea how many cities we would have to travel to throughout the country, how great would be the variety of executives we would meet and how deeply our own lives would be affected by them.   Our odyssey spanned three years, taking us twice across the country taping executives in New York, Chicago, Cleveland, St. Louis, Seattle, Los Angeles, San Francisco, Tacoma, Washington and New Orleans.   We talked with our people in all kinds of places and at all kinds of times—in spacious houses, in an apartment, in skyscraper offices, in cities, suburbs and residential districts, mornings, afternoons and evenings, amid crowded terminals and in isolated places with the phone cut off, during breakfasts, at lunches and at dinners, drinking and not drinking, listening and listening with cups of coffee and wreathed in cigaret smoke.

And after each foray, laden with tapes and notes we would return and my associate would have our gifted friend, Natasha Audrain, transcribe the tapes and rush the transcriptions back to me.   So the pages of transcriptions piled up and between trips and at night I would struggle with the chunks of lives we had entered—the sound of voices on tapes, the memories of faces and moments with people we had come to know and to care about.   These self-revelations and examinations of all our subjects were as stirring, exciting and exhausting to the interviewer and the author as they were to the subjects themselves.   Several of those whom we were privileged to have as subjects told us this act of probing was one of the most important and fascinating experiences of their lives and that they had learned more about themselves and their own motivations, feelings and the quality of their existence than they had ever known before.

What, then, motivated these men and women to go into this experience?

To understand this, it is necessary to know the criteria for selection of these subjects. First of all, we did adhere closely to our main criterion: These men and women had to be purely corporation people—not entrepreneurs, small business men nor professional men within a corporation. Theirs was entirely the world of the big corporation, and while there is much more mobility in the executive life today, the mores, customs, traditions and rituals of the big corporation still dominate their lives.

But they were also a special calibre. These lives are not average or common; they are representational. We had to select subjects most of whom had the gift of self-examination, who were perceptive, thoughtful and interested in the world in which they have lived, and who were articulate and intelligent enough to convey its essence. Most of them were thus quite far above the average, and their contributions and insights are, therefore, more truthful, perceptive and valuable than we could otherwise have hoped for in such a study. Thus also they were predisposed to serious and revelatory self-examination, and, having satisfied themselves that the study was worthwhile, they committed themselves wholly and completely and went into this self-examination with no reservations and no restraints.

We feel deeply our respect and admiration, our love and our obligation to these subjects. We had the rare privilege of entering deeply into the minds and feelings and lives of superior persons and in doing so they have to a degree changed our own lives. Obviously the true authors of this study, then, are these persons who told their stories, who gave of their time and thought and knowledge, who allowed their experiences to be recorded, all with complete frankness and without censorship, so that the world of the corporation might be better understood.

As to the study itself, we must point out that our material is as given. It is, in a sense, raw material for the use of sociologists and others studying the life styles of our culture or for those interested in going into this world. We will have more to say on this later. Now please share with us our journey into this influential and somewhat mysterious area of our civilization. . . .

PART I

We start with a young man and a young woman who are slowly and uncertainly moving into the morass of the corporate world. We then move to a middle manager who has gotten deeper into the life and then falls by the wayside. . . .

I

"I Have Come to a Crisis in My Career and in My Life. . . ."

A young executive reaches a turning point

Bob Blake is a well-favored, crisp, cool man in his thirties, clean-cut, with a personality that makes an immediate impression. Yet, as will be seen, he is a man who stumbles through a crisis in his life scarcely aware of what is happening to him. He represents in a particularly chaotic form the shifting sands of corporate life at the beginning of a career. His egotism has partly blinded him to his effect on others. We first saw him in his office at one of the regional headquarters of the huge corporation in which he had begun his career—a man on the way up—on the way up, that is, until . . . but the story is not over yet.

My name is Bob Blake, Robert C. Blake, and I'm thirty-six years old, not bad looking, well paid and had been generally thought of as a comer. I work for a huge, progressive corporation similar in size and resources to IBM or Xerox, and I feel I play a valuable part in my company's business. I am, or was, a manager in charge of a district, merchandizing complex electronic equipment and I had come up far and fast. Let me go back to the beginning, then, and tell you how it all happened. . . .

First, I guess you could say I was a high school drop-out. I was born and brought up in a little town in Westchester, New York, where my family had lived for seven generations—kind of an unusual background. My father was a salesman for a small food company. He never made much money but we lived in a beautiful $85,000–$95,000 house, built by my grandfather before my mother was born, so there was no mortgage on it. We just inherited it—a beautiful piece of property. Looking at it, you'd think we had a lot of money but we just managed to make ends meet. My mother's side was the old family part. My grandfather was a judge. I have an older brother—seven years older, now married with two daughters.

One day when I was thirteen-and-a-half years old, I overheard my parents discussing the problem of putting my brother through Syracuse University and still being able to make ends meet and pay my allowance, which was then about two dollars a week. I've never taken money from my parents from that day on. That overheard conversation was a turning point in my life. In school, I'd never been pushed by my parents and never got very good grades. I was held back in second and sixth grades because of illness. In the seventh grade I changed to a Catholic school. Meanwhile, I was working, first in a clothing store in town, then in a junk yard fixing cars. I built cars, I caddied, I played golf, I was a waiter, a bartender, a maitre d'—all to get money. I enjoyed picking out and buying my own clothes. I never really relied on anybody and I guess that was because my parents never really took great interest in my schoolwork—you know I had college to come. The seven years difference between me and my brother I think made quite an impact on me. I never really got close to my parents or my brother, except now my brother, who's a teacher, and I are closer.

He used to keep harping on this education thing to me and I rebelled. Again, I've always known me—I've never had to go out and search for myself. I've always known what I wanted and that I'd never starve. I could always make it regardless of what I did. So, much against my parents' will and against the advice of a lot of my friends—we lived in a town where 98 percent of the children went to college—I dropped out of high school. I was 19 years old and in the eleventh grade and I dropped out to work.

First I worked in a men's clothing store and then I looked around and decided: "OK, the draft is gonna get me," which it did. Probably for the first time, I turned to somebody in my family, my brother, to ask what he'd recommend. He said: "If I were you, I'd go into the Air Force because you'll get a lot of education there." Well, that probably wasn't what I wanted to hear at the time but for some reason I did decide to join the Air Force and get my military commitment out of the way. I joined on December 2, 1957 and on that night, my life changed.

I went down to 39 Whitehall here in New York and was sworn in and somebody turned around and said: "OK, you group of 70 guys are going to take the train down to San Antonio to the Air Force base. I expected to fly for the first time in my life—I'd never been in an airplane before—and I was looking forward to flying in Texas. What happened behind the scenes, then, I don't know, but I was put in charge of 70 people on a two-and-a-half-day train ride down to San Antonio, and I was given all their military records. These were the DD #4 forms, showing record of enlistment and they had everybody's background on them. Well, late at night on the train in bed, I started looking through the records of these 70 guys I was with. This is my first time away from home, it's just before Christmas and I'm going down to Texas; I've never been away from home at Christmas. I realized that night that out of 70 people I was with, I was the only one who hadn't finished high school, and over 90 percent of these 70 people had one or more years of college. I saw the light. I said: "By God, you'd better get yourself an education."

I'd always had a knack for personnel work, so when I got down there I went through all the testing and that kind of thing. On about the fourth day I said: "All right, I want to go into personnel administration," and they said: "No way. You don't even have a high school degree. "I said: "I want to take the test." I took the test and I got into the school. The school happened to be in San Antonio, so I stayed there for six months, came out number one in my class, became part of the Strategic Air Command and went up to Forbes Air Force Base in Topeka, Kansas. I went to school at night at Topeka High School without anyone even knowing it and got my high school degree, my General Equivalency diploma. I got promoted all the way up to airman first class, which was as high as you could go without re-enlisting at that time, and got every award possible in the service.

Among these awards was one for the most innovative room on the base. I paneled my own room and made all my own furniture. I threw out all the government issue and it kind of started a tradition. The Air Force was lenient in that sense and they let people do what they wanted to in their own room after my case. At first they'd said: "You can't do this—this is government property." I said: "I'm bettering it, not worsening it," so that became a policy. I also wrote a number of Air Force policies out at the base. I got a lot of write-ups because of the incident, which relates back to something that's come out before, and that is that I have a big ego. No question about that, because I do.

Anyway I came out of the service and decided I had to go to college. I figured no accredited junior college is going to take me, so I looked around and found a little college in Vermont which at that time had 78 students living in farm houses. I went up there for a personal interview with the founder of the college, who is quite well known. He's the only man living who's founded four universities in the United States and Europe. At that time he was about sixty-five, I'd say, and I hit it off with him. I told him my background and he said the college there was designed for people like me and they welcomed veterans. I guess the ratio of students to instructors was about 3 to 1. The town nearby had a population of about 700 but there was no place to go except the local bar to meet everybody.

So I went to that college and found the change—getting back to the books— quite a challenge. I drove down from this little town in Vermont to the town where my family lived in Westchester to the men's store there to work every weekend. I drove down every Friday night for four years straight. They paid me enough to cover college together with my own borrowing from the government, the National Defense Loan, which supplemented that income. I found the college extremely good because of the closeness of student to professor. Some of the professors were outcasts from other universities, because they didn't like the structured life, so many of them were very, very qualified. They wanted to live in Vermont, where they could maybe write a book, if they wanted to, be on their own, live out in a shack or a log cabin.

It must be understood, of course, that this college was not then accredited; it was a junior college. Well, after my first year there it became a four-year college. I became involved in 18 or 20 activities throughout each year I was there. I initiated the student government, I initiated the Judiciary Board, I got involved in just an awful lot of activities within the college to help it grow. I wanted to become part of that college.

After my third year there, majoring in economics, I wanted to kind of round myself out and decided to see if I could get into Cornell University for a year and take industrial and labor relations. Everybody said there was no way, but the college president said: "I'll write you a letter, but remember we're not accredited and you may not have a chance even though your grades are very good." Well, I got accepted, but did terribly at Cornell. I couldn't keep up—I was in way over my head. I passed but with poor grades. However, I was accepted by a big famous corporation (not the one I'm with) out of the School of Industrial and Labor Relations to work in their employment area in New York as an exchange. I'd work there for four months and then go back to Cornell. This was quite an honor, since they only take one person out of the entire group. That was basically done on my first and only interview with them.

So I helped handle the relocation of the corporation headquarters from Manhattan to a suburb. I was doing the interviewing, testing and placing for all those people who refused to move out of New York and relocate. These people ranged from clerks all the way to programers and accountants. This was really my first experience in the business world per se. I guess I was chosen mostly because I've never met anybody I couldn't get along with, whom I couldn't sell myself to or come up to or down to their level. I just never had that problem.

At this time, one of the most rewarding things in my life happened. I came home one weekend and there was an envelope in which I found a diploma from the Catholic high school I'd gone to dated back to 1957, the year I should have graduated. It was signed by the principal and the priests who were there at the time. Someone had taken it upon himself or herself to find out that Cornell had accepted me and they felt I deserved a diploma. They had drafted it up and sent it back to Ohio where the principal was to get it signed so it was authentic. It just had a very short note which said, "We felt you deserved this." I was just completely dumbfounded. I actually broke down and cried, for that's the one thing I'd wanted and worked for so long and felt I'd never achieve.

So I went back to the little college in Vermont and got my degree with honors. The college was growing and was on its way to being accredited, but there were no scholarships up there. So on the day I left—this is kind of a funny story, I guess—I set up a scholarship in my name, the Robert C. Blake Scholarship in Economics. In order to get it you had to have a 3.5 average and participate in not less than 32 student activities over a two-year period. This was because I wanted them to find somebody like myself, willing to dig into the life of the school and really help it and the faculty and everybody else there. It's only been awarded three times, I think, in the last nine years. But it's still up there and in my name. Most of the people think I'm dead now. I was president of the alumni association for two years and I've been an alumni association officer for six years. I basically started the association, I guess. I'd been on the college's board of trustees also. I've always had a great many outside activities even now.

So I graduated and I'd had this experience with one big corporation. I could have gone back there and, with what I knew in that area and friends I'd made, I think I could have gone up. But I wanted something new, some new challenge, and I always preferred to take "the road less traveled," as Robert Frost wrote. Incidentally, Robert Frost used to walk around the college up in Vermont and I'd met him a number of times when I was there. Once I asked him under a bending birch, one of the trees on the campus, if he'd write a toast for my brother that I had to make at the reception. He did, but I subsequently lost it and I could shoot myself for this. I don't even remember the toast. He died two or three years after he wrote it . . . but to get back, I've always taken the road less traveled, not necessarily because I chose it; it ended up that way. I went through the school of hard knocks, things not going the way you'd like them to go, and I'd always recover and come back in a lot of cases. I didn't want to be helped by anybody, so I went back to the men's store after graduating from college and I said: "OK, I'm going to look around and find a new company where I can spread my wings, learn, not be structured, where I can meet people"—and this automatically meant selling.

I interviewed a number of companies. Nothing turned me on. A friend of mine came along who was working for this great big high technology corporation. I didn't know anything about it, but he said: "There's an opening in the financial branch. Why don't you come down and interview for it?" So I did. I walked into this man's office, sat down and we exchanged all the formalities of a normal interview for the first two minutes. Then he said: "What do you know about this company?" and I said I know a friend of mine who works here and he told me this is a good company. The man looked at me and said: "Take a copy of the annual report, go out and read it and come back when you know something about the company you're applying for." I do the same thing today. If a guy comes to me for a job and he doesn't know anything about the company then I send him right out the door. I realized I'd done a very stupid thing, and I thought, "Forget it, there's no way they're going to hire me now." But I read the annual report and I liked what I saw, so I went back in, and they hired me.

I started as a marketing assistant, the first level there leading to a sales representative. A marketing assistant works for a sales representative and I did this until I was assigned to the sales marketing school down south. I came out second in the class as far as ability and my presentations were concerned. Each man makes a presentation and sees himself on closed circuit TV. I came back to the New York area, did well for about six months and somebody, I guess, spotted me, saw something in me that he wanted and brought me over to the banking area, where I represented our products in banks. Then I was promoted again.

In these early jobs you moved through a prescribed course. There's little or no politicing. You just do the best you can and you move up. You come out of school—the company school—and you get a territory. Then you either sink or swim. I didn't sink. I had a bad area but I did well. I learned about my customers. I knew my products. I knew my own company. I knew how to get along with people. I knew what people and businesses in my accounts needed— and that was it.

I'd been interviewed together with others for this territory. The others had more experience and there were people on our team who have a lot more time in the company and a lot more knowledge and experience. One of them had been with the company thirty years and was obviously well off from handling his major accounts. In a year I had his job because he retired. That had been one of my goals. I wanted to be the one who handled these big customers. As I said, there were no politics involved that I know of. Nobody stood in my way or specially favored me. No one tried to keep me down. I'd heard there were politics in big organizations like this, and we'd seen some but not in our area. A big hot-shot manager breezes into New York and in 90 days he's gone. He'd either reached his level of incompetence or someone didn't like him. But it didn't happen in my area.

On the other hand, nobody favored me specially either. They're men who are marked out by management for key positions early in their careers, and they have it easy. They have a protector, someone watching over them to bring them to the position they're being groomed for. Unless they screw up badly, they've got it made and they don't have to struggle so hard. That didn't happen to me. I earned every position I got, and I alone decided where I was going.

At last I came to a point in the company where I realized I ought to get into another area—the service area. I wanted to become a top operating executive, but I wanted to be the best manager I could. I wanted to know everything about my job. In the corporation, the big areas for me were marketing and the second big area was service. The corporation was known for its sales in the high technology area and for the fact it serviced its equipment, because as with products like those put out by IBM or Xerox, servicing the machines and equipment is of major importance. Now in our corporation, this was so also, but in our corporation marketing has little appreciation of servicing. The manager from marketing says to his service people: "OK, you're in charge of seeing our equipment is serviced. You've got 80–100 people working under you and I don't want to hear any bitches from customers on our service. I don't want to hear from you. And keep down the cost." All that manager wants is profits. He wants to go out and sell because that's where the money comes from. Sales makes money; service spends it, production spends it. For every dollar of sales, 15¢ is spent on servicing. If we could cut that down to 10¢, we'd make a lot more profit.

So I took a transfer into servicing. I wanted to know their problems. I took this step sideways and I'd like to think management realized what I was doing but I doubt they did. Still I did a very good job here, which surprised some who didn't think a man coming in from sales could understand service problems. But it was here for the first time I ran into a man who held me down. What can you do? You can't do much. I'm not the kind of guy to try politicing. I never bad-mouthed this man. Still I never said anything good about him either. I just told the facts when it was necessary. When anyone asked me: "How's Roy," I'd just slough it off saying: "I guess he's doing all right." But this man was a pretty tough manager. He wasn't people-oriented. He managed by objectives without really considering people which was not my philosophy at all. You change your objectives to adjust to the proper utilization of people. However, this man only lasted here a year and then was promoted into another job. Another manager came in and we hit it off well.

You may wonder why I wasn't promoted to that job. First of all, I was probably not the most qualified person in the area. I'd only been in servicing for about a year. There were more experienced people. Secondly, I wasn't so sure I wanted to go up in that part of the company. My commitment to that servicing area was for 18 months and so I held to it, which I think was right. But I have to admit I was becoming bored with the job. The reason was it had no more challenges. I had such a devoted group of guys that had been with the company so long and knew their jobs so well I could disappear for a month and everything would operate as if I were there. They liked and respected me and I liked and respected them. I just had a real smooth-running group. So I didn't really feel needed. However, after 22 months, I was finally promoted with a 20-percent increase in salary.

It was an area of the company outside of its main business, away from its basic bread-and-butter products, so it had its dangers. I had to start to learn this area. My basic objective hadn't changed. I wanted to get into top management, but

I wanted also to know everything about the business before I did; and I will. I don't think I've reached my level yet and I intend to keep going till someone tells me I'm not qualified and convinces me I'm not. But I expect to go up. I don't think you can plan ahead very far—maybe two years. So I'm going straight on and, if someone stands in my way, I'm going around him. I've always kept up my outside activities. I've made good contacts in the company, among them the president. When I was invited by the Chamber of Commerce in connection with one of my outside activities to go to the Orient on a mission, this corporation sponsored me and the president of our company personally congratulated me. He knows what I did. The corporation is very progressive in community and social welfare activities, and our president personally takes an interest when someone does a good job in these areas. So I am not without a contact or completely unknown in the company, though I'm not trying to say I can go to the top any time. I have to say again they're not grooming me for anything. I have no godfather or sugar daddy that I know in the company, as do some. But if anyone were very unfair to me I believe I would go to the top, and I have reason to believe my immediate management knows it.

But, of course, if worst came to worst, I'm single and I can walk out and I won't starve. I have no wife and children dependent on me. Still, while this may be a plus if you had to quit, it's a liability in the corporation not to be married. For example, when the company interviews for a manager, based on a scale of 100, 25 points are valued on the plus side if you're married. Management feels that a person who is married or has been married is more stable; has his feet on the ground and knows where he's going. If he's single, it's sometimes felt he may not be manager material. Of course, there are single managers in the company, but I know that I was the only single man promoted to my position and I'm probably one of the few at this level in the company who's single.

I have to say also that it's a disadvantage in other ways not being married. I don't entertain in the company. I don't spend time with other families. If I were married, certainly I would have my boss and wife down. I would have people and their families that I would have established very close relationships with even outside the office. I'd have them in my home, let them know what Bob Blake is really all about. Yes, marriage is very important—and not just for business reasons either. I'd never get married just to get on in the company. There're other much deeper matters.

It's true a single man can devote himself to his work but his motivation isn't complete. He likes his work the way I do, but here I am, I have a good apartment and money and I can come and go when I want, but there's nobody to do it all for. I haven't the motivation. Supposing I have a wife and a house with a mortgage on it in the suburbs and three kids, wouldn't I have a lot more motivation to get on and to bring home the buck? There's another thing. I can't divorce myself from my work when I leave the office. I get up and I go into the office at 6:00 because I can get more done from 6:00 to 8:30 in the morning than I can between 9:00 and 5:00 because of the telephones, meetings and the everyday humdrum routine of the office environment. Of course, as a single man I can get up at 5:30 in the morning if I feel like it and go to the office. I may not leave the office till 7:00 o'clock at night or 9:00 and I can do that in my environment. But am I happy with myself coming home at night? No, I hate it. I come home at night and sometimes cry. I really do. I want to discuss a problem I'm having, and there's nobody to discuss it with. Of course, the job is hard on families. I try to see that my men get home on time. I want to arrange our office work so a man can get his work done in eight hours. There are times when you have to work on weekends, take your own initiative and do the work out of hours—there's one time on a big account one of our engineers worked 23 hours straight—but that's rare and I don't like to see it especially where a married man is doing this. But me—I live with my job 24 hours a day and I hate it. It's not what I want. I want to be able to come home tonight and put my arms around the girl I love—Cathy—and have kids and play with them.

Last night, for instance, I was provoked by something that happened on the job. I called Cathy up—she lives nearby—and said: "What are you doing?" I still don't see enough of her anyway as far as I'm concerned. Twice a week isn't enough. So I said: "Listen, why don't you invite me over and I'll bring a pizza and we can sit around and have it with the kids?" She has children by a first marriage. So I come over and we sit down and eat the pizza and I fixed the TV, which took about two hours, and we moved around furniture, since Cathy was redoing her apartment. So my mind wasn't on the job. All my problems left me. My hands weren't clammy and wet like they are now, thinking of what happened these last two weeks, how my life's suddenly fallen apart. But before I go into detail on what has happened to me, let me sum up on a few thoughts about my life and my career.

First of all, here are some feelings about the organization itself. It's hard to be noticed in a big company no matter what they say. I feel I'm doing all kinds of things and nobody notices it. When I had big exposure and my name in the papers a couple times because of my outside activities and there was an article on my trip, I thought there'd be some reaction to it in the company. But there wasn't. My people have trouble getting through me, I suppose, to be noticed by higher management and I have trouble getting through my managers to be evaluated by higher management. I suppose, it's nobody's fault. Nobody's trying to keep you down except in rare cases. It's just something to do with the needs of the corporation. If they need you for some specific thing, they notice you soon enough. If they don't, you're forgotten. At least that's the way it seems to me sometimes.

Secondly, in spite of what's just happened to me, I think somehow it'll come out all right. I'm going to tell it as I feel it now with all the bad and the turmoil.

You get to a point where you have to take it on the chin, you have to pick up the pieces of your life and go on. I've always made my own way. I've always been independent. I'm making more money than my father is right now and I think he and my folks are proud of me. If the worst happens here, though, in this crisis, I'll have to start all over again. But I still think somehow I'll make out. . . . So now we come to this terrible two weeks of my life. . . .

There had been rumors about what was going to happen for some time, but while I'd been anxious, I felt I could only go on doing the best I could. I'd loved this job, this territory, and we were going along very successfully. I had some six supervisory people and 80 field engineers reporting to me. It was the biggest and best assignment I'd ever had. The rumor was, though, that there was going to be a consolidation of territories, and that mine would be merged into an adjacent one. If this happened, obviously I'd have nowhere to go but down. On Tuesday I heard it was official. Needless to say, I spent the next two days in total mental anguish.

On Thursday I received the call. It was from my boss, Joe Bannion, the regional manager, and he said: "Bob, can you be on the plane to Washington, D. C. tomorrow?" I knew then the time had come.

I came home that evening a nervous wreck. My stomach was in pain, I had a headache and I had no desire to have any food. The only desire I had was to sit down with the one I loved, Cathy, and discuss the entire problem and try to find a solution or at least get this off my mind and have someone to talk to. Cathy had been aware of the problem or the forthcoming problem that might exist. However due to a problem in her mind and certain priorities that she had, I was placed obviously low on her list, which disturbed me quite a bit. The one thing that I wanted was to involve her in my problem.

I called Cathy when I got to the apartment, only to find she was not at home. This was unexpected and I left a message to have her call me. From approximately 8:00 o'clock that evening until 11:45 I was in a state of deep, deep depression. I realized that I just had to speak to Cathy, the one person that I truly loved, so rather than going into the bedroom and trying to get some rest, I took a sheet and slept out on the living room couch for fear of not hearing the phone ring. Finally, she called, and being quite upset as I was, she was very interested in my problem, however did not feel she could come over to the apartment, even though she lived nearby. I became quite emotional, cried and asked her to please come over, I just had to talk to her, I just had to see her. She said that would be impossible at that time for what reason she gave I don't know. But had her priorities been where I wished they would be, she would have been there in a matter of seconds.

Be that as it may, I got off the phone and still felt quite bad. I had a drink, took a Valium, sat down with a yellow pad and tried to outline just what might take place organizational-wise. At about 2:00 o'clock in the morning, I received a phone call from another man in an adjacent territory caught up in this political shake-up and who was obviously going to be demoted. However, he was in a different position from myself. We had a long talk and he was probably even more depressed than I was, which may or may not have been true, since I'd never felt so bad in my life. However, his crying on my shoulder straightened me out. At 3:30 in the morning, I had to try to come up with something to save my job. I sat down, put my head together and came up with a plan to break up my territory. From a business aspect, it was a good idea. I would lose some manpower but retain essentially the same job at the same salary and it would provide a place for the other man who'd been merged out of a job. I finished the proposal on paper, established people, organizational format and dollar installed base at approximately 6:00 o'clock, at which time I showered and got dressed and wrote a card to Cathy, stating that I very much wished to see her as soon as I got home from Washington to let her know how things went.

I got out to Newark Airport and took the shuttle to Washington, got in the car and started driving down to the regional headquarters on the outskirts. My mind was completely clear and I could see what I had to do. However, I felt very shallow and empty inside. I had always done things for other people and I especially wanted to do this for Cathy. However, I knew that she was not aware of this or if she was she didn't want to be.

I arrived at my boss, Joe Bannion's office, at approximately 10:15. I will not get into details of our conversation. However, Joe explained what the circumstances were, that he didn't have much choice and that I would probably have to take a step down unless I was willing to relocate. I said I would though I didn't particularly wish to move. At that point he asked me if I had any alternatives, and I told him of my plan.

He enthusiastically endorsed the plan, and the other displaced manager who came in later, having been called in like me, also enthusiastically endorsed it. He as much as I wished to save the New York area. The solution saved both our positions and solidified the new territory into a much more workable set of segments in terms of number of people and span of control of all managers concerned.

So Joe said he would see if the company would buy this plan on his trip to California on the following Monday. However, he felt 90 percent sure that this could and would happen. Needless to say, when I arrived home on Friday night I was quite pleased at the way everything had turned out and had high hopes that they would work out the way we had proposed.

I came home expecting and hoping to find Cathy at home. Again when I called she was out on another date, which upset me a great deal because I'd spent all the time planning, working and everything else that ran through my mind only for her. I know this sounds stupid to a large degree, but there's no doubt in my mind that it's the truth. I've always had to have someone to work for and do things for, and having been in love only four times this meant a great deal to me. Four years ago my third love, my fiancée, was killed in an auto accident. Unfortunately, the affair, love affair, so to speak, was, is definitely one-sided and priorities are not where they should be. Living with this, the weekend was not good. Saturday, Cathy and I did have dinner and spent a most enjoyable evening, one that should have been spent many many weeks before. However, I guess she did not wish it that way.

As I mentioned before, Joe said he would call as soon as he found out exactly what the plan was going to be. Monday and Tuesday were quite depressing in one sense since I didn't hear anything. Apprehension obviously grew and rumors began to spread around the territory as to what was going to happen.

Late Tuesday I received the long-awaited call. Joe told me that the plan had been approved to break the territory up in any manner we wished and that he wanted to have a meeting with all the managers who worked for me and the other displaced regional head so that we could formally announce the split. This meeting was called and to be held in my office on Friday, which I thought was absolutely terrific. I was ecstatic about it because everything had stayed in its proper perspective. My job and everything looked absolutely terrific. Joe arrived in our territory on Friday, as he stated he would, and everyone arrived for the meeting at 1:00 o'clock.

What transpired at that meeting was quite unusual. Joe went in and spoke with the line managers first, leaving the other displaced regional head and me out. He then came out of the meeting after an hour and spoke with the other displaced head for about 45 minutes alone. He then called me in. He said he had problems that he had not foreseen and had made a decision not to divide the territiory according to my plan. He would have to go back to regional headquarters and give it some more thought.

So needless to say, everything was back exactly as it was the week before. No decision was made. Everything was again up in the air. My input obviously was given considerable thought but for one reason or another, Joe changed his mind and was not willing to explain why. Thanksgiving and the weekend were spent with a great deal of tension.

Monday was a relatively uneventful day at the office. The senior members from California, the operational headquarters of the division, as well as the Washington regional group were due to fly in later that evening. About 4:30 that afternoon, Joe Bannion flew in from Washington and came into the office. He had a couple of offers that he spoke to me about with which I was not at all impressed. One would have been staying in New York and taking a demotion, which I refused. The other would have been a staff coordinator in Washington, D.C. for the territory, which may or may not have been a great opportunity but I did not wish to pursue it to any large extent, based on the fact that, as he told me at the time, it was a created position. At about 6:00 we went out and had some drinks and then went down to the Inn where I had arranged for a seminar for customers to take place on Tuesday morning. That was one of the primary reasons why the head of our whole operation, Ray Halpern, was flying in from California. Ray Halpern is the Man, the head of the division producing and marketing this product on a national scale.

Joe and I had some more discussions but basically to no avail since he was trying to talk me into various other positions that were not important, not decision-making types of functions in my opinion. About 9:00 o'clock that evening, Ray Halpern arrived and we sat down and discussed products and customers and things of that nature in a group of eight or nine people. I had not had the opportunity up till then to speak with Ray Halpern relative to my situation, and he got me off to the side over a drink and said: "Look, we want to have a little discussion tonight"—meaning a discussion with my previous manager and the other people who were involved in making this decision—leaving me out of it. These were the people he wanted to talk to that evening. So about 12:00 o'clock that night they went into a huddle in their room, and I decided to spend the night at the Inn, since I was in no condition to drive from the Inn to my apartment in New York.

Needless to say, I did not get much rest that evening and did not partake of the seminar which I had arranged that morning. Ray was in to give his presentation, introduced himself as the head of that operation both to the customers and to the Washington people who were there and I simply tried to sleep as late as I could. I didn't feel very good about the situation, since it was my territory and I was not there to welcome the customers I knew. However, I was there at the hotel, which made things a little sticky.

However, at approximately 12:00 o'clock when the meeting broke up for lunch, we got together and again the parties involved went to the hotel room and had another huddle. I was told that Ray would speak to me at approximately 2:30. Well, you can imagine how I felt—down, depressed, nervous—so I went up to the bar at noon after having a substantial breakfast, not having eaten in three days, and had a couple of drinks. I didn't want to overdo it. I wanted to have more but I was afraid to. So about 2:30—well actually it was later than that, it was about 4:00 after the seminar ended—they came upstairs in a group, and we were all sitting around kind of shooting the breeze. Then Ray came over and sat down with us and he asked me if I would come over to the far table at the end and huddle. So I ordered another drink and Ray had his drink and we walked over to the table and sat down.

The first words that I recall out of his mouth were would I be willing to relocate, and I obviously said yes I would if it were an opportunity for me. Then he continued with an explanation of the job he had in mind, which was basically as a product manager for a product I was aware of, and of which there were a few around the country. This new product is being tied in and is similar to a presently existing product in the market place, and my job before the last one had been as a field service manager devoted to the servicing of this allied product. Therefore, my knowledge of the product was more than anyone else's in the field other than those people who would be in production. So he asked me if I would accept the challenge of coming out to Los Angeles and being the coordinator of this transition program. I said yes, I would. I felt that was right up my alley and was quite pleased with the offer.

I had been out there approximately two months earlier and had heard about this position that was going to become available. However, I had no idea that it could come my way. So it was decided at that time that I would accept the job, that I would relocate to California—that was on a Tuesday—and that I should fly out to California the following Monday to find a place to live. Since there would be no one in the home office in L.A.—they would be at a users' meeting in Hawaii—and I would just spend three or four days with some friends out there. He suggested further that I return on Thursday to spend the weekend back here and then come out that following Monday to speak with him on his return from Hawaii.

So I went out to California on Monday, spoke with some friends of mine, found a lovely apartment right on the water and basically did very little of anything. I found the apartment the second day and Wednesday I pretty much had to myself. On Thursday I flew home. My primary reason for coming back, of course, was to spend as much time as I could with Cathy. Again that didn't develop the way I had wished it to. We did go out on Friday night. Saturday night she had a previous engagement that had obviously been made between Thursday and Friday, since we had a date for Friday *and* Saturday. She changed that when I got home, which I thought was quite inconsiderate.

However, Monday I flew back out to California and got a little bit more involved in my new job. In my own personal opinion the twelve or fifteen people I met who run this product area are totally inadequate, inept, inactive and basically have reached their Peter Principle, their level of incompetence. Of the fifteen people, there are only three who are decision-makers, who can say yes, no, do this and do that. The others not in this group are people like myself who were either district or regional managers and have since been given very responsible positions in the home office on the staff level. I personally would not be surprised to find this entire division being sold in the next year, the way they've reorganized and packaged the division into a very nice salable commodity for another organization. That would obviously have no effect on me as I am part of the mother company and not an employee only of this division. So I have no worries about its being sold. That would probably be an advantage to our mother corporation.

I do welcome this opportunity to go to California. I think the change in environment, the change in mental outlook, the opportunity to work in a staff position, to effectively write and to implement plans out in the field, to see these plans either work or not work, and basically to put myself on the firing line with a great deal of exposure will be basically beneficial to me and to my career. One of the best ways to get ahead in a company is to be exposed, to let people know who you are and what you are. My ultimate goal at the present time is to do this project in southern California as best I can. I would assume that the job will last approximately two years and at that time I would go back out to the field again—in what capacity I do not know.

I do have a number of questions in my mind about this new opportunity, though. I'm used to working with effective, decision-making type individuals. I've made up my mind I'm not going to change my attitude. I'm going to do what has to be done and I'm not going to take any shit from anybody. I'm going to do it, and, if they don't like it, then I'm going to find myself in trouble. It's not worth being somebody you're not. I know my capacity. I know what my abilities are, at least to a limited extent, and, if worst comes to worst, I feel I'd probably be very valuable to another company. At this moment I just basically feel uncomfortable. I'm looking forward to going out to California and getting into it, but the things that I've seen out there and the type of people I'll be working with do not impress me so far. I don't know how I'll be in a staff job.

Finally I have to face up to the situation with myself and Cathy. It seems now that she will not go with me. It seems now that this part of my life has come to an end. I would like to hold out some hope for myself in this situation but as of this moment it seems that it's not to be, and somehow I must make a new life for myself. This, I guess, is the final blow.

These last two weeks of agony have done something to me. Things had been going along so well and suddenly this happens. Maybe it's made me not so sure of myself or of anything any more. I feel I am not quite so sure of others to the same extent as I used to be. What the future will bring I don't know. But I still feel, and I have to feel this, that somehow, despite everything, I'll land on my feet. . . .

*   *   *   *

Obviously, Bob Blake is the odd man out. The others can be taken more seriously. They will be more aware, more sensitive, more intelligently committed. But what happened to Bob is a good illustration of the uncertainties and terrors that can attend the beginning of a career. When we last heard from him, he was successfully meeting the challenges of the new position; his fears of the staff job had vanished and he had resumed his upward climb. He was trying hard to make a new life for himself. He still dreams of Cathy, still misses her, still hopes somehow she will relent and make her life with him. He still wants to get married, have children, have someone to work for, but he is making new friends and seeking new emotional interests. And he is still being tested through his struggles in the organization.

We turn now to a far more challenging beginning—that of Jane Killian, as she runs away from home to St. Louis and moves slowly, uncertainly but, with her ambition, inexorably through the corporate thicket to the threshhold of an executive position in a large bank. . . .

2

"On the Day I Became an Assistant Vice President, They Gave Me a Corsage. . . ."

A woman executive penetrates higher management and learns a few things about making it in a man's world

When a friend first introduced me to this officer of one of the largest banks, an executive with 60 people reporting to her, it was something of a shock. Jane Killian is slim and attractive. She is 28 and looks like a girl of 23. She is quiet and composed with a pleasant manner but, if one looks closely, one sees a slightly aloof, amused smile.

I'm afraid I don't look like an executive. My name is Jane Killian and I'm twenty-eight years old with long blonde hair and, they tell me, a disturbing figure. But I did not sleep with anyone to get where I am. Quite the contrary, I tried to keep my personal relationships separate from my business relationships. Also, I don't pretend I can speak for women, although my experiences in the business world, I would say, are very representative of the experiences women who want to get anywhere would have. You really want me to begin at the beginning? All right, I'll try to be completely honest with you.

I was born on a farm in upstate New York, the oldest of six children. I never say I was born on a farm—I'm not sure why, but I'm sensitive about it and it seems to give the wrong connotation. My parents were not uneducated. My mother had the chance to go to Vassar, though she didn't take it. Besides, who ever heard of a bank executive born on a farm. I always say I was born in a small town in upstate New York.

It's very difficult to describe the kind of childhood I had. Oftentimes I would like to think it was happy because I had many happy experiences. I was very close to my brother—he's two years younger than me—but when I try to remember exactly what was happy about it, I realize that overall I would have to say that it was unhappy.

My relationship with my parents was strange. I remember my father as being very authoritarian. We were never allowed to show emotion in our family. My parents never touched hands or kissed or showed emotion toward each other or us. As a matter of fact, this would be considered some sort of weakness—unmanly—which was strange considering I am a woman. But it was something you did not do.

Even though there were six of us, it was as if we were two families. There were three older and three younger, so that my sister, four years younger than I, was in a sense the youngest child and the favorite. She received a lot of attention and my brother and I resented her. As children, my brother and I used to constantly receive beatings, because we were supposedly beating up on her.

One thing I always remember as a child was that I was very independent-minded, which was very frustrating to my parents because they didn't know how to force me into doing what they wanted me to do. We were isolated. Our nearest neighbor was two miles away. I never got to play with anyone else except my brothers and sisters. At that time, of course, there were only three of us. We did have then someone who took care of us, a sort of maid-type person. I never remembered much about her except one instance when I wouldn't do something she wanted me to do—I think it was go to bed—and she tried to frighten me by telling me God was going to strike me with lightening if I didn't go to bed in the next five minutes, which scared the hell out of me.

I think one of the reasons why I became so independent-minded and so aggressive is that my father wanted a boy first, and unfortunately for him I turned out to be a girl. So, until my brother was old enough, he used to treat me as though I were a son—take me fishing with him, and so on. I used to do everything with him. Even when my brother was born, it was my brother and I as though we were one. We used to do all kinds of "manly things," much to my mother's distress.

I think I was about seven years old, when I first decided I wanted to run away from home. One of the reasons was that my father demanded perfection. If the school bus arrived at the door before we were standing there waiting for it, that night when we came home we got a beating. After one of these incidents, I decided the solution to the whole problem was to run away from home. I tried to convince my brother to come with me. We would go to my grandmother's. But my brother, being the logical one, said we'd never get away with it; they'd track us down. Wherever we were, they'd find us and it would be worse, much worse—they'd beat us even worse if they found us. So that time he convinced me not to run away.

But I finally did. It was when I was in high school. My parents couldn't understand why I ran away from home. It was on a Sunday they finally located me that first time and I had run away from home on Friday. You see, I was very active in sports because that was the way to get out of the house. I'd go to basketball games, I used to twirl the baton, I played the oboe, and I always had to go to concerts and things like that. So that was one of the ways I got out of the house. But this particular time, they decided they didn't trust me and they were sending my father with me to bring me home. It happened that after this certain event I was supposed to go for a coke with my friends. So I decided there's no way I'm going to tolerate this. My father said to me: "I expect you here at the car when the game is over." Well, I would have loved to have had a movie camera to shoot the expression on his face when he got back to the car and I wasn't there. I'd left. I'd run away. I only told one girlfriend. She had just moved twenty miles away. The whole school knew she had moved but didn't know where. We had this whole thing planned. It was all so beautiful! So my boyfriend drove me to her house. My mother started calling everywhere and my father called the state police—they sent out a three- or five-state alarm or whatever. Finally, my little sister squealed on me and said I'd been sitting in the school bus with a certain boyfriend, and it was this boy. They called him up and they threatened him. The police threatened him three times. They told him they knew he knew where I was, and if he did not tell them they were going to put him in jail. This poor, naive guy was only seventeen. So they scared him half to death. The third time they called him, he told them where I was. He was the only one that knew. So my parents came and got me. I went home and up into my room and my mother and father were, of course, very upset. I knew if my father had found me on Friday night, he would have killed me.

But since this was Sunday, they'd already started feeling guilty about it. Well, instead of telling me: "You are going to go to church," they said: "Jane, would you like to go to church?" So I gave them a very dry, "No, I'm not going to church." Then after church: "Do you want to come down to dinner?" "No, I don't want to come down to dinner." So before they'd bothered me. They used to bust into my room and read my mail. I had no privacy. Anyway, today they knocked on my door: "Jane, may we come in?" So I thought: "Oh, this is a joke." So I decided I'd play it up too. They asked me why I ran away from home, and I said: "Because I'm unhappy." "But why are you unhappy?" I said: "Because of the way you are." Since I wasn't about to talk too much, they started offering reasons for why I ran away from home. "I know you wanted to go out with Chuck and we wouldn't let you." I thought: "This is it, this is it. If I say yes, then they'll let me go out with him and I'll be able to get away from the house." So I said yes, but it was a complete lie. Then afterwards I got to go out. Then I could always go out with this guy. It was so marvelous because I played them up. Played their own game.

Sometimes, looking back, it's sad to have to take advantage of people. I've done this game-playing in business too. I have this theory that if people can accept truth, there's no need to lie, but unfortunately there're a whole lot of people that can't accept truth. When you find that out, you tell them what they want to hear, and it works. Still, it's affected me, too. It's made me in part what I am today. . . .

But finally I did run away again and lived with a girlfriend and her family that summer until I went to college in September. I guess that was how in a sense I finally left home for good. It was strange to show up at college, my boyfriend having taken me and everybody else's parents having brought them. It was a strange, strange feeling.

Even when I arrived at college, though, I continued to be very independent-minded. I never joined a sorority. I didn't make a lot of friends. I had a few close friends but I wasn't the cheerleader or queen of the St. Patrick's Day Ball or anything like that. I did, however, become a member of the women's student government. I believe I was more a leader than a social joiner. I remember one incident on the women's student government—which is ridiculous when you think we had separate student governments, one for women and one for men. The men's organization, of course, was the predominant influence on the university. One of the things we wanted to change was the curfew hour, which I think was ten or eleven o'clock weekdays, and one o'clock weekends. We tried the proper route, going through channels, petitioning the dean of women and the president to change these rulings so that we could have the same curfew as men—for whom there was none. Naturally the response was no, without any explanation, which I seem to remember as part of my childhood. My parents always said no without any real explanation. Just because they were the authorities, you had to abide by their rulings. Interestingly enough, the following year, the women's student government decided not to abide by this ruling and sponsored sit-down demonstrations, camping overnight on the president's lawn. That very same year the rules were changed and there were no more curfews for women, which I think says something about society—that unfortunately we have to be forced into change. Change is not readily accepted. You have to convince people to change either through force or economic means.

The subjects I took in college I now consider most beneficial to me were philosophy, math and Russian—Russian mainly because it separated me from the masses. Only about six students in the whole university took Russian. I enjoyed math because it's very logical and philosophy expands your mind, your way of thinking. Actually, although I hated English and history, which were at that time combined, and my English professor acted as if all freshmen were going to be English majors, I learned something very valuable in the course, particularly how to write a letter in a clear and concise manner, using as few words as possible. That's helped me the most in that I probably write better business letters than anyone else in my department or that I've encountered in business.

The other significant thing about college was that I suddenly realized I was confined to a liberal arts course. The university didn't have the business curriculum I wanted and it didn't have a music major which at that time was one of my considerations. So the only thing left for me to do was to latch onto someone—to marry. So I "fell in love," left college and eventually moved to St. Louis to be with this boy. At that time we were engaged. I lived in St. Louis for two years, until I realized that the reason I had wanted to marry this boy was to escape college, escape having to go home and escape having to work at a mundane job with no outside interests.

So now we begin the story of my fabulous career. I lived in St. Louis for two years and the first job I had was an inventory control clerk, adding and subtracting on silly little cards all day long. Despite the fact I had some college education, there was nothing for me in St. Louis. The fact you were a girl meant you were going to get a girl's job—that's what I had, a girl's job. During the year I was there, they had several openings in the accounting department and I asked to be transferred there. They reacted as if that were absurd, as if I were some kind of monster. The only thing they seemed to believe I could do was add and subtract. I did it well, and did it fast and efficiently, so there was no reason to transfer me. It's the old rule—if you're too good at your job, you're stuck there. No one wants to promote you because they're going to be losing a valuable employee at a very dull job. So I decided to leave.

At that time I was a coward and afraid to tell them why I wanted to leave. So I had my roommate call up and tell them I was called out to New York immediately because my father was ill. I found another job with an insurance company two blocks away, and during this whole time I was petrified since I was sure I was going to run into someone from my old job. I worked at the insurance company, which was a bit more liberal in that they had a woman in charge of personnel who allowed some women to come into the company above the entry level positions. So I went into the accounting department, I believe, as an accounting clerk mailing refund checks to customers who had overpaid or who were canceling their policies. I did this so well and so fast that I took on another accounting clerk's job when she left and did both jobs—at the same salary. Eventually I decided that the only way to get ahead was to learn everyone's job. So I would finish early in the day, about three o'clock, and then offer to help anyone else with something they had to do. Most of the people were quite pleased I was willing to help them, not realizing my goal was to learn everyone's job and make myself so valuable they would have to give me an increase and a promotion.

I started corresponding with customers, analyzed accounts which had problems, some of which were computer errors. I worked with some of the programers and helped them figure out what was wrong with their programs—from the output standpoint. I explained in clear and concise terms exactly what was happening, such as the program doubling the amount of the refund check or of the policy itself. At that time they were converting to a new computerized system. So I eventually learned everyone's job and as they would go on vacation, I would fill in for them. After I realized I knew everyone's job, I went to my boss, the company's treasurer, and explained I wanted an increase. I believe this whole process took about six months. He said: "Well, certainly. You're making $295 a month now. We'll put you in for a $5 a month increase and that'll be $300." I explained no, what I actually had in mind was more like $30 a month increase. He looked at me as if I had gone mad. He referred me to the head of personnel, who told me, very patronizingly, of the salary she had started at five years ago. She said I was very young and simply could not understand the way business worked. Actually what I wanted was to become supervisor of the accounting department, but after my discussions with the personnel head and the treasurer, I realized that anything more than a $5 increase was going to be unconventional and unheard of, and that I was doomed if I stayed there. So I left.

I went to another insurance company, but I only stayed a week. I remember I walked in and I got the $30 increase a month that I'd asked for at the previous company. I sat down and about two-and-a-half hours after I had been there, I realized the system they had was in desperate need of improvement and I made the recommendations to my superior, an older woman. She told me this is the way things had been done around there for many years and who did I think I was—a young kid coming in and telling her how to run her business. I sat there for a couple of days, did it the way I realized was more efficient in half the time it took everybody else to do their job. She then started screaming at me. I went to the personnel department, to the man who had hired me, and explained to him I had a better method of doing the job. He explained to me that since she was my supervisor, no matter whether I had a better method of doing it or not, I had to follow her orders. I immediately walked out, deciding that St. Louis and my whole life up to that point was one disaster and I was going to give it a try in the big city.

Now we come to chapter two. I'd always wanted to live in New York and I felt it couldn't possibly be any worse. Hopefully there in the big time people would be more open-minded and I would be given an opportunity to prove myself and to use my ability. I arrived in New York and stayed for a month with my roommate from college who had moved there with her husband. During the first two weeks, I started looking for a job. In St. Louis I had been snapped up at the very first interview. In New York it took me two weeks and I couldn't believe it. I started feeling very insecure, started wondering what was wrong with me, but then realized it was just a more complicated world.

The first job I landed in New York was with an insurance company. When the job offers finally came, there were three of them at once, the result of my first three interviews. During that period of job hunting, I didn't know what I wanted. All I knew was that I wanted a job where I could find advancement. In some interviews, they tried to persuade me that being a receptionist or a typist was a job where you could get advancement. None of this was very convincing. I finally ended up with a semirelated accounting job in cost analysis and budgeting. It seems to me I started at $95 a week doing basic accounting work and someone else doing the actual cost analysis. I started asking questions and being very inquisitive and I realized what they were doing was not complicated and not something I couldn't do.

I spoke to my boss about it and he had a couple of openings, so he moved a person up and I took over this man's job and became the cost analyst. As my boss recognized my potential he started bringing me along, getting me involved in budgeting, allowing me to branch out and start writing reports and initiate some innovations. My boss was one of the most politically oriented people I've met and I disliked him intensely, but I have to admit I learned a lot from him. I learned more from him in the two years I was there than I have in all of my career thus far.

In any case, from the inception of my career (if you could call it that) with that insurance company in New York, I had received two promotions. I think I was finally making $130 at the end of two years. Then this man was hired into the department at the entry level position I had come in at and at that time he was making $2,000 more a year than I was at my present level of the measly $130 per week. So I went into my boss' office and I said I'd just discovered that "there seems to be a discrepancy in salaries." It so happened that the man had the same background—two years of college, he was the same age, he had almost exactly the same liberal arts background, the same work background—an exact duplicate of mine.

I told my boss that I knew this man was making $2,000 more than I was and I was supposedly two levels above this man—Why? His answer was: "Well, you have to understand this man is married and has a child to support." I said: "But don't you realize that's discrimination?" He said: "Oh really, Jane, I mean— that's ridiculous. You just can't possibly think that, now really!"

Well, you have to understand this man. It wasn't only his blatant discrimination. I'm afraid this is still not uncommon, but, as I said, he was a politician. He was constantly down in the board room explaining this marvelous new budget he had and what fantastic improvements. . . He knew nothing about what he was talking about. Every time they would ask him a direct question, he'd get on the phone and he'd go: "Jane, could you come down and explain this to me?" I thought: "A real asshole."

What irritated me about this man, though, was his talking about the peons who worked for him. Unfortunately that's the way management thinks a lot of times —my people, the workers, the peons—almost like slaves. Now a couple of years later, sometimes I find I too use these phrases, this "my people" idea, and it's very upsetting to me—being infected with this kind of thing from the hierarchy.

But to get back to the situation I found myself in with my measley $130 a week and this entry level man, two levels below me, making $2,000 a year more than I was; I was so infuriated after my interview with my boss that I went to a lawyer. I wanted to sue. There had been a number of other things the man had said that were very discriminatory, blatantly so. I explained my case. The lawyer agreed I had what he considered a very solid case, except that I should be aware of the ramifications of my winning such a suit. He explained to me that his daughter had been in the same situation. He represented his daughter and she had won. What would happen, though, he explained, was that there would be a sort of underground blacklist that would be circulated among companies, that I would be labeled a trouble-maker and that I'd *never* get another job. Now, true, the company couldn't fire me, but they could make my life so miserable I wouldn't want to stay. So I had all these things to consider and I began to realize the best solution would be to leave the company.

Oh, incidentally, at that time, the company was going to move to California, and they asked me to join them. They asked a very select group of employees to go to California with them and I was one of those asked, which I thought was very funny. The thing that ran through my mind was: "Why shouldn't they? Why not ask me? It's cheap labor." In any case, I began looking around for another job.

Now we move to chapter three. I went to an agency, and they tried to place me, and convince me I'd be a good programer. I'd been in jobs up to now that I really hadn't wanted, jobs that were dull and didn't present opportunities for advancement. All I knew now was that I wanted to get into the business world, into a large corporation and that I wanted to advance. I was very fortunate in that there was a big bank that was starting a new department. I went for an interview. I think I must have been the first person the man who saw me had interviewed, because he was so nervous. I interviewed him more than he interviewed me. I felt very sorry for him. He was so uncomfortable about interviewing me and I seemed to have so much more poise than he had that it was embarrassing. In any case he hired me.

And one of the first projects I got into as part of this new department was a systems-type job in an important area. Their set-up was so archaic in this area that I was lucky, because no matter what I did, it had to be an improvement. The man who was in charge of the whole department, however, said to my boss: "I don't want any dizzy dame coming into my department," and my boss went through the whole explanation of how I was such a serious-minded, responsible young woman. There would be no problems with me. When I met the department head, I was so frightened that perhaps for the first time I put forth a more businesslike attitude than anyone else. I was petrified he would think I was a dizzy dame. Naturally, he came from the old school and to him a woman was just cute but dumb. He took a very patronizing view toward me and treated me as if I were an idiot.

So I wore my hair up and back in a bun. I wore these cute little navy blue dresses with short sleeves and straight lines—always A-line dresses—never anything flamboyant, never any wild jewelry. I was always very plain—almost no jewelry, almost no scarves, nothing to look fashionable.

Then one day he started to realize that I was intelligent, that I did know what I was doing, that I wasn't just the cute, quiet little thing he wanted, and that was almost the end for me. He started throwing everything at me all at once. He really poured it on. I was so frustrated that I used to lie awake at night trying to figure out exactly what was happening in that department. What was he talking about? He used to throw around buzzwords, which he knew I wouldn't understand, and never attempted to explain them to me. But I persevered and finally got to the bottom of it. I came up with some very solid recommendations for improving the system, all of which he disregarded and said he would never have time to read.

You have to understand these organizations. At this level, all they want is not to have the boat rocked. When you think how I had betrayed this man by not being just cute and dumb, and then compounded this crime by not buckling under the onslaught of his unexplained assignments, you can see that what I had done was unforgivable and that he would never be able to bring himself to take any of my recommendations, especially if they were any good.

Fortunately for me, however, the president of our company decided that this was a potentially profitable area which could be marketed by other areas of the bank and that it should be made into a more substantial division. They, therefore, brought in new management, and one of the vice presidents who came in decided that I would be a very valuable member of his team and he asked me to join his new group. He had found my recommendations made sense.

I thought about it and decided that this would be my opportunity. I was going to make demands, and one of the demands was that I become an officer. Not an assistant manager, which was the lowest level of management at the officer stage, but an assistant secretary, which is the title they give the next level of officers. All the women who became officers, of which there were two in our department, had come in as assistant managers, while the men began as assistant secretaries or above. I wanted to be on the same level as the men. So I explained to this vice president that I would not accept the promotion to an assistant manager and that I would come in only at the level of assistant secretary. He gulped a bit and said he would see what he could do.

Well, I don't know what transpired above, but the terms were accepted. I was promised my officership in March and finally got it in May and became an assistant secretary. My boss, I think, recognized that I was probably the most valuable member of his management team, and yet he was very concerned about the egos of all of the other men; and this was sometimes very frustrating. For example, he did not want to put out a new organization chart, which would show me in the position of authority in that department, with some 15 or 20 people reporting to me, a few of them middle-aged men. Another gambit he had was to muddy the lines of authority. He would tell someone who was now to report to me that he could come to him for awhile. To another he would suggest remaining in his old relationship reporting directly to someone else. In one case, a woman who supervised a section reporting to me seemed to resent it when I asked her to do anything. Finally, she came out with it, saying: "I don't see why I have to take all this from you, a young girl, when I'm supposed to be working for so-and-so." I looked at her, and then I said: "Come with me," and we went into my boss's office and I said: "Who does Mrs. Green report to?" He gave me a tired, world-weary look and said: "You, of course—why do you ask?" We went out, and the poor woman said: "Nobody ever told me I was working for you. You never get told anything around here." I sympathized with her and spent some time trying to establish a friendly relationship with her so we could work together in a pleasant atmosphere. Another time, one of the men reporting to me, a middle-aged man, came in the office and sat down and said to me frankly: "I have to tell you this. I don't like working for a woman." I said to him: "I appreciate your frankness, but I've worked for a lot of men and I've managed to survive it. So let's see if we can get this job done together. I'm not going to get in your hair and I don't want you to get in mine." This man eventually became a friend and a good associate.

So now we come to the last chapter up to the present. It was promotion time again, and I knew I had at last broken through the barrier. I received the call from the senior vice president, walked into his office, and he immediately started making jokes. He began by pulling a long face and saying very seriously, "Jane, the board of directors with only one dissenting vote, has elected you an assistant vice president." I said: "You mean someone objected?" and he laughed. It was a joke, because I believe the vote has to be unanimous to reach this level. The second thing I realized was that this was the "women's month," the month when they elect women or promote women to officership. Yes, they really do have a women's month. You will read the official bulletin they put out and you will see that 60 percent of the newly elected officers that month are women. Then you'll see that the next five months they're all or almost all men.

I had said to my boss that I hoped if they ever promoted me again they would do it in an ordinary month, not the women's month. Now we come to the third thing, something they thought was very cute. They were going to give all the women who received promotions to officership (there were six of us, but I was the only one elevated to assistant vice president) a corsage. They weren't going to give the men boutonnieres but they were going to give us corsages!

So now the senior vice president says to me: "And as a reward for being promoted, we are giving you this corsage in lieu of a raise." He found this very humorous. So I decided to go along with the humor and I said: "Here, Mr. Keyes, you keep the corsage; I'll take the money." The poor man didn't know what to do. Here he was making these tremendous jokes and I was breaking protocol and making a joke back, but my joke wasn't very funny; it seemed to have bad overtones. So then it was very uncomfortable, because I didn't know whether I should sit down. He didn't say: "Sit down," and I was standing and half-sitting, and I decided the hell with it, I'm just going to sit down. So I sat down, and I figured that when he was finished with whatever he had to say he'd tell me to leave.

He told me how much money I'd be getting with this new promotion and everything it meant, and he tried to be friendly by saying: "All right, Jane, how long have you been with the bank?" He said that he had had all kinds of good reports about the outstanding work I'd done. I said to him: "Mr. Keyes, I've been with the bank for four years." He said: "Oh, that's remarkable for a girl—why, I think that must be a first!" I started to laugh, but I could see he was very serious and that he was about to be very upset, so I sort of muffled myself. But it was too funny that this man was sitting here telling me, wow, this is tremendous for a girl, when what he was probably thinking was: "Oh my God, I just did it, and I'm responsible for this!"

It just so happened on that day that a friend of my boss's was in the office while I was in there, before the senior vice president called me down. I was rummaging around in my boss's closet looking for some papers and this guy, Jim, walks in and he goes: "I must say, Harry, you have the prettiest girls around here!" I turned around and said: "Girl, girls, where do you see girls!" I said: "We can't hire girls. Women work here, not girls. It's against the law to hire children." So he laughed and Harry goes: "O-o-oh, here comes the Women's Lib speech again." It was like a joke. So the call comes upstairs that the senior vice president wants to see me downstairs. So I go running downstairs and he gives me the corsage and everything and I come upstairs and I set the corsage on the table and then I just burst out laughing. They were both still there, and I said: "I must tell you what happened. Mr. Keyes said to me that that was very, very good for a girl," and Jim said: "I hope you gave him the Women's Lib speech." And I said: "Oh, right."

I sat there and I thought about it, and I let the corsage sit there for about fifteen minutes and then I thought: "You know, I'll wear that damn corsage, because if I don't, there will be a whole lot of people that will be insulted." The other women were wearing their corsages, and it would have created so much resentment that I just put the damn thing on. And that's how I became an assistant vice president.

Now I want to say something about this career so far. I love this job, that is, I love the work. I come in at nine, and I very often don't have lunch or if I have lunch it's usually at my desk. Then I work sometimes until seven or eight. I come home or go out to dinner and have a glass of wine, relax, and then very often around eleven o'clock work for a couple of hours. Then I go to sleep. Most of the work that I do in the office from five to seven or at home involves the real hard-core type of management work, planning and trying to resolve potential problems before they arrive.

Of course, a lot of management work is human relations, dealing with people, helping them get through functional problems, helping them put out brush fires. Some of it, more and more of it, involves contacts, relationships with other executives and customers or potential customers on a social level. And as a young single woman, there are things you must watch. You don't walk into a room full of businessmen with their wives, for instance, and the women are there as wives—you don't walk in as a sexy dame and start flirting with people. You walk in with a very serious attitude, and you can look sexy if you want to, but you have to have a very serious attitude and you talk business all night long. Occasionally, if someone's wife disappears for awhile, you may make a comment that you like someone's tie or something they get a personal charge out of, an ego boost. But it doesn't affect your business image. It's really very important as a woman to keep things on a business basis, especially in such a staid type of business world. This, of course, doesn't stop anyone from looking at you and saying: "I wonder who she slept with to get where she is now? He must be pretty high up!" I have about given up on trying to stop the speculation as to whose girlfriend I might be.

So let me sum up briefly. In this type of corporate world, I've found three kinds of people—both men and women. The first kind is the old timer, the people, mostly men, in authority. They may be very able but they like things the way they were and they don't appreciate women trying to move into executive positions. They like women cute but dumb, and while they'll pay lip service to letting women rise, they'll consciously or unconsciously try to keep them in what they consider their place. A lot of them call their wives "the boss" and they're very cute about it. But that's different because a woman's place is in the home, not out here in the business jungle. That's no place for a nice girl. Like my boss that I told you about; when he found I was able and intelligent he started to throw everything at me to break me down.

There was another man who used to do something even worse. He'd lie to me —or tell me half-truths—or he would be devious and not tell me the whole truth about what was happening. So I would take it down and be very interested and I would be very sincere and pretend that I believed every word he was saying. Then I would go around very subtly and find out what was really going on. One of the advantages I had was that I was young and most everybody else who was at entry level positions or below were also young and they could relate to me. So they would tell me what was really happening. I would lie awake at night and I'd figure it out and all of a sudden I'd jump out of bed and write it down; and I knew this man had lied to me.

So the next day, I'd go around, after having worked it out and written it up, and I'd say: "Excuse me, Mr. Coleman, but I seem to find a discrepancy. Do you remember . . ." and I'd repeat everything to him that he had said to me. He'd say: "Yes," and I'd say: "Well, this is what I found out is really happening. . . ." He'd say to me: "You know, you're a smart cookie." He just couldn't say anything else. He was so embarrassed that I'd caught him in a lie, that he would say: "I have to go to the bathroom," or something just to excuse himself and disappear. He'd have to recover from it, you know. But, of course, they're not all like that. I just got a particularly bad one.

Then the second kind of people in this corporate world are the young old-fashioned executives, almost all of them men also. These executives may be young or they may be really middle-aged, but they've reached their limits and they don't want anyone to rock the boat. Maybe they were the "silent generation" or from the McCarthy era. They don't want to make waves, and they resent a woman who has brains. They feel threatened by her, unless, of course, she's a secretary or in some other lesser woman's type of job. On my way up, I had a boss like that too. I'm not one to go screaming discrimination in general. I don't do that. I really try to analyze the situation and if I really think I'm being discriminated against or one of those reporting to me is being discriminated against because she's a female, I used to go in to this man and give him my reasons. He would always say to me: "Jane, you're much too sensitive." That's the key word with a woman. Now would this man have said to another man: "You're much too sensitive." No, of course not. That's a woman's trait—being too sensitive.

Finally, the third kind of corporate executive coming up are the young people, people who are of college age or just out of college or about my age in their late twenties. This type of man really accepts women. They would accept me for what I am—they'll accept my ability. If I'm good, they'll be the first to say I'm good. If I've done something wrong, they'll be the first to tell me that too. So in relation to the young executives of my age, it's more like a game of chess—he moves, I move—but we know that we're both intelligent and we're making moves, but it's fair. I'm not being discriminated against because I'm female, and they don't feel threatened by my accomplishments.

Now as for the corporate world as I've seen it, it's quite complex. For instance, in my career, I've stumbled on what I believe must be a major fraud. I was looking through a contract which had been made by our company with a supplier, and as I was analyzing this contract, I began to see that it was a very, very bad contract from one crucial standpoint. That contract inexplicably tied us into this supplier in such a way that, because of the circumstances of the equipment being highly technical and requiring complex programing, we would virtually never be able to get out of the contract. We could never afford to put in brand new processing or to redo the whole thing. Every three years we were bound to pay this supplier a huge fee to continue, and it would be impossible for us ever to get out of it.

I got to wondering how this could happen, and then it dawned on me. Of course, somebody upstairs or somewhere in the company had been paid off. That could be the only explanation. No one in his right mind would have passed or approved such a contract unless some sort of pay-off were involved, because this was such a blatantly bad contract. I sat down and started to mark up the copy of the contract, and I started to think about the circumstances, and then I could see to some extent what had happened and who might have been involved. It was a very hot potato. It was way above me.

So I went to my boss and I laid the contract in front of him and I told him about it. He said: "How could this have happened?" and I didn't say anything. We sat and looked at each other, and we both knew what had happened. I said: "Maybe our outside auditors ought to look at this contract," and he nodded. I left it with him and I haven't heard anything about it so far. But you do hear a lot of stories about dishonesty from time to time. I heard of one that involved a bank vice president. They caught him in some flagrant fraud. Now banks don't like to publicize these things, so they just let him go. They did it in such a mealymouthed way that all he had to do was walk across the street to another bank, where he's now vice president. You hear these things from time to time, but I have to say most people I've known in the corporate world are honest. Most are straight-shooters where it comes to being ethical. At least that's my opinion.

All right, now I said I'd be honest with you, so I have one last thing to tell you before we end; something I've left out that I've never talked about. I guess I left it out because maybe it's the key to what I am and who I am, a key to the fundamental thing that's motivated my life. I've told you about trying to make it in this sort of man's world, where you often deal with men stupider than yourself or often run into these situations where, no matter what you do, they're going to try to keep you in your place as a woman. Well, I'm ambitious and I'm very independent-minded and I have to be free. I have to be treated equally, and finally I'll not be put down by anybody. So I'll tell you about it. It was when I was sixteen. I tried to commit suicide. . . .

It was this way. I was a senior in high school at the time I was telling you about when I tried to run away. Everything seemed like it was falling apart. I couldn't cope with anything. My parents were demanding perfection, and no matter what I did, it never seemed to be right. I could never be perfect. They never gave me praise for anything. So I did this very stupid thing. I couldn't see my way out. I had tried running away from home and that hadn't worked (You remember that three- to five-state alarm?) and they found me. So I tried to commit suicide. I did it this way. I went up to my mother's room and rummaged around and I found this bottle of pills. They turned out to be Excedrin, and I think I took about twenty of them or something like that, which was all there was in that bottle.

Well, what happened was I woke up the next morning with the worst hangover you can imagine, and I kept thinking well why am I here? I'm not supposed to be alive, and the next upsetting thing was what to do with this horrible hangover. So I hadn't told anybody what I was doing, of course, because I was serious, but miraculously I guess I lived through it without any medical help at all.

At that time I was somewhat religious because I sort of believed there was a god. You know, in high school I really believed in God because my parents were very religious and they forced us to go to church. And as you might have guessed, by now I was rebellious about that too. I didn't want to go to church and they would drag me there. And then when I started wearing make-up and I tried to sneak out of the house, my father would grab me and drag me to the sink and wash my face. Everything was just piling up on me, so I tried to commit suicide. Oh, I always used to escape to my room. I didn't want to have anything to do with my parents. We lived in a very large house, fortunately, and I had what was the master bedroom, so it was a very large bedroom—much larger than this room here in my apartment. So I always escaped there, and that was home to me. And I read a lot and I did things I wanted to do. In my room—my home. Oh, I was talking about the suicide. . . .

Suddenly we had this terrible blow-out. I came home from school and I said I was going to this boyfriend's house. His mother would be coming home from work fifteen minutes later. And I said I was going to listen to some records, and my mother says: "No, you're not going to his house alone." "But, Mother," I said, "his mother's coming home in fifteen minutes! Well," I said, "I'm going anyway," and I walked out of the house and I went there. Well, my mother got hold of my father and together they came and dragged me out of his house, and you know it was terribly embarrassing to me as a child; it was humiliating. So I said: "I hate you; I hate you both," and "I wish you'd just leave me alone; please just let me go away—I don't want to live here anymore." At that point, I told them: "If you don't let me go away, I'll commit suicide." And my father said to me: "You'll never commit suicide—you love yourself too much." And I said: "Oh ye-a-ah—guess what, I already tried!" Well, as you remember, my mother didn't have any drugs or anything but she did have this Excedrin. So they said to me that I couldn't possibly have tried to commit suicide, and I said: "Yes I did, go check your Excedrin, Ma." So they immediately both ran upstairs to the bedroom and found that the bottle was empty. And my mother went, "Oh, my God!"

Well, the next day they approached me very subtly and said: "All right, Jane, we talked to this doctor and this doctor recommended a doctor that you might see." And I was very pleased. I knew this was going to be the answer. The psychiatrist was a woman. She said to me: "Jane, there's nothing wrong with you— you're just independent-minded." She said my parents were much too restrictive. We went three sessions, and she said: "I'll try to explain to your parents that they have to give you freedom." Well, the first two times I went alone. The next time she pulled in my parents; she told them what she had told me. That was the last time I went to a psychiatrist. My mother and father were not ready for that. They couldn't accept the blame for any of it. But I always remember this woman—she influenced me very much. She taught me there was nothing wrong with me, that I just needed freedom. I can't be put down, I have to be able to go my way. Today I'm still like that. I have to be free and equal. I'm ambitious. I have to go up. This is true in all the parts of my life.

You ask me whether I ever want to marry. Yes, I definitely do want to get married. But I will not marry a man just for the sake of marriage. As I said, I've considered it at one time and I realized why I was about to get married and that it was an escape, even though we were compatible. But I think you must marry the right man and get married for the right reasons. One is that you are compatible, that you have the same interests, that you are going to grow together. It's very important to me to be on an equal level with a man. A man can never be greater than me nor less than me in the sense that I don't want to dominate a man, even though I very often do, nor do I want a man to dominate me. So it's very difficult.

It's not only difficult in my emotional life. Today I'm an assistant vice president in a big bank. I'm already running into trouble with those above me. I don't know my place. But I'll keep struggling. I'll keep pushing up until I get to the level that will fulfill me—perhaps as president of a smaller bank. Right now, though, I'm useful here, and I'll stay if they give me any kind of break. If they give me any kind of break, I'll go up even though I'm a woman. I'll go up and reach the level of my capacity. Maybe I'll even find a man I can admire and love, who won't feel threatened by my career or my success. I don't know. I hope so. . . .

*   *   *   *

Despite a rough start, Jane Killian will make it. Her ambition is strong enough; her looks compelling enough, and her competence deep enough to overcome the obstacles.

Now we come to one of those who cannot make it, who committed the first fatal mistake: He should never have gone into the corporate life in the first place. The corporate world as viewed by those from the outside seems often not an exciting, challenging or varied world, but a world most truly represented by the experiences of men like Howard Carver, a closed world, a world of conformity and fear, a world that can and most often does break good men. . . .

So we turn to the corporation as seen by those who consider it a dangerous place, a ratrace, a place of constriction, politics and ruthlessness—a wasteland. . . .

3

"Mine Has Been a Career in a Wasteland. . . ."

A middle manager feels that his career has been a failure

Howard Carver sums up and represents most of the hatreds and frustrations that we found in this study. Of the men we spoke to and interviewed, who felt the corporate world was a wasteland, not one would consent to allow his frustrations to be taped and presented just as he expressed them. No one wished to permit his voice to be heard alone, even in disguised form, so Howard Carver is a conglomerate of several individuals, each of whom in one way or another found his life in the corporation desperate and unrewarding. These men felt trapped. They were there largely because they considered that they had invested too much of their lives in their careers to throw them up and try to start all over again. They also felt trapped by a scale of life which could only be maintained on a corporate salary, and generally they felt it was too late to make a change. Oddly enough, this kind of executive was extremely rare and difficult to find, since people who hate a life style rarely stay in it. This, then, is Howard Carver, a man in his fifties, in a fairly good, comfortable position, rather bitter, and with a sort of love-hate relationship with the company.

I'm tired. I have to admit it. You get tired of the intense stupidity around here. It's been a long time. I look around. Oh there've been some good things—I won't say there haven't been some bright guys among the general clunks—but the fact is I should have gotten out long ago. Now it's too late—there're the mortgage payments and alimony and support and I guess I have to say it's comfortable here and where else can I get the income.

I'll bet you get a lot of horseshit in this study of yours, a lot of the rewards-of-achievement stuff and wanting to contribute and the opportunity-to-serve stuff. Well I'm going to tell it the way it is for most of us—well, for a lot of us—who don't go for all the crap dished out. Have you ever read our recruiting brochures or listened to the speeches by our eminent president? "We are meeting the challenges . . ." or brilliant insights like "The future lies before us . . ."

My God ... and here we are in middle management, a bunch of middle-age drudges, a lot of losers. . . .

You think I've gotten pretty far up for a loser? Well, all you have to do is step on the creeping escalator and keep your nose clean and you go on up with the rest of the drudges and morons. On the way, I've seen guys who could barely tie their shoelaces reach positions where they could sit on their fat asses and make life miserable for everybody else. I just got out of such a situation. They promoted the idiot and now he's got more people to make miserable.

I could give you a collection of the stupidities our great company cherishes. There was our punctuality neurosis not too long ago. I don't think they could get away with it today. They decided to put time clocks in headquarters (Incidentally, we make the damn things among other more complex equipment.) After all, our great leader decided—he was the heir apparent for some years of the gray eminence who built up this corporation into its billion-dollar prosperity and our present leader shared his propensity toward moralizing—that if they could punch time clocks out in the plants and warehouses, why couldn't we do so here at headquarters?

Well, you should have heard the furor. Unpunctuality was sinful and we were going to be protected from this sin. Even our most servile vice presidents were outraged. Most of them were putting in ten-hour days as it was. I was in personnel at the time, and the turnover in the middle management ranks from this one act was fantastic. Well, we went along this way for almost a year. Then someone estimated that counting the cost of the clocks, the timecards and the paperwork involved in keeping them, and our turnover and recruiting expenses, if the executive staff were all late every day of the week, that still wouldn't equal what we were spending to keep track of their punctuality. So morality fell to economics and they took the clocks out. The stupidity quotient in our top ranks at that time had reached a new high.

I guess what I object to most is the wastage of human resources here—mine included. I've been passed over twice now so I guess you can say I'm bitter about that, and it's true I am. But I look back at even the good times and I think mine has been a career in a wasteland, where so few of our talents are used and even when we contribute to the overall good of the company, so little use is made of that good.

I've been cursed with a fairly high IQ and stupidity does something to me in the guts, so of late years my feelings of frustration have gotten worse. A lot of the men can get used to it. I can't. Well, why didn't I get out, you may well ask. I guess I didn't have the guts when I needed them, and before my marriage broke up, I had a lot of obligations. My wife was extravagant and I had to struggle to keep up to what she and her family were used to. I come from people who never had much money. My father was a high school teacher in a small town and we were always scrabbling. Then I married the belle of the ball—my wife's folks were pretty big in our town and I had to get us out where

I could keep my end up. The terms of that scale of living were earning a pretty decent salary and going up a bit. Ours was a bad marriage going nowhere but I wanted her and I wanted to prove something. This company gave me a chance. It has a lot of prestige. The company had a plant near our town and a lot of the executives belonged to the country club there. Being in a corporation like this opens a lot of doors.

No, I don't want to talk about my childhood. It was all right but it's not germane to what I'm telling you, and I'm not sure I'll even let you publish this no matter how you disguise it. Anyhow let me get it off my chest. There's nothing special about my childhood anyhow. I did well enough. At the university, I did brilliantly. I suppose I could have stayed on and gotten my master's and even a Ph.D., but with a new social wife I couldn't see myself sitting around living off scholarships and her parents for the next four years. I started off in sales engineering, believe it or not. That's where this company is particularly strong, but you get too great a dose of engineers, particularly production engineers, and you're liable to develop a very low opinion of the intellectual capacity of the human race. I started out having to prepare instruction manuals for very complex equipment, which meant interviewing engineers, and a more inarticulate bunch, barring some of our dumber top executives, you will never see in a long career.

I suppose I started out young and eager like most of us. I lived in a town where the power of the corporation was very evident, and even at a young age I suspect I had felt there was something vaguely sinister about corporate life. But this feeling quickly evaporated after I started working. I found the job interesting, though frustrating in an odd way and I was promoted pretty fast. Our plant or works, as we called it, was a beautiful place, looking something like a university campus with fine landscaping, green lawns and topiary borders. It was, as the recruiting brochures pointed out, "a good place to work," and of course a lot of the town's prosperity came from the works—its payrolls, mortgages on homes for employees and other business opportunities. Furthermore, top executives mingled with the town's social elite at cocktail parties and other events and the company contributed generously to all town needs and organizations. So my making good early at the works helped me a little in the eyes of my wife's family. I was finally promoted to administrative assistant to the general manager, a big heavy, burly man with a warm voice and fatherly ways.

Our works was responsible for rather sophisticated equipment and there was an "R & D" laboratory associated with it with the usual pipe-smoking, bumbling, academic types assigned to a new complex product. I became the liason between the general manager and the laboratory group, and this indirectly led eventually to the most interesting and productive job of my whole career. But before that and the next two moves, I had better tell you about the disaster in my life and get it over with. It concerns the break-up of my marriage.

It isn't that I don't like women. It's probably the opposite; I'm too attached to them. My mother was an ambitious woman, I'd say—basically cold. She somewhat looked down on my father. As I told you, he was a high school math teacher and he liked teaching, but high school teachers didn't make much in those days. My mother thought he ought to try to get into school administration, and become a principal or something. The principal, a man named Richards, was always hanging around, and knowing women as I do now I suspect there might have been . . . well, let's not go into that. Also there was—and I'm still not sure of this—there was supposed to be something at one time, I believe, between my father and one of his students, though if so it must have ended suddenly because I'm sure my mother would never have put up with that.

You know it was kind of embarrassing going to the same school where your father's the teacher—at least I found it hard. It set me apart and if there's anything you don't want when you're that age, it's to be set apart. You want to be like everybody else. So I never got to know my father very well and I guess I considered him less important, and that's very hard on a kid. So we see a kind of world where women are dominant and ambitious, and, now I come to think of it, that's the kind of world I seem to have grown up in. When I turned to the girl I married, maybe this was the pattern I was following. I have to admit it, though, Lillian was a beauty—auburn hair, graceful and sensuous, and you couldn't see the steel underneath that velvet exterior. You couldn't hear the ambition behind that soft, sexy voice. I don't think Lillian was very sexy but maybe I just didn't bring it out. What turned her on was power, and you could see (how well I remember that stillness) her attention, all her beauty begin to focus in any gathering on the man who had the power; mostly older men because that's where it lay. I think this was unconscious on her part, a deep-seated orientation of her nature. I never should have tried for her world, though. I wasn't really cut out for it. I wanted to get somewhere but I guess I would have been more suited to the academic field. Yet I wanted Lillian more than anything in the world. I might as well say it since I'm not going to let you print it. I couldn't sleep nights, thinking of her. The dreams of her were with me all the time. It was a terrible attachment, like a sickness. She was everything I ever hoped for.

When I got to know her, I sort of sensed her coldness and ambition and with all that she was something of a snob, but none of this made any difference to the intensity of my desire. I didn't have the family for her but I was the brightest guy in our class and it looked as if I were going places. You see me now, a middle-aged drudge with glasses and a receding hairline, but I wasn't bad-looking in those days. I was clean-cut and looked as if I could be a well-off eastern prep school type. So briefly Lillian did turn that incredible, quiet gathering of all her beauty and power on me, and I was lost. All right, I'll say it, since I'm not going to let you print it. I was lost and it about ruined me. I suppose I've never recovered from it. I never married again. Oh there've been others. I have a very fine relationship now—she's in personnel in the company, a divorcee, and we've been going together for some time. But I'm leary of marriage and well, you know how it is . . . I still follow Lillian's meteoric rise, though. She's married now to a very rich and powerful politician and I'm waiting for the inevitable. If he ever begins to slip, to lose either his wealth or power—looks very unlikely at this time—I know it'll be "Goodbye, it's been swell" from Lillian. This is her third marriage. One of the interesting though sad satisfactions I've had in the years since we've been apart is the observation of what happened to the guy she left me for, the hotshot in our company, my former boss, who was going to set the world on fire but developed a slight drinking problem after his promotion and their transfer.

Now I don't feel any satisfaction in it anymore even though this guy was always, underneath his genial exterior, an arrogant, insensitive bastard. It's not hard to visualize what happened to him. As I told you, everything started while he was still my boss and in the beginning I admit I liked him. But what I couldn't understand was, even though he was rumored to be going places, how Lillian could stand his physical presence. She was beautiful and elegant. He was a big, crude bear of a man, a cigar-smoker with a phony fatherly air about him and a lot of that false geniality people like him use to get their ends. He was something of a man's man. He liked smoke-filled rooms and locker room stories and a lot of noise and back-slapping. I don't believe he had too many brains either, though he did have force of personality. Still I have to admit I liked him in the beginning; he was fair minded and a decisive boss. He also seemed to have toned himself down somewhat, eliminating some of his crudities, but it took me awhile to catch on. I thought it was the pipe-smoking "R & D" guy that she liked to talk to that she liked. I should have known he wasn't even in the running. He was like me without power in the company, not on the inside track. I should have realized it from the beginning.

When I think back, I remember now seeing that sudden quietness when Lillian first met Carl Boorstal, my boss. I remember her focusing her attention and beauty on him and his reaction even in the midst of that loudness and the "Little Lady" nonsense he smeared all over Lillian. After all, he was my boss and, though I hated this in her, she always tried to further my interests in this way. But I thought it was an act with her since her fastidiousness would ordinarily have ruled out anything with a big, loud, lumbering, middle-aged cigar-smoker like that. But I realize today Lillian had no capacity at all for real love or disinterested love. I suppose she might have loved her father, the banker, one of the worst cold-hearted bastards in town; a guy who scarcely even bothered to talk to you unless there was something in it for the family. Now that I think of it, I guess my own stupid ambition—which, thank God, I've outgrown now—stemmed from Lillian and maybe my mother.

Anyhow, it's the old story: The husband's the last to catch on. You know something I've learned in life is, contrary to what the sages tell you, what everyone believes to be true usually is true. I tended to discount a few disturbing rumors that reached me. I thought it was the "R & D" guy that she liked. I suppose also it seemed incredible to me that Lillian could even consider a boor like my boss, although he did have presence. Now don't misunderstand me: The rumors were that they were having an affair and this I am almost certain was not true in the sexual sense, if only because Lillian, although in appearance beautiful and extremely sensual-looking, was and probably still is rather cold. More important, I believe she would not lower herself to have an affair with a man unless no other tactic would work for her purposes, and the stakes were much higher than they were here. Old Boorstal wasn't that much of a bargain and besides she had him by the nose almost from the beginning. No, the rumors were wrong there, I believe, and thinking back now, unless I am much mistaken, I'm pretty sure I didn't need to worry about coming on them in some bedroom or catching sight of her car parked outside some motel. I think she was leading him around the party circuit and assessing his potential. She had written me off. So what she finally did was to tell me very calmly one evening that she had decided to make her life with Carl, that she loved him and no longer loved me, that Carl's promotion had come through and he was being transferred to the main offices in Chicago. She said when the divorce came through she would be joining him there.

I won't bore you with my reactions. I'm not too proud of them. I did about all the wrong things you can do with a girl like Lillian. I pleaded with her. I cried. I promised her everything in the world. I did everything that, had I been in my right mind, I would have known would disgust her. She hated weakness. She responded cruelly to it. It brought out all her latent sadism. Maybe I'm exaggerating. I don't know, but I do know poor old Carl probably, like me, got very little from Lillian when things began to go sour. The only thing that had really ever turned her on with me was success. The hottest sexual bouts we ever had were the evening I was elected a councilman in town and the evening I was promoted to assistant to the general manager. I used to lie to her about my prospects and about possible promotions because it would bring in her that sudden intense stillness, that rise of lust. I'm sorry about this. I know this must seem disgusting, but the truth is this woman was the most nakedly venal woman I've ever met, and it was not something she had developed or put on, it was built into her—it was she. Sex was success and success was sex and to have sex with her you had to have success. It haunts me yet—that sudden stillness, that focusing of her beauty when she saw a man with power. It was like the freeze of a beautiful predatory animal just before crouching to spring. When I dream about her, I dream of myself suddenly come to power and that sexual stillness in Lillian and me turning away in scorn, rejecting her. . . .

But that's enough of that. Let's go back to the company. After a period

of drinking, insomnia and depression when I almost lost my job, I was transferred to the regional marketing office near Syracuse and I worked there in a
frenzy for the next two years. Then I was assigned to a special task force, put
together at one of our biggest works near Trenton on a possible new product
being developed. This—I have to say it—began the best time of my life. This
product was a completely new, almost revolutionary kind of thing and we were
trying to develop it in the greatest secrecy. If it had worked out, it would have
been one of the biggest breakthroughs in our field, and we had some great
people assigned to it. I was alone now living in an apartment in town and I
threw myself into the work. I'd found something that seemed to me really
important and worthwhile to give myself to. I was with a group of great guys,
really bright, savvy guys—two of them are now up at the top and all have become successful in one way or another and that's how I know they'll never
really let me go here. I was once one of them. Anyone who was on that task
force lived through an exciting, frustrating, heartbreaking, great period. We
worked ten, twelve hours a day, sometimes seven days a week. I had no ties
at this time and I'd come in nights sometimes to work out cost projections,
sometimes Sundays and there'd be one or another of our group there. That
thing haunted us. We knew if we could only solve some of these problems—
engineering mostly but economic and marketing also—we'd have something that
might revolutionize the field and open a whole new market. For over a year it
looked as if we could do it. I was immersed in manufacturing and supplier cost
projections. I slept and kept all my papers at the apartment. With only a minor
and rather sordid episode or two, I had had no personal life since Lillian; I had
been, as they say, a burnt-out case. But I was giving all my time and thought
to this project and it was bringing me back to life. I began to look better and
feel better. I'd been rail thin, shabby and run-down with the drinking for a
long time. The hard work saved me, took me out of myself. I began to care
about something again. I looked forward to getting up in the morning and I
hated to go to bed at night now. Most of us on the task force were so sure
we could make it.

Then two things happened. A competitor developed a piece of equipment
somewhat similar in operation to the one we were working on, though ours
would have been much more sophisticated, and secondly a recession hit our
major markets. For the first time our profits took a bad tumble and the storm
warnings were up throughout the company. If we'd had a management with
just a little vision, if we'd even had a management with some guts, our project
might have survived and we would have weathered the storm to bring it through.
But we had . . . well we had the kind of management we have now—a rather
pronounced shortage of brains and no guts. The cry was cut our losses, cut our
losses, cut out everything that's not selling. Take a big bath now and look good
later. Our project which could have done so much for the company, which

might have become a strong part of their future, was one of the first victims. We were wiped out almost overnight and the members of our task force, our great team, were reassigned. I ended up over in a costing section at one of our regional offices. . . .

I look back. Things haven't been the same for me since that time. I don't want to bore you with my own nonprogress, but I do think it might be instructive for you to see how a dynamic corporation like this really bumbles along. We're often cited as the sinister, multinational octopus, a huge conspiratorial entity plotting to take over the world for our own mysterious purposes, so powerful that ordinary people—customers, stockholders, even governments can't touch us. It is to laugh. True we do make a useful and important complex piece of equipment used everywhere, but as for our sinister conspiratorial power, anyone who's seen us operate from the inside is not so much disturbed by visions of our taking over the world as by curiosity as to how we've managed to survive at all with the way we stumble around. I suppose we know enough to make and sell our products and to price and maintain them pretty well and that's about all we know. We waste more time in petty internal politics, our own people scrambling for the goodies of promotion and favor and our top management in jumping whenever anybody—customer, stockholder or the government—says boo that we hardly have time to react sensibly to anything let alone decide how the world should be run. The few times we have tried to do anything outside of manufacturing, selling and maintaining our junk we've gotten into so much trouble, we've even had to reshuffle the management and run around looking for scapegoats.

Let me give you a few examples. At one time our great leader got a sudden access of social conscience and decided that social responsibility and support for the arts were the great public relations approaches for corporations. So among other things, our company undertook to sponsor an extremely expensive symphony series on television, a series you may well remember because it pre-empted Sunday evenings, driving out a far more popular situation comedy. We also had a less than banner year, and at the next shareholders meeting a big stink was raised about the company's wasting shareholders money on a lot of pinko do-gooder community projects and on that expensive symphony program. Our chairman made a beautifully dignified reply to these idiotic protests and then proceeded to undo everything by trying to cancel the program, which got the corporation into a load of the worst possible publicity from music lovers and the press. Having done something good by accident, we didn't have the guts to stick to it; so we got it from both sides.

You may also remember the big furor about our contribution to the campaign fund of that egregious crook the American people in one of their dumber years put into the White House. The corporation's management had been making contributions to both parties for years as part of what they considered a sensible policy of social insurance and support for our political structure. When it came out that the contributions exceeded legal limits, we had a parade of embarrassed top officers slapped with fines and threatened with prison, and the company was pictured as a sinister force helping engineer the election of this shabby, power-hungry incompetent, thus attempting to enslave the American people and destroy our democracy. Again this is a big laugh. Our top management may be dumb but they are not ambitious to take over our political system or anything else outside the company. And they're not especially sinister except in their capacity for company in-fighting. They mean well for the company and want the company to be loved, and if anyone's going to destroy democracy around here, it's the American people—you and me—and not some clumsy organization trying to operate at a profit and meet all the pressures of community service and good citizenship imposed on it just to keep operating. We may—like U.S. Steel—poison the atmosphere, but as soon as the community or the government decides to make us clean up if we want to stay in business, we're going to clean up, because our first goal is to stay in business—to do what we were set up to do—and our second is to make money out of it. So if we've got to play footsies with shady characters or with dictators or other governments abroad to stay in business, we play footsies. Like the artist whose sole morality is to get up in the morning and keep his brushes clean, our management's sole morality is to see we stay in business short of murder, treason, larceny and acts of God, and anyone who sees sinister motives in that need only stop buying what we sell or tell the government to pull the plug, and we're gone—our 100,000 people are out of jobs and some similar organization with similar motives but that you like better will have to take over to supply the world. We've had some arrogant, tyrannical top managers in this company but they're not in a position through this organization to take over the U.S. or the American public, let alone the world.

One more point. Corporations do lobby and lobby hard to get special breaks for themselves and their industries and sometimes they use bad tactics—bribes, women, threats of hell fire—but so do our other honorable institutions, schools, the military, the scientific establishment, the arts and so on. The use of these stupid tactics varies with the amount of money and power invested in these areas, but regardless of the tactics, at different periods of our society's evolution different institutions are held in higher esteem than others and therefore get away with more. Right now business and our corporation are out of favor, and believe me we are squeaky clean. Our gray eminence of a chairman has outlived his usefulness and is jumping around desperately to try to hold on to his job. He won't make it—he's seventy and the new shibbolith is to get rid of 'em at sixty-five. He'll be the last to hang on after the retirement curfew. Our board of directors is getting impatient and we'll soon be seeing a changing of the guard.

So you can see it isn't on moral grounds that I don't like corporate life and

feel I'm living in a wasteland. I'm not that naive. It's on entirely other grounds—
it's the awful wastage of human life in this kind of set-up, the aridity, the petty
politicing and the scary power scramble. The fact is, the company, the bureaucracy, can only use a small part of a man's capabilities and yet it demands so
much in time, in loyalty, in petty politics, in stupidities. I don't know whose
fault this is; I think it's the fault of the system, but since this isn't going to see
the light of day, I'm going to be perfectly frank about the people in the company I've had to deal with since those days on the task force. I'm not saying
they're all idiots: I've had some good friends here and there're some outstanding
men at the top. But the ratio of morons, time-wasters, time-servers, petty
politicians and scared rabbits is so high here that it's discouraging, and I'm beginning to feel only little bully boys and smart operators can claw their way
through middle management.

However, I've got to say it: I made one bad mistake a few years ago and I
think it's this that's virtually ended my career here. Oh, I'll stay on, but I'm
not going much higher and I'll never get to where my capacities would ordinarily
take me. I said something in anger and my career was over. To understand this,
you have to go back to the situation I found myself in after my reassignment to
the regional costing center. At that time I was a hot number and the section I
was assigned to should have been glad to get me. But unfortunately for me, it
was headed by a slow, lumbering time-server, R. I. Henty, a thick-set, sad-faced
man with stomach trouble whose chief concern was that things should not move
too fast or get out of hand. He was sitting on what would ordinarily have been
a pretty useful function, providing cost information on several components and
subassemblies. But since nobody could get anything out of us, some of the
plants had built up their own costing groups and were circumventing us, sending
pro forma requests and figures for our analysis but putting together their bud-
gets on their own figures. We could never be blamed for anything because we
never quite came through with anything anyone could blame us for. Our section was one of those little bureaucracies that spent its whole time trying to protect itself from criticism and avoid doing anything that could possibly provoke
criticism, so of course we were useless. We existed because we looked good, as
if management were protecting itself and getting as much reality into our costing
as possible. Our existence gave the impression that our costing was standardized
and objective.

Anyhow I was desperate. The atmosphere in that section was numbing. I
grew to hate Henty and he me. I took it out in unnecessary witticisms, he in
picayune criticisms of everything I did, which was little enough. He was also
sitting on any possible raises due me, so my cries for help were directed at one
of my old buddies on the task force who had become head of personnel at
headquarters. After my third plea and threat to quit, he got me a transfer to

his own division, personnel, on a temporary basis, while he and some of my other friends who had gone up looked around to see where they could use me. It was a respite, a lifesaver.

Being on temporary assignment, however, is at best a bad situation. You're really in limbo. You're out of phase. I was forty years old, and I'd had a couple of bad breaks and I should have gotten out. But it wasn't that easy, and you can't do it halfway. There were still possibilities here; I thought or I guess I rationalized on this. But here I was rescued like a drowning kitten from that R. I. Henty backwater and my stay in personnel was a refuge before the second storm.

It was while I was there in personnel I made this bad mistake. Anyone who was on that task force was known to top management and specifically to our chairman. We had been an elite group. I had not realized it but all of us had been under scrutiny for future positions of responsibility, as they termed it, and my folder had apparently looked no worse than anybody else's. I believe I had been known up to that time as a man who had pulled himself together from a marital disaster and done a very creditable job. This is all conjecture based on hindsight. But what I did do, while I was in personnel and looking around for an assignment, was to circulate among top managers to see whether there was anything for me in various areas. My big mistake, I believe, occurred one Friday evening after a hard day, sitting around talking to a vp named Rolly Spofford. Rolly was one of those guys who oozed charm. I don't know whether he had any ability or not but he could charm the birds out of the trees and he was one of the easiest men to talk to I've ever met. I think this was my downfall. I said a few things about the company that were more honest than tactful, but I said something about our revered chairman under the influence of Rolly's warming personality that was absolutely idiotic. I said: "When is our old has-been going to retire, Rolly, so this company can catch up and come into the twentieth century?"

There was only the faintest hesitation before Rolly leaned back in his big chair behind his beautiful big desk in his big corner office and laughed, but some instinct in me told me I'd done it. Later I asked my friend in personnel. "Yeah," Mel told me, "Rolly's one of the Old Man's fair-haired boys. The Old Man brought him along, though I don't think he's particularly pegged for anything higher."

"Then," I asked, "if the Old Man retired, Rolly would lose his main support?" "Well, it wouldn't help Rolly along," my friend answered, "but he's pretty well set now anyhow," and I knew I'd blown it. I knew I was through. I told Mel what I'd done. Mel sat back and rubbed his hand over his face. "Jesus Christ, Howard," he said, "can't you keep your mouth from going off! I was hoping we could get you something in merchandising, but if that remark ever gets back to the Old Man, your goose is cooked as far as going up in this company. I've got a good offer for you from budget and planning and I think you'd better take it. It's not as high as I'd hoped to get you, but if that remark gets back to the Old Man before I've placed you, you're really in trouble."

That's how I blew it. It's been ten years since that day and while I've gotten on the escalator and gone up routinely, all the good posts have eluded me. The guy I report to now has just moved up, A. C. Banyon, one of the all-time assholes of the world, a typical petty bully. Never did a thing in the twenty years he's been here but live off better men's brains and try to push around anyone he could get to. He and I had called a truce early on because I wouldn't take any shit from him. The big boss of our area was one of those on that task force and A. C. has never been sure how close I am to Bill Barker or whether I might carry tales out of school on him. So A. C.'s been my friendly enemy for the three years of our uneasy association and now I have his division, though he's still there above me. That's probably as far as we'll both go. It's just possible they've plotted me to move sideways and up to A. C.'s level in another area, however.

I made that bad, that stupid statement years ago. I kept my lip buttoned since then and my nose clean for quite a while after that, but now I know I'm never going up to higher management and I'm willing to tell you how it is. I'm not dumb enough, though, to let you tape me or crystallize my frankness for the world. I've got a few more years before I can even take early retirement, and you'll get no release on anything from me. I hope I've been honest with you at least and let you know how it really is, because I imagine you've got plenty of the usual crap in your interviews by now. I tell you frankly I think our present management stinks and we're living off the last generation's brains and dynamism. I object to the increasing remoteness and pomposity of our higher management and the increasing loss of human contact. I object to the loss of that family feeling that the company once tried to foster. Everything is becoming less human and more impersonal around here. But for me, well, I made a blunder. I should have gotten out long ago. I didn't have the guts and now I'm here for the duration. My personal life is pretty much over too but I don't miss it the way I used to. I have a friend, a divorcee, a quiet understanding girl considerably younger than I, but we are of different generations and for me marriage is out of the question. Lillian took it all—whatever I had to give—and while in that instance I admit my taste in women was lethal, I'm not about to foist a burnt-out case on someone else.

So I've looked at my life and the corporation which has taken so much of that life with considerable sadness and misgivings. I've looked around and seen others—some who've made it and some like myself who haven't—and I can see, not malevolence, not conspiracy, not a sinister force operating in the world for its own hidden purposes or trying to bend the public to its will nor, on the bright side, as so many would have you believe, a hard-working fulfilling existence, a set of challenges and excitements that can command the best of truly good men, but a trivialization of human effort and aspiration in a chaotic and mindless drudgery, a sidetracking of valuable human resources, and, for most truly intelligent men who have so much to offer, as I once did, in the end a career in a wasteland. . . .

PART II

What is this life really like?
Here are executives who are
getting there, who are feeling
the strain. . . .

In a time of an expanding economy like the 60s in America, young executives came up fairly fast and there was a cult of youth and quick executive development. People like Bob Blake and Jane Killian could move up into management slots on fast timetables. In the contraction of the early 70s, all of this changed. The belief in youth in management faded; lower management jobs were frozen; markets were contracted; territories merged as happened to Bob Blake, leaving young tigers in limbo, and the time span for apprenticeship in lower management lengthened with more drudgery and less opportunity for testing capabilities.

The early hazards along the way in this world are many—moving into the wrong field in the company so that the job is eliminated when times get tough, falling under a stifling or neurotic boss, failing to gain the right competencies, lack of ambition—because as one moves forward he or she is judged by attitude, loyalty and drive—and finally lack of a plan for one's career. But one of the worst hazards, one of the saddest, is revealed by Howard Carver—surviving into middle management in a life style one hates. . . .

We turn now to middle and higher management—men beginning to move deeper into their jobs, the hours getting longer, the good part of corporate life revealing itself: interesting work, adventure, a dawning sense of one's usefulness and authority, increasing recognition, a sense of achievement. We see Anthony Rossi, who can't wait to get in in the morning, Joe Hardy, our black executive, who in a sense has conquered the establishment, and Dave Danbury who, even though he never reached the top, has found fulfillment in the corporate life. . . .

4

"I Love Every Minute of It! I Can't Wait to Get In in the Morning...."

An entrepreneur in the corporate world tells how he goes where the action is

Anthony Rossi is a youthful-looking, dynamic man in his early forties, and vice president and general manager of a 40 million dollar instrumentation company that we will call General Instrumentation Corp. He has moved up through a small plant in the south to a giant forest products company, World-Wide Products, Inc., and from there to General Instrumentation, where he pretty much runs the show. He was an upwardly mobile, take-charge man in every one of his assignments. He seems always to have been a little too young for the assignments he was able to take on and to have had to work out his challenges under the aegis of an older and in one case a more conservative, less cooperative superior, until he finally reached his position of top operating responsibility. One would not have guessed that he lost most of his stomach in this upward climb. He was operated on for gastric ulcers and two-thirds of his stomach was removed five years ago, but he is back more than ever in the thick of the fray. He exemplifies quintessentially the work ethic in America. Work is what he lives for. He loves work and he is not afraid of risk. He has had his dark moments, but he cannot be kept down. And there is a certain pleasure, a sort of joyousness in meeting challenges that seems to be his hallmark. One feels that he will go on and on as long as challenges exist, that that is the way he wants to live his life—to be always where the action is.

I have confidence in myself—I believe you will see that. The one thing I think sets the pace in the corporate world among the people who move up and those who don't is the degree of confidence a person has in himself. I have a philosophy I guess you could call it: "Don't beat yourself." I've been defeated once or twice—things haven't always worked out—but I don't defeat myself. I take a challenge and make decisions and then I go to it—I don't agonize over it. I don't beat myself!

Let me tell you a story. A lot of us in upper management went to these management training courses in this huge corporation I used to work for. In one of these classes, I remember—it was a class in statistics, I believe—the instructor says: "I want to ask you a question. If you were talking to a guy and you knew this man could back it up, would you flip him for $100,000? All those who would raise your hands?" There were 20 of us there, all upper management, and only three guys raised their hands, I being one of them. This instructor says: "Only three out of 20!" He turns to me and says: "What's your reason for flipping this man for $100,000?" I answered: "Where else would you have an even chance of making $100,000 in about ten seconds?"

You see, what all those 17 guys who didn't raise their hands were thinking of was losing, while what the three of us who raised our hands were thinking of was winning, and this is what that instructor was trying to point out. That's my attitude. I'm not saying that I'm naive; I'm not saying I don't lose sometimes. I do, but I take the odds and I can usually make it stick. I don't beat myself. If the odds beat me, well ok, but I never beat myself.

I guess my story begins in an old southern city, a city that has musical traditions, where I was born and grew up. My parents were immigrants and we were poor. My father worked in a diner and we lived, so to speak, on the wrong side of the tracks. But we were a close enough family—I have two beautiful older sisters—and like a lot of ethnic families we knew who we were and where we stood. My parents respected each other and we respected them. The only thing I can say that represented a real handicap was that we were what nowadays you'd call a "culturally deprived" family. My father never went to school and my mother only went to eighth grade. They were as good honest people as you could ask for but they didn't know anything about music or art or anything of that sort. There were no books in our house and no real intellectual stimulus. Today I am a history buff; I got into music early and I collect paintings, but this came from two great teachers I had, one in elementary school and the other in college. They were the biggest influences on my life. They changed my life.

The first one, Miss Delafield, I met when I was 11 years old and in the sixth grade. She taught me everything. I studied history with her. She taught history in such a way that it gave me an abiding interest in it. Although I've not taken a formal course in history since the eighth grade, except for senior American History, I bet I could go to college and take a Ph.D. examination in it. A day never passes that I don't read history—and all because of Miss Delafield. She taught me how to write; she taught me history; I know more of geography than most people because of Miss Delafield. About five years ago, a remarkable thing happened. I was working for a great world corporation at that time in the southwest and I was talking to a man who had recently been transferred in. We talked back and forth and he asked: "Where are you from?" and I named the southern city. He said: "Did you go to school there—to grammar school?" I said: "Yes, I went to a small grammar school in a bad section of town" and I named it. He said: "Did you have a teacher named Clara Delafield?" I said "She's the best teacher I ever knew. Is she still living?" He said: "That's my aunt and she's retired but she's fine." I said: "When you write to her, tell her you ran into one of her former students and that Tony Rossi said hello. . . ."

So a good teacher can change your life. I could recognize to this day anyone who had been in Miss Delafield's class by the way she taught us to write in a certain style. I could look at it and say: "Anyone who writes like that must have been in my sixth grade class or the letter must be from Miss Delafield!"

The second teacher who had a major influence on my life I didn't meet until my senior year in college. He was a chemical engineer and head of the department, but before we get to him let me tell you something about my education earlier and in college. I was pretty good in school. Even then I guess I was what you'd call a take-charge guy. I remember when I came through for Miss Delafield in a reading class when we put on a demonstration for the PTA. I was a better reader so I was training those who couldn't read. We were reading about the eruption of Mt. Vesuvius. Then in high school—and we were in a particularly tough section of the city—I did even better. I finally became president of my class in that school, of the senior class, for the fact is that even when I was in school, when we got into groups and somebody had to run it, it always fell to my lot. I could get things moving the way they should, so by the time I was a senior I was president of about everything there was in the school.

Then I went to college, to the state university nearby, and that was a different story. World War II had just ended and suddenly the universities were crowded with GIs going on the GI Education Bill. You couldn't get into the courses you wanted—not in sequence anyhow. I was going to engineering school so I had to take some freshman courses, when I could get in, some sophomore courses and some senior courses—you had to somehow squeeze them in or you wouldn't have them in time to graduate. So I was working so devilishly hard, taking so many hours sometimes that it was even illegal. One time I was in class for 36 hours a week—that's almost 8 hours a day. It was murder. I remember that's when I gave up reading the funnies. Certain things had to give way and that was one of them. I haven't read the funnies since then.

In these engineering schools, you know, the chemical engineering school is usually one of the smallest. You'll have a great number of civil engineers, a smaller number of electrical engineers and a very small number of chemical engineers. I was in the chemical engineers group, the smallest department, and it was headed by a man named Casey Kramer, a chemical engineer and, of course, a Ph.D. He was ancient, about 45. He was a gruff, sort of taciturn man and he'd sit there looking over his glasses at you like this—kind of quizzically. He was the department head but he also had regular classes. It just so happened that there were three different courses of study you could take and in the early years it turned out I had the two courses not taught by Casey, so I didn't really know him until my senior year. That year I took some engineering design courses from him.

Well, let me say at once I was not a distinguished chemical engineer and I was having a terrible time in Casey's classes, in math classes and in a lot of my work because I was so overloaded. I was carrying such a weight of classes that I could do only what was essential just to get through, to get the essence of it. For instance, some of the professors gave credit for work done at home. I couldn't do it, and I just didn't do anything except what would keep the project moving— and the project, of course, was-getting a degree. So my grades were down and I sometimes lost confidence in myself because I was trying to take so much. But while I didn't do well in Casey's classes, I got to know him briefly outside of classes, and it was what he made us do that changed my life. We thought he was nuts at the time, because instead of just taking courses in what we were majoring in like everybody else, Casey made us take courses in art appreciation and in music appreciation, and these courses changed my life. That art appreciation course was one of the best courses I've taken in my whole life. It gave me a lasting interest and understanding of art. I never miss an art show.

Well, I got to know Casey better because of a project I was pulling together for a college engineering fraternity. We were going to have a spaghetti feed, and I decided we also needed to do something unusual. I knew that Casey played the viola in the city's symphony orchestra, so I asked around our class to see if there was anyone else who could play instruments with a view to putting together a little performance that evening. Well, we got together the most awful group of musicians you can imagine. Casey played the viola, we had a guy playing the drums, and a guy playing the tuba. It was a real mishmash, but we whacked out a few themes and it went over big in front of the students—a lot of them married and attending with their wives. After the thing was over, Casey came up to me and said: "We enjoyed that," and I answered: "It was fun," and that was the first time I think Casey'd really noticed me.

Later he told me about a meeting the professors had had and they'd taken a poll on the students and their futures and they'd decided that of the guys in the class I'd probably be the first to become a vice president. I don't know whether that was true or not, but of course I was always into things. Anyhow this man had done a great deal for me.

So I graduated with my degree as a chemical engineer, and I was exhausted. I had been carrying this tremendous course load and I had already begun to get an ulcer. Now that was over and I completely let down. This period of my life was spent catching up—just fooling around, going out, doing all the things I'd missed doing, working just enough to bring in something so I could take it easy, sowing my wild oats.

Now we come to my first corporate job. It was a chemical company, doing about a six million dollar a year business, and my job was a good one for a young fellow starting out—it was solving technical problems, and this plant had a lot of them. Now I'm not a great engineer—engineering isn't my forte—I'm more a manager. I like to see a project, explain it, pull the resources together—that's my long suit right there. But when I started out I had to work on these technical problems and some of them were most interesting. The plant was one of the first in the U.S. making ammonia and urea and it had been designed from an insufficient pilot plant, so we had our share of troubles. Management would take an engineer and say: "OK, buddy—here's your problem. Solve it." This means, first, you had to identify the problem; then you had to come up with the solution; then you had to get the solution implemented and it had to be the right answer.

If you had a good sound project, you could step right up even as a young engineer and ask for the money you needed to put the project across. Of course, spending money was relative—spending 20, 30, 40 thousand dollars was a big deal here. We really had to scale our projects. The real problem with engineering is that you sit down and think about a problem. You believe you've thought it all through—the designs that will carry it through—and you find you've left out something essential or you've made some obvious wrong assumption or . . . well, I've seen some classics in my time. Once a fellow was designing a big log rolling system, which depended on logs going into the water and resting on the bottom of the vat to be picked up by a big drag and brought into a feeder. You'll say: "But logs don't sink to the bottom; they float." So here's a guy with a big drag and logs that float and you'll say: "That's stupid." Well, it happens all the time, like the architect designing a building without bathrooms.

Anyhow, I was with this company three years and the problems were horrendous and we were working 14, 15 hours a day, every day—364 days in the year. I never worked so hard in my life. I was 27 years old and another young fellow and I were about the only ones left who could take this kind of schedule. The others were breaking down under it. The department head had a heart attack and two other executives had nervous breakdowns, so one day they brought in a fellow as our new boss. Now this was perfectly wise and proper. This was a 40-year-old man with experience, but I thought I was going to get the assistant department head job. I'd put in all that time and worked myself to death for them, but what they'd offered was a big increase in salary. Now you can't tell a 27-year-old smart-ass anything. He wants what he wants. So I said: "Look, I understand you want me to teach this new boss how to run the plant?" They said: "That's right." So I said: "OK, fine. I'll do that in the next few days because next week I'm leaving."

They tried to get me to stay, but as I say, no one can tell a 27-year-old smart-ass anything, and I left. Now my next job was a lucky one. It was way out of my field. I'd been in production and this was a sales job, and as experience I wouldn't trade it for anything in the world. I went to work as a sales engineer for a process instrumentation company. It was a typical salesman's job. I had a territory and there were a number of plants and process industries in the area and I had to set up periodic calls with them to try to sell them process instrumentation, heat controllers, flow controllers, and so forth. I wouldn't take a million dollars for that year I spent punching doorbells. It was tough on the family, though—by this time I was married. I'd leave Sunday night and come back on Friday night, but I learned a lot about organization and the problems of salesmen.

Now let me say something about my marriage—it's one of the greatest things that ever happened to me and my wife is the best friend I have in the world. You remember I'd been knocking around town after the heavy schedule in college. I'd been exhausted from the course load and studies and getting that degree, so I wasn't doing anything important after that, just knocking around, having a good time, chasing girls and all that, and I'd taken a job just to get a little money. I didn't have any special ambition. I liked problems or challenges—yes, but I didn't have any real motivation. Now in one of those passing jobs I'd heard about this girl before I'd met her. They'd thought highly of her in that company. She was a southern girl from Tennessee and they used to talk about her in that company as she used to work there and had a husband who was very ill. Then her husband died, and she had decided that the most important thing she could do was to rear the child, a baby son. She had a little social security money, so she had decided that what she would do was to take home secretarial work so she would be able to stay with the child. The company liked her so much they gave her work to do at home and she could bring it back to the office on completion. That's how I met her—at this company when she was bringing back her work. We started to go out together, to go to dinner, and I tell you ... I love children, I still love children—the only thing I miss now that our sons are grown is that there're no babies, no children around the house. I can't go by kids without stopping and fooling around with them and giving them some kind of talk. I tell my wife now: "Sue, I married you because you had Marty." That was the baby she was supporting then and now our son has just graduated from M.I.T. this June with high honors. We have two more sons of whom we're very proud. But still, I wish we had some children around. Anyhow, Sue and I were married and it was the best thing that ever happened to me, because all at once I began to get ambitious. There was something to work for and I had motivation. Also I had a wife who could tolerate me, could stand the kind of pace I went at, could stand my ambitions and the long hours I worked, and could stand the fact that I needed and need very little sleep, not more than about four hours a night. I've always had an edge on competitors because of that. I can keep going all night and have many times and then lie down and drop off for ten minutes or so and be fresh and ready to go again. Sue was the kind of warm, sympathetic, independent woman who could stand a man like me; who'd always be able to rustle up something for me to eat, no matter when I came home, who could take care of the children and then if I got in at midnight would be there to talk to me and get me a meal. My God, how lucky I've been!

To get back to this career, such as it is—and I'm in the middle of it now—I'll have to take a look at it with you as I'm telling it, because I haven't had time to look at it much on the way up. Things have been too hectic. Anyhow, I stayed with that doorbell ringing, sales engineer job for about a year. Then I had a chance to get back into production. There was this small, privately owned company of about 100 employees making fiber boards, and it was being miserably run. They desperately needed somebody to straighten it out. So I was offered the job and I went in as plant manager. It was my first real total managerial job, and I couldn't have been happier with it even with the backbreaking hours. I really went to work. You remember the 14-hour days of that earlier job; well, this one had 18-hour days. I worked every day like that, every day—it didn't make any difference. I hardly ever got home. Well, I kept up this pace for about eight months and made some very substantial improvement in operations but we still weren't making any money, so the owners of the business asked me to sit down and work up a report on what I'd need to really put that plant into shape to make a profit.

So I took a day off. I wrote the report. I submitted it to them. Now this plant was small and what I asked for essentially was about $150,000 to refurbish it. You must understand that the owners are reaching into their own pockets for it, this is big money, and that's where the money was coming from in this case. Then the big white angel came flying in, the angel in the form of a huge multibillion dollar corporation on the Pacific Coast. It turned out that we processed something they wanted, and the big company offered to buy one shift of our products. So the owners said: "We'll sell you the plant." The big corporation looked at it and to them it was petty cash, you see, so they bought it, and with it, they bought me. Now World Products, this corporate giant, asked me what I needed to put the plant into shape, and I submitted my list. They asked: "Would you like to make these additions?" I said: "I would love to make them." They asked: "How about this?" And they said: "Let's do that also." But I answered: "That $150,000 was for essentials." They said: "Why don't you take $250,000." So I said: "OK." We spent the money. The plant turned around. They asked me if I wanted to go to the West Coast, to their research division to work. So I came to the West Coast.

This was my first experience in a really huge company. This company was so big and complex, had so many divisions and interests that it was hard to get a handle on it. Out in that little plant down south, I had been a one-feather Indian. Bringing me into headquarters on the West Coast I was still only a two-feather Indian, maybe, but very far from being a chief. Since I'd had practical experience in business, I had been brought in to the "R & D" division as a business evaluator. I found myself a hard-driving, practical, entrepreneur kind of guy in a nest of slow-moving, pipe-smoking academic research types, and the change was dizzying. It was like trying to claw my way up for air in a sea of molasses. My job was to help review research plans, that is, to look at some of the research projects being recommended for implementation and tell whether they were economically viable or not. In the last few years I had been working 14- and 18-hour days and here I was sitting in this nest of academic, contemplative researchers, moving at what I considered a truly glacial tempo. My days were now from nine to five and I was taking vacations, when before I hadn't had a vacation in five years. Here we had the usual 240 workday year, while the year before that I had worked 344 days and the year before that 364 days, and I'd never had two days in succession to myself. Now don't get me wrong, these research men weren't incompetent or lazy or anything like that; they were an interesting and capable lot, though a bit impractical and disorganized, but their tempo was so much slower than mine that I was feeling guilty all the time, especially with those eight hour days and vacations. I wasn't used to that.

Another thing, I hadn't been brought in because they needed me so badly. It's not like a small outfit, where every man is virtually indispensable. They had a hundred men like me who could run that little plant down south, and they'd put one of them in to do it. Then they had to find something for me to do, and while I believe they felt I was competent and a pretty good man, they had a lot of good men and I was no big deal to them. But this was one of the finest companies I've ever known and they felt a responsibility to people, so they felt they had to do something with me. Now they didn't have to ask me to come to the West Coast. They could just have left me in the plant, and if I wanted to when they put their man in, I could get unhappy and I could leave. But that isn't the way they did things.

So there I was out on the West Coast in a research and development group, and in spite of the slower tempo I was happy and taking it easy, working only the eight-hour-day and taking vacations. There were a few other privileges you got in the research division. You got to go to a national convention each year, which in effect amounted to another week of paid vacation. Some of the men would go to Pheonix or to Chicago or to Honolulu or just a little way down to San Diego, wherever their convention happened to be that year. So one day I am reading a mailing on this big machinery show in Germany, and after all that's in my area, so I said: "I'm going to plan for a trip to Germany." I'd always wanted to go to Europe. The rest of the guys said: "You've got to be out of your mind. Nobody goes to Europe. The company's not going to sit still for you to go to Hanover." I answered: "Why not? It's a legitimate convention in my field, isn't it?"

Now as I told you, I never beat myself. That's my philosophy. I don't second-guess myself. I don't defeat myself like the guy who says: "I'd sure love to go around with that girl, but she probably wouldn't even look at me." Well, how do you know if you don't try. So I sent in my application for approval, and it came back approved.

So I came home to talk to my wife. I said: "Well, Sue, I'm going to Europe." She said: "When do we leave?" and I answered: "We're going together all right and it'll be in another six weeks." Then I looked at her soulfully in the eyes and I said: "Listen, you know we may never go to Europe again. We are going to do everything there is to do while we're there." So we made provisions to take care of the children and in six weeks, we took off. We did everything and saw everything. We didn't sleep at all; we just covered everything, and, amazingly enough, that trip became a turning point in my career.

On the business side, one of the things I was doing during that trip was looking over machinery and processes throughout Europe, in Hanover, France, Norway, Switzerland and back through France and again into Germany. So when I got back, I wrote a report on my findings. I explained the economics of those businesses and told them there was a business opportunity for our corporation to license some of these processes for the United States. They took a flyer and decided to license one of these processes, and it worked, so they decided to set up such an operation.

Now here's where you run into one of the problems of being in a big corporation. This had been my idea, my baby and I knew most about it, so I thought I ought to manage the new enterprise. I was sure I knew how it ought to be set up, but the company thought otherwise. I was only about 33 years old so they brought in an older, experienced, salesman type and set this operation up on an elaborate scale. They gave me a good job as technical manager, but the whole concept was flawed from the beginning.

Nevertheless, we gave it all we had. I worked for three years in that business and let me tell you I put my blood in it, and this was literal because after awhile I ended up in the hospital with a bleeding ulcer and had to have this operation that took out most of my stomach. All the time, I felt the concept was wrong and that we had gone about it the wrong way. In fact this was one of the lowest points of my business life. You see the company had had two choices. They could have believed a brash young guy like me or they could believe a mature, suave executive like the man they put in charge, and they made the natural choice. Now the man they brought in was a good salesman and he was used to doing things big, and he wouldn't take recommendations from someone who'd seen this kind of thing before—namely me. So we started out like General Motors, instead of starting small and building it up gradually. I'd seen this sort of attack before. But the business couldn't stand that kind of overhead, and though we worked ourselves day and night, we couldn't make it go.

I remember in the beginning, two weeks after I'd learned that I wasn't going to get to be in charge of the operation and I learned about the guy who was, I had tried to quit. But the company put me in a position where they wouldn't let me go, because they knew I was essential to the business, and they were kind of patting me on the head and saying: "Look, young fella, you're a bright boy; we like you. Come on, let's be realistic. This guy knows what he's doing." Two years later after we'd worked our guts out, it was no good. They had been wrong. This man hadn't known what he was doing, and the thing collapsed. So there I was—talk about low points in your career—sitting there, frazzled, exhausted, frustrated, at the end of my rope, I said to myself again: "I guess I'll have to leave the company." Then along came my old mentor, one of the division heads who had run among others things that "R & D" group, and he said to me: "I've got a job for you. I want you to come back to headquarters with me as a division engineer."

So this was my first major promotion, just as I was at the end of the line. "Now what I want you to do," this division head said to me, "is build the division made up of some of these little half-assed plants making this product and see if we can't put it on a sound footing." Harry, my new boss, was a very taciturn, a very spartan sort of fellow. He said to me: "Tony, we've got to do something about that plant you just left, the one trying to make that product we licensed. What should we do?"

I replied: "I'll tell you what we can do. We take this piece of equipment . . . ," and so on. "Then we do a big long report, and if management goes for these changes, we'll be able to do great." Harry said: "Let's do it."

I went out, got on my charger, worked up the changes into a recommendation report and he presented it to the board of directors. That was his job. We got the money, went out there, made the conversion, started up again, and the plant began to do great. That was a whirlwind year of activity. Then Harry says: "Tony, I think we need the same kind of plant in the east. So I went out and hired consultants and we started looking for plant sites in the east, and we found something that was just better than gold. We found a major source of low cost raw material, the biggest in the east. I went down and talked to the chief shareholder and owner of the company, an immensely wealthy guy, and he said: "I'm sorry. I'm just about to sign a contract with another company. I've been negotiating with them for about three months." I replied: "If you're a gambler, go ahead and sign that contract. But if you'd like to bet on a sure thing, sign with us. We're one of the world's biggest companies and I can work out a deal for you that will show you in black and white what we can buy from you over the years. But it's going to take me about two or three months to work it out and cost about $30,000 or $40,000. Now if you're willing to wait until we work it out and take a chance with us, you'll sign now with me. If not, go ahead and sign with the other fellow."

He signed the contract with us. We put together a plant in the southeast. We started construction on the plant and the market went SHUUUT—right down to the bottom. Harry and I sat around in his office back at headquarters and he said: "D'you think we ought to go ahead with this plant now?" I replied: "Harry, you know how these things are. The market can't stay that low. There's just no way it can. It always goes up. So if we build now, we'll be there when the upswing comes. We'll be right there to meet it." So he says: "Let's build it."

We went at it hammer and tongs. A plant like this usually pays out after three or four years. This one paid out in 18 months. It was a phenomenon. After the first six months it operated, we hit the market on the upswing. So now Harry begins to get much favorable recognition from the company. They were saying: "Look at what Harry's division is doing!"

Then I built a third plant, or rather rebuilt another plant that had been studied for ten years, and nobody could point the way to go. So when I took a look at it myself, I said: "It's obvious we have only three ways to go, but I don't know which of the three any more than any of the other guys who've been looking at this. Still, it ought to be simple. I will put all three side by side, make profit and other calculations and there's got to be a winner: it's got to be number one, number two or number three."

So I set up a model, put in the judgments and assumptions of the experts, and it was amazing. When the three numbers came out, I got calculations with minor differences such as 14.2, 14.6 and 14.7, not really enough to argue about. But there was a second test—trying to put the absolute income with the total income from the investment, and when you did that, one just stood out like a light from all the others. You could invest one million or two-and-a-half million or four million to beef up that plant, and on the one million there just wasn't enough modification. On the four million, you'd make about 6 per cent but on the two-and-a-half million the incremental investment hit about 22 per cent and this was pay dirt.

Harry was promoted to vice president after 30 years with the company. Now Harry knew what I'd done but I don't think the company realized that I was the guy who did it. However, my job was enlarged. One of Harry's areas was that of research and new business development and one thing he had been preaching a long time was that we could make quite a bit of money out of licensing some of World Products' technology. So he called me in one day and said: "Tony, I'd like you to be licensing manager for the corporation." I answered: "I can do that." He went on then: "I want you to form a group, put the licensing operation on its feet and see what it can do."

I began to lay the groundwork for a licensing department. First, with the help of a wonderful girl who started out as a secretary, I made a survey of where we were in licensing at the time. We found a whole lot of things; we had licenses in the wrong places, the wrong kind of licenses and so on. We put it all together. I would tell this girl: "Put this on the computer." She'd say: "I don't know anything about the computer." I'd answer. "Neither do I, but put it on anyway." We got computer reports: who had paid, who wouldn't pay . . . She really organized it. It was fun getting it going. I'd say: "I think I'll go over to France for a few days." There was a lot of traveling for this enterprise, Japan, Europe. We really got it going, and we put it on a very profitable basis. All this was gravy for the company. I learned a lot too. Between my trips abroad selling licenses, I was attending the corporation's management schools, and in one of these classes I was attending there was this consultant talking about creativity and he was saying: "Live big and do what you're supposed to do and do what you think you should do . . . " and so forth. We had a break and during the break I walked up to this man and I said: "Mel, you know I tried to sell licenses to a guy and I sometimes give him what he wants, and then the guy says: "I don't know . . . " and he acts as if he doesn't trust me. I said: "I tried to be straightforward and honest and he knows that I wouldn't do anything to hurt him. I couldn't in the position I'm in, but then he acts as if he doesn't trust me—why is that?" Mel says: "It's not you he doesn't trust. He doesn't trust himself." So I answer: "Yeah, that makes sense."

I learned another thing too. I would sit down and try to negotiate with a guy. I would talk to him about signing a licensing agreement and I'd say: "Do you want this thing exclusive or not?" He wouldn't way anything. I'd be doing all the talking. Now you don't learn anything doing all the talking. So finally, I got to thinking about it and I'd say: "These guys are afraid to talk; they're afraid they might say something that I'd hold them to." I would sit down with people that I'd never seen in my life before, and they'd be scared of me, as if I were a bear, because I represented a big powerful company. Now I'm pretty professional about putting people at ease, making them feel comfortable, and I'd make these two points: When we enter into this negotiation, I'd say: "Remember one thing; you can say anything you want to and there's nothing I can do about it, because the only thing that counts is when we put what we've agreed to down in black and white and we've signed it." Secondly, I said: "I'm not going to let you make a mistake. I can't afford to. It's got to be as good for you as for us."

These techniques, if you want to call them that, worked. I used to conclude license agreements in an afternoon that used to take others a year to conclude. So the company prospered in this area. I remember being at a convention of a society of professional people in this field and one topic was selling licenses, and one of the men there from a big processing company like ours gets up and says: "We had a very good year. We sold four licenses." Another representative of a big aircraft company remarked: "We had a bad year. We didn't sell a single license," and then a third man from a big company gets up and says: "We had a pretty good year. We sold five licenses." So in this kind of show-and-tell session, I got up and said: "Hell, I've signed 22 license agreements this year so far." Someone else said: "You've got to be kidding." I answered: "No." He asked: "How big is your staff?" I said: "Just me and one girl," and he said: "I don't care whether they're big or small, that's one hell of a lot of licenses!"

So in two years, we signed 54 license agreements and we brought in about a million dollars to the corporation. So for two years I did this, living the life of Reilly, traveling everywhere and negotiating in fifteen to eighteen countries, and it was fun.

At this time, our president had undertaken a huge acquisition, and the company was rounding up men who had experience in various areas to get the various units of this acquisition into production. When my card was put into the computer for the manpower inventory, there in the background is something that says "chemical engineer." So as they were looking for engineers for getting some of these plants into production, my name fell out. The next thing I know, Harry calls me in and says: "Tony, how would you like to get together a team and make a study for us that can tell us whether the corporation should go into the chemical business? After all you're a chemical engineer." I said: "Basically, I'm a manager, not an engineer, but it sounds like an interesting proposition."

So I put a team together and I was placed in charge of it and we made the study. The results said that this looked like quite a good opportunity for World Products. So they said: "Fine, we'll let your group market the chemicals the company already produces and see how that works out. Then we'll take the next step."

Now I saw this as a big opportunity both for me and the company. The company had been in the chemical business for some time, processing chemicals for their own products, and I could see how this marketing group could become a division and could grow into something important. I'd become the head of the division eventually and end up as vice president. Well, let me tell you, this became one of the biggest disappointments of my life. I ran into a political situation—the kind everybody runs into, I guess, in corporate life, even in as politically free a company as this one was.

We had a number of executives in the actual chemical plants and processing areas who had been there some time. They were basically chemical engineers, and they knew a lot about the chemical aspects of our products, something about running a plant but nothing about running a business. They thought they should be the ones to run this marketing organization I was building up. So suddenly I ran into stonewall opposition. My group was really meeting stumbling blocks. We were budgeted to make around $1,000,000 for our first full year of control, which would be a very good performance if we could make it. Well, let me tell you. There were five of us in this marketing group and we attacked this thing at the throat. We built up relations throughout the industry;

we made trades and exchanges and we marketed. I tell you, we really pitched in, and by the end of the first full year, we'd made $2,200,000!

Now after that performance, it seemed to me the next logical step was to form a chemicals division to pursue the opportunities available to us. I waited and I waited—and suddenly I realized it just wasn't going to be that way. Politics took over. It was, of course, partly me. I'm brash; I'm a pusher; I'm an organizer. I like action and I like to be where the action is, but there was a powerful executive upstairs who found me hard to swallow. So they were going to go slow. They were going to let me season. I can look over my whole career and I can see that the young smart-ass guy who left his first job because he couldn't take over was still there hidden under all that executive savvy. It was at this time a board member of one of the fine old companies who supplied our huge conglomerate with certain intricate equipment approached me. I'd been with our worldwide corporation now for 14 years, and I knew if I were patient and weathered the storms and moved at the pace they set there, I'd end up a vice president. But this was an enormous, complex company, it had a great reservoir of talent and this might take years. The years could be full of challenge, sure, but would I always be where the action is? Would I ever get to actually running the operations I wanted?

The offer of this much smaller supplier was very tempting. I would have large stock options. I would be running the place, actually running it as executive vp. I'd have part of the action. So after some long, serious thinking, I finally said yes. I knew if I stayed, I'd be in a personality conflict with one of the World-Wide Corporation's very powerful executives, that I'd suffer hostility, and that I'd have a pretty long wait. So I announced that I was taking the new offer.

So here I am—and I now know I made the right choice. I'm the operating head of this company. I'm in community work now—I guess I get that from my mother who did a lot of charitable work just to help people. I'm trying to help in the rehabilitation or to put it another way, in the saving of people who are coming out of prison. One of the big problems of people coming out of jail is that there're so many things stacked against them, they're pretty apt to be back in again shortly. When they come out they have no money, they have no job, and they have no position in society. They're given a suit of clothes and fifty bucks and told: "Go out and sin no more."

Well, I do have mixed feelings. I think most people who are in prision should be in prision, but there are some who are saveable and I think somebody should spend some time and effort helping them. Now also I am into one or two other commercial projects besides running this company, and these provide me with plenty of action. Basically, I guess I'm an entrepreneur. My goal? My goal's to be where the action is. I can't tell you really where I'll be ten years from now. I only know I don't need much sleep and I hope I'll be where there are interesting challenges. I love what I'm doing. I like to put projects on the road. I like to organize, to get things going. I love every minute of it. I can't wait to get in in the morning. . . .

*   *   *   *

After the hours of taping, we spent an evening at dinner with Anthony Rossi and his wife and a friend in their beautiful home overlooking the bay. We watched the sun set over the water and the distant lights of a bridge sparkle on in the dusk; a breathtaking view, one of the most beautiful in the country.

Anthony Rossi's wife is charming and seems to have adjusted to a life without children (their sons are all away at college or have married and left home) and often a life without Anthony himself, for he has always been a man on the go. He has other business interests outside his main corporate job as an executive and he pursues them with the same excitement and pleasure. He needs only three or four hours sleep at night, so he has time for all he wants to do. Here is a man not basically fitted to corporate life yet who finds pleasure and challenge in it. I remember the verve and laughter as he reminisced about the multibillion dollar company he left for his present corporation. "It isn't all beer and skittles," he was saying, "but there's plenty of challenge and fun!"

We move next to another man who had faced even heavier challenges and found them satisfying, good years with the bad, and who has finally thrown in his lot with the corporate life and is building his world around it. . . .

5

"I Had to Come up a Long Way Where Black Wasn't Beautiful. . . ."

A black executive tells how he made it

Joseph Hardy is well over six feet tall, handsome, self-assured, with an attractive agreeable smile and a powerful handshake. I had met him after speaking with a number of other younger black executives who were upwardly mobile within the corporate life style, but I knew immediately Joseph Hardy was the man we were looking for. He is a man of such obvious superiority in appearance, personality, intelligence and ability that it may be difficult to see how he could be representative of the dilemma of the black executive in a white world. Yet even though today the superior black executive has become a highly fashionable commodity, his very superiority, it seemed to me, highlighted the many subtle aspects of this dilemma.

If one is poor, underprivileged, uneducated and from a bad environment, being black in a white world is just one more among several desperate handicaps. If one is superior, handsome, able, determined, highly intelligent and aware, the dilemma of being black in a white dominated culture begins to reveal itself in less obvious, unexpected and insidious ways. Joseph Hardy's story shows what these experiences were in the later half of the twentieth century.

In the middle of the battle, you can't suddenly wonder; you have to know where you're going. I'm a very valuable commodity. So my story, I guess, is the story of making it in the corporate world—not just making it as a Black but making it as an executive; going where I want to go, and in the process getting to know who I am and where I'm at. . . . Let me start by saying that I have learned to rely on myself, I do know who I am and I do know where I'm going. All this was bought and paid for, and sometimes the price was high. I'll try to go back to the beginning and show you what I mean.

I was born down south in Georgia, one of five children, the second child and oldest son. My father was one of many kids. He was born in South Carolina in 1906. His stepfather made him an offer when he was in junior high: either go to work or get out. My father didn't go to work in the fields; he got out. His desire at the time was to be a Pullman porter, which was a pretty big step in those days. That was all there was. So there were two female teachers who lived together and allowed my father to live with them. He shined shoes, waited on tables, did odd jobs, did a little bit of everything that was necessary.

I believe he even boxed a little. I heard him tell how if he was able to shine someone's shoes he could buy some peanut butter and crackers; if he didn't he didn't eat. He was eating out of tin cans. He had a pretty rough time. So I had to really admire him, because it was his determination to make something out of himself that got him to what he achieved.

So with these odd jobs my dad got through high school and these teachers he was living with insisted that he not at that time become a Pullman porter but that he should go on to college. He got into a black college and got a degree in engineering. He then went on to get his masters in engineering at the University of Indiana. There is another stop there—I'm not exactly sure—when he went to theological school and became an ordained Presbyterian minister.

There're certain ways you have to behave in order to achieve what's due you, what's fair. Sometimes you have to get it the hard way. I remember looking at pictures in *Life* in the 1940s and 1950s and seeing Blacks chained to a tree. When I was in the service in 1965 outside of Fort Bragg, North Carolina, I'll never forget the tremendous billboard that showed a Ku Klux Klanner on a horse and said "This is Klan Country." Now that's in the 60s in 1965. I remember an incident at a gas station and restaurant in Georgia. My wife was with me and she wanted to go to the restroom, but they didn't allow Blacks in the restrooms at that place. I had my officer's uniform on. I knew I was going to Vietnam but I couldn't accept that contradiction. She couldn't pee when she wanted to pee, and yet I was about to go overseas to fight for this country. So I said I have to take care of this problem first and if that's the way it was going to be, that's the way it was going to be. My wife, by the way, decided she didn't have to go to the bathroom as badly as she thought, but I told her: "You go pee!" My wife doesn't ordinarily take orders from me—she'll tell me what I can do with myself, but something in my tone of voice frightened her and made her decide she better go in the restaurant.

Then at the gas station two of the men were standing there, ugly looking customers. Well, I reached in the back seat and took out my twelve-gauge shot gun and just sat there while she went to the bathroom. Then she came out. I looked at them. They looked at me. The guy finished putting gas in the car and we left. Yes, there has been change. I'm sure that wouldn't happen today, and the rate of change is improving rapidly. But now I think we are in the most difficult stages of the change—we are dealing with change in areas that are extremely sophisticated, where very slight handicaps now affect whole careers. . . .

But to come back to my dad, even though he was the greatest influence on me as a child, he is one of the most strong-minded, stubborn and—I guess the word I want is inflexible—men I've ever known. He's strong-minded, which is great, but he's inflexible, which is bad. I think the environment has taught my Dad to be absolutely determined, if he hoped to succeed.

There are numerous lessons that I learned from him. I can also say that he is probably the most intelligent man I have ever met. He uses words on me even today that God only knows what they mean—just pure brilliance. I don't consider myself particularly bright, certainly not brilliant. There are mules in this world and there are geniuses. I'm not a genius. I'm a mule. A genius can do in one hour what it takes me two. I just have the determination to put in the two hours.

My mother was a school teacher and a beauty. She was born in Virginia, has blue eyes and very light skin, what they used to call in those days "high yeller girls." I have seen her picture when she was young and I mean to tell you if my father didn't have her, I would have liked to have her for myself. She was raised by my uncle who died fifteen years ago at the age of one hundred and thirteen years! He had been a Pullman Car porter, which was the elite job in those days.

But the fact was my father, my brothers and sister and I had to come up a long way where black wasn't beautiful and it's done something to all of us. I see a lot of my father in my sister. My sister is determined as hell in the same way I am determined as hell. It's like that situation in Georgia. In fact, there is no doubt in my mind that all of this came from my dad. I remember when he went to Pittsburgh he put the old shot gun in the back seat, because under no circumstances was anyone going to get at his family.

But we all had to prove ourselves. When I was only a small kid and we were moving around so much I was always a new boy in the neighborhood, and I was always picking myself up off the ground in those days and starting to fight from there. Then I started to get some size on me and I must say I was pretty well able to handle myself. In New York I got into a few situations with six or seven at a time—it got pretty rough. So I guess you could call me a bad-ass boy scout, because with it all I had pretty good manners. I acted like a gentleman. I wouldn't back off of a fight, but I was courteous in those days. My wife tells me she wishes I was the same man now as when I married her; she says I'm not so much of a gentleman as I used to be. Back in those days, I didn't use profanity; I didn't smoke; I didn't drink; I didn't do anything. I was a good, clean-cut fellow, but I knew how to fight, and I learned never to run away.

I guess it was an incident in Cincinnati that first brought this home to me. There were nine or ten of them and they had a baseball bat. I guess I was a new kid or I'd done something they didn't like, and they chased me home. I got in the house and my father looked at me and he said: "You ran." I'll never forget that, because that was the last time. I've never run since.

In the service in other situations I found myself volunteering or assuming my position because of that type of image of what a man was. I remember one situation where the commanding officer of the base camp said everyone would go out on patrol, and I had the option as commander of a platoon the size of an infantry company of letting the jr. lieutenant lead on patrol my men who had never been in combat. But I couldn't have faced myself in the mirror if I had, so I said: "no, if my men have to go, then I have to take them." So I think it flashes back, remember, when the ten guys . . . and I ran. But you can't run.

You learn about prejudice, about discrimination early, of course. You can face up to the obvious ones like that time in Georgia and the things you read about where they cry out at you and at any human being, but how do you handle the subtler ones. For instance, when I was growing up, I had this friend, a white boy named Johnny Binns, and he'd come to my house a number of times. We'd always accepted him and I'd treated him as my buddy and taken him to my room. So one day I went over to his house. His mother had me wait in the basement. I was very disillusioned. I guess I was in the fifth grade then, the cowboy and Indians stage.

Now my father didn't want me to leave home. He wanted me to go to college nearby—to the city college. It was about this time that I met my future wife at the high school. One of the guys made a bet that he could get a date with this girl, before I. Challenge. Well now, she hadn't been friendly enough even to give me her name. So I remember one day I came by and her next door neighbor's little boy, who was about ten years old, was sitting on the stoop. I said: "Iley, young feller, do you know what's-her-name, this girl next door, what's her name now?" He said: "Irene. "Yes, Irene," I said, "Thanks." I marched up to the door and knocked and said: "Hi, is Irene in?" Well, her cousin came up, and because I had stood up there and said "Is Irene in?" she just assumed I knew her. She said: "Sure, come on in. Have a seat." Irene walked into the living room and there I am sitting there. I said: "Hi, how are you?" Well, to make a long story short, she thought I was a big dummy.

Well it was important in those days that I was good with my dukes, because I had gotten in bad with one of the gangs. I was just in my first year of college in the city. We lived in a bourgeois black neighborhood. Jackie Robinson lived there. Here are two examples of what happened. I went to a waistline party. That's a party where you pay so much an inch around your waistline. It was for teenagers and held by an Episcopal Church in its basement. My wife's father was chaperoning it. He was a policeman, a detective. I was standing around and a guy named Willie, from a gang called the Hollis Bishops came over and stepped on my foot and said: "Hey, you got the bottom of my shoe dirty. You better apologize." I said: "You can go to hell," and a few other things too.

So we sat down, and about fifteen guys came around the table. Well, my father-in-law came over and forced me to get into the car and go home. I was really mad. These kids had knives, but I was still mad as hell. So the next day, I was walking down the street with two buddies. We were going to play cards—a simplified version of bridge—good boys' stuff, and who do I see but Willie and a few of his buddies from the gang leaning up against the car. So I walk in front, casually, and right in the middle of them, I stopped, leaned over and grabbed Willie and smacked him left and right. I was fast. Then I told him if he ever embarrassed me again, I'd kill him. I said: "I know where you live. You get me, you kill me, because I'll be sitting on your doorstep." Crazy. Totally crazy.

Anyhow, we continued, played cards and later we were coming down this main drag—one guy on a ten-speed bicycle of which he was very proud—when we look up and see about twenty guys there. We turn off the main drag and start to run, but there we are facing another bunch of guys. So we're surrounded, and the cry goes up: "Burn the bastards!" which means shoot them. Then the zip guns started to go off, bang, bang, bang. Well, we're not a gang—OK? They're a gang. The guy on the bike was so scared he ran right into one guy with a zip gun and almost broke his arm, and I never saw so many back yards and fences. But when I got home I was in a cold fury. I thought it was time to go deer hunting. I ran upstairs, went to the closet, got my deer rifle, loaded it and when I got down, who was standing by the door but my father. He took the gun away from me.

Well, that kept me out of trouble. About a week later, Saturday, my parents had gone out to the store and about seven I hear a knock on the front door. I got my deer rifle. I loaded it. Did you ever see a deer rifle? Well, there's a lever action. It has seven shots. I'm not cold-blooded like that, though. If I were at war then I don't consider it killing. It's a job. But I just stepped down the front step and I ejected about three shells. Did you ever see high jumpers? Well, these kids didn't open the gate. They leaped over the fence at one time, all in unison. . . . So that's the type of era in which I grew up. You could get killed or worse, you could kill somebody else. I was lucky.

So I was starting off at city college. I didn't want to be there. I wanted to be away from home, because Dad still regulated my activities. I really didn't do a lot of work, but I was getting an education, the education I wanted and thought I needed. I joined a fraternity. I learned to drink; I learned to rap; I learned to jive with the girls. So while I had marginal grades at school, I passed the course of life. But my father was upset; he was disgusted with me. I wanted to get away, and I was fighting with my father, fighting physically. My father weighs 240, 250 pounds. Well, one day, my Mam had asked me to do something. I had refused and I guess my dad felt I was getting too sassy. My father came up to me—he'd never raised his hand to me before—and suddenly he swung. Well I was so surprised and shocked I had a motor reflex—you remember I was used to counterpunching. I instinctively blocked his punch and before I realized what had happened, had jabbed and then came across with my right. I knocked him over a chair and broke his leg.

I'd never raised my hand to my parents before and here I had really hurt my dad. I was really shook, and I was concerned with what he would do to me. Well one night I came home late and I'd been drinking a lot. My father and brother were laying for me. My father's got a baseball bat and he goes after me and they give me a beating. So that was it. I told my father: "I'm leaving here." He said: "Well, look, it's kind of late for you to get into any other college, but I have a friend who's now head of a university and I'll call him up." So I was at last on my own.

So the first year at that college I said: "OK, I'll be a good boy now. I got what I wanted—great." The second year, though, I started to get bored again. I was known as a pretty smart sort of fellow. I did my work. I was interested but I wasn't really challenged, and now I worked out a sort of a balance in life to get fairly good grades while on the other hand starting to enjoy life a little bit again. After all, there was no point in being dull about it. So I managed somehow to work part time, to get myself a little piece of a car, a house off campus, and all the things I hadn't done before, I got out of my system. So I not only understood life but, man, there wasn't anything you could think of to do I hadn't done, some of which I'm not too proud of. Let me say this—and please excuse my frankness but you wanted me to be honest—if it had a skirt on, I tried to make it. I went through the students and the faculty and the school's secretary. I got it out of my system. To a point, though, because in my senior year, I had some close shaves and I sweated out a few situations. In those days I also ran thunder road. I used to get moonshine, gallons of it. Once in awhile the dean would stop by my room. He'd never ask any questions and he always got a drink. I learned to deal with the faculty too, and campus cops—sure—they'd all got a drink.

I graduated and I was ready to get married. One thing I didn't put into perspective, though: my wife—I call her a Black Jewish Princess—really is a fine person, a fine girl. She balances me out. She's a lady. I had seen a lot of girls, for one thing, when I was in college as an undergraduate and I was tired of playing the male-female game—trying to do this with her or that with her to get even, or maybe using her or being manipulated or trying to manipulate. I was turned off by not being able to be honest. When you were honest, you were exposed, you were vulnerable, and you could get hurt. So you became cruel; you played the players. The girl who became my wife was different. She was honest. I didn't have to worry about lying or cheating.

I want to say something about Blacks that I found when I first went into this tough, white, corporate world. There weren't many, but they were as bad as the Whites who were threatened by a Black man's rise. Sure, there's no problem when Blacks have these unimportant, low-pressure jobs, but all of a sudden you see a Black in a job that's on the same level as your own and what does that do to your self-confidence, your self-image, your ego? I've seen white guys go into a frenzy over this and frankly I can understand it, and it has to be dealt with. I think you are beginning to find this thing less and less and not with the really big man. I find there's a difference between the middle manager, the bastards in the middle, and the president, for instance. The president has no problem, but I haven't met many Blacks there who've put this thing into perspective either.

Here I'm talking about vanguard Blacks going through the corporate world now. Now there're a hell of a lot of slots; there's a hell of a lot of underrepresentation within the ranks of the corporate structure. When you have Blacks in the bottom of middle management, why in hell should they be trying to destroy each other. It's unnecessary; it's a waste. There's room enough for all.

In the high technology company I work for now, which used to be lily white, there're seven levels of management to the top. Though it's high technology, complex equipment with outstanding service engineering, it's really a marketing company famous for its clean-cut, high-powered sales engineers, and it has complete dominance in its field. When it decided to hire Blacks, it went all out and it got a fair number of us in administration and marketing, but to survive here we had to be competitive. But I'm getting out of synch. Let's go back to 1964, the year I was going to graduate from college. We can come back to this later.

As I mentioned, ours was an all-Black college and I'm sure when I graduated I regretted that I didn't go to Princeton or Yale or some other big league school. I somehow felt a little inadequate—not personally inadequate, because I could do the job on an intellectual basis. But somehow I felt I was looked down upon as coming from an inferior school. Later going to business school took care of that. But that year, 1964, was a big year for me. First of all, I didn't know what I wanted to do. I didn't know whether I wanted to be a college professor or go on and be some kind of engineer, since my major was math and physics. I was also a gung-ho kind of guy, as you've probably gathered, and I used to lead a special group of ROTC around in the morning doing exercises and running. Neither I nor anyone else in those days was against the Vietnam War, which had just started with people taking shots at our boats in the Gulf of Tonkin. I was designated as a distinguished military graduate and had a chance to receive a regular army commission equivalent to coming out of West Point. Those were my options.

But one day in April of that year I just happened to be going to the business office of my school—its placement office, in fact—to pick up a date. My date, Emily, happened to be there to be interviewed. The interviewer comes out and says: "Well, Emily's going to be here a little while. We're running behind schedule." So I'm sure my face reflected a look of annoyance and disappointment, and I'm sure it was not an ideal situation for an interview. But this man says: "By the way, are you a senior?" I said: "I'm a senior," and then he said: "If you had such-and-such a grade average, I'd have interviewed you." I answered: "I do have such-and-such a grade average." He said: "Have you ever considered working for this company—have you ever considered becoming an executive here?" I said: "Are you shitting me? Com on, fella, how many black executives do you have?" He answered: "None—that's why I'm here," and I said: "Bullshit."

But with a hurt look on his face he said: "Well, look, since you're going to be here anyhow (I didn't necessarily agree), why don't you take this little exam. Emily is going to take it." So I agreed to take the exam. But being the wise-ass and rebel that I was—there were three parts and there were 15 minutes allowed for each—I did the first part in about seven minutes, sat back, lit a cigarette and smiled at him across the table. He sat there and started to burn. He thought I wasn't very serious—which I wasn't—that I was really putting him on, yanking his chain. Well, the same scenario was repeated on the three parts of the exam. I got to the end and I'll never forget the look on his face as he reached into his pocket to whip out his red pencil and prepare to give this wise-ass what he had coming to him. He pulled out his marking easel, put it down on the exam and went down the first column. He found nothing wrong. He went down the second and he found nothing wrong, and then he got down the third ... To make a long story short, he found only one answer wrong, and his mouth drew open and he said: "Will you come to New York? Are you free?" Well, it was ironic, and to top it all, Emily flunked the test.

So I told the interviewer I'd have to check my schedule, because I just didn't believe there was a future in business. I didn't think business was sincere in that way. This was the time of Martin Luther King so I think there was starting to be some concern on the part of business. I think most large corporations, even this one that had been known for its clean-cut, Brooks Brothers-suited, lily white crews of men with their white shirts and black ties, were sending their recruiters out to do their thing for America, to hire the more intelligent Blacks, if you'll pardon the sarcasm.

But anyhow after playing games about the date, I decided I would go to their headquarters, because after all . . . a free plane ride and so on—well, why not? I got there and they took me on this tour to see what a representative, for example, did. The representative is the backbone of the company. He's a sort of sales engineer assigned to a territory who is in charge of one or more of the company's accounts, and except for top management and the "R & D" group, these men are the elite. Most of top management have come from the rep ranks. They take an intensive technical education and training course, go out into some territory and serve and develop one or more of the company's customer accounts, then, if they're good, move up to territory manager and finally to district director. From there after some service in administration or as head of a plant in manufacturing or head of an office, they may move into general management as an assistant vice president and eventually, if they're destined for the top, vice president and executive vice president heading one of the corporation's big areas throughout the world. In our tour besides the recruiter and the rep, we had a territory manager with us. They took me to a restaurant for lunch after the tour and we had a couple of martinis—as I say I was always able to hold my own and never turn down a drink. In the conversation we talked about the realities of careers, what a representative did, how great the job was and all the rest and then after these specific things were covered, there was a deathly silence around the table. I was uncomfortable. They didn't know what to say to me. Then one of the old geezers, a rep of about fifty, about to ride off into the sunset, says: "Say, Joe, why do you think it is that a lot of people don't like Jackie Robinson but everyone likes Roy Campanella?"

I said to myself: "Holy shit, here it comes. Here I am a college grad, coming up for a job and if I was white, if I was anyone else, they wouldn't ask me such an assinine question at a job interview. I debated whether I was going to be nice or nasty and I said: "Well, they're not really serious about this—it's just conversation. It's been a good lunch; they paid for the trip, but anyhow here goes." I turned to him and said: "You know, I'll tell you. Roy Campanella is one hell of a catcher but he's not much more than a catcher. But Jackie Robinson, he's something else. He could do your job in the territory and the district director's job and the division assistant vice president's job probably a hell of a lot better than any one of you could—therefore, he's a threat."

This old geezer's jaw dropped about six inches. The district director looked at me and he sort of dropped his head—he was one hell of a nice guy—and then he turned to the rep who had spoken and the look on his face said: "Well, you opened your big mouth and I guess you put your foot in it."

I realized, though, I'd been too candid. I realized I'd probably ruined it, because there are certain norms and certain kinds of behavior. You don't rock the boat, whether you're black or white. If you want to be a captain, you've got to live through being a lieutenant. If you want to be a major you've got to live through being a captain, and at our company at a certain level you've got to face up to this or else you'll have a great future behind you. I said to myself: "Well, it was a nice trip, but I guess it's the end."

So we finished the tour and went back to the recruiter's office and I was shocked as shit when he said to me: "Joe, what do you think? Would you accept a job with us?" I said: "Are you really serious?" He said: "Yes." I said: "Well, let me ask you something. Do you want me because of my ability or do you want me because I'm a Negro?" That's the term we used then. The change to Black took place about 1966-67. In those days, black was an insult. Black hadn't yet become beautiful. Well, I'd asked a very naive question—I'd never ask such a dumb question today—and there was only one way the guy could answer. He answered: "Joe, we want you because of your ability." What else.

I would have answered the same way. Then he made me a salary offer of $7,500.

That's how I got my job. I'd turned down my regular army commission and I'd turned down the chance to go to graduate school. This seemed to me a pretty good offer and I thought about it and I decided to take it. Those were the days when not many Blacks went into corporations or into business because they didn't believe there was a future for them there. Hell, you know there are some theories that Blacks are inferior mentally. Oh, maybe so. I don't know. I think it's academic, but Blacks are at least as smart as Mr. Skinner's pigeons. Mr. Skinner's pigeons were taught to peck for corn. When they pecked one button, they got corn. When they pecked another button, they didn't get corn. Well, I think Blacks had learned that pecking the corporate button wasn't going to get them any corn, so not many Blacks had gone into corporations.

But I started to work, then, in June of '64 as a managment trainee. It was supposed to be a fast track. You go through all the early steps, training, a development program, going out into the field and seeing what people actually do and actually doing it up to the first level management. Then you go through these steps for a year and a half to the second level management when you get to a point where you are very proficient, and then, based on performance and ability to achieve numerical objectives, you find yourself in the harbor of competition ready to be promoted to the district level.

So there I was, a trainee, one of the first black marketing trainees. There weren't many of us. In fact, I came to the company to process some papers and met a personnel man who told me there had been only two other Blacks before me, neither of whom made it. I asked: "Why didn't they make it?" and he said: "Well, one of them fooled with the girls and the other fooled with the money."

Then he went on to inspire me and tell me how rough it was going to be, that there were a lot of people who weren't going to like me. I later found he himself was one of the biggest bigots in the company. But he seemed very sincere, and finally I said: "I promise you one thing. I will not quit. You'll have to fire me."

I then went into training, and suddenly I was confronted with some big blanks in my experience of life. It was awkward. I wasn't used to that kind of world, to the sensitivity that was exhibited there by everyone. The black culture, the black norm is a lot looser. I wasn't like the bourgeois Blacks, the Jack-and-Jill Blacks, those who thought they were the up-and-ups and who lived in Georgetown. I came from a milieu that was basically black even though I had the benefits of a mother and father who had been educated and had the impetus from a white culture. But suddenly relative to Whites I was starting off with a big handicap—I didn't know the rules of the game; I didn't know how to weigh each word. I didn't have the sensitivity, the natural tact. I didn't sense things. I was uncomfortable. To make it worse, I was always the one singled out.

I'd be sitting in my group of 12 trainees and one of the vps of the company would come in and say: "Hi, fellows. . . ." He would go around and introduce himself and ask the fellows their names and he would say: "Hi, Joe, how are you? I've heard all about you." Well, you know it's a pretty natural thing for a top man to do that in this paternalistic company. "Hey, we got a Black! That's great! Let's go down and check him out;" like checking out the stud.

And there was another thing, any questions about Blacks were directed to me. Was Martin Luther King right? Was he wrong? What do Blacks think about this, about that? It's like saying: "Why all of you Blacks are alike—if one thinks it, they all think it." We are not really separate; we're not unique; we're not individuals. It's like saying you pick any white man like Barry Goldwater and say he's the same as Ted Kennedy, because after all they're both white, aren't they? It's very uncomfortable.

In training, first you take a formal technical course in the company's equipment. Then you take some courses in psychology, in communicating, and in dealing with people. You get some of the rough edges knocked off you. You're now going to start as a management trainee, an assistant to a rep, and when you've served a few months you're ready to become a rep yourself and be assigned to a territory. Or you can go into maintenance or billings and claims or onto the manager's staff in one of the plants or warehouses or to any one of the far-flung worldwide offices because our foreign business—pardon me, our international business—had become just as important as our domestic business, as far as the company's profits were concerned. But the way to go up fastest was to become a rep, developing and serving one or more of the company's accounts. You had to have been out in the field if you were ever to get any place in the company.

Being a rep's assistant is a real training job—very lengthy, very demanding, very tedious, and very specific, due to the nature of the standards we're measured against. You can't beat them. They take random samples. They list them on customers' contracts, and if you say you were going to do something by such-and-such a date, first of all you have to meet that date; then your two-day commitments, your three-day commitments—it's all so specific. Well, it's got to be done—no if, ands or buts. If it's not done, it's an error. In a statistical sample basis you don't have any leeway. Either you did or you didn't do it. It's all right there.

So I learned the routines and that was no tremendous thrill; all the administrative work, the billing and collections, and then I went out under an experienced representative to his accounts. I finally finished the apprenticeship and did OK. But the appraisals—yes, the appraisals. I got one of those that said: "Joe did this, *but* . . . , the "OK, but" type of appraisal. Well, to make a long story short, I struggled along as a management trainee and kept getting my ass chewed. My rep supervisor kept telling me to tie my necktie tighter and to tie it to the right and to tie it to the left, and he'd say "Jump!" and I'd say, "How high?" But I wasn't going to quit.

Well, you can imagine this was hard on my wife. I was getting very hard to get along with. I remember my boss's boss taking me out to lunch and saying to me: "Hey, I'm glad you're trying very hard, Joe, but why do I have so many problems with you that I don't have with the average trainee?" How could I answer? The kind of thing I was getting was too subtle; you could never explain it so you sounded rational. But the fact was I exceeded all my standards, all my requirements, and the time came when under my ROTC contract I had to go into the service. So I went in to see my boss, and now it was all different. My boss told me: "Joe, you've done a tremendous job; you've exceeded all your standards. I want you to write your own appraisal and I'll sign it."

Now it's Christmas and I was in New York after going through basic training. I decided to stop by at the swanky office headquarters of the company and see the personnel guy I had once promised I'd never quit. I was now an officer and in uniform. Well, I stopped by his office and I thought he'd be glad to see me. I thought he'd say: "I was wrong about you, Joe. I saw that appraisal: what a fine job you did!" Not at all. He greeted me rather cooly. I said: "Did you see the appraisal of me?" He answered: "Yes." I asked: "Could I see it?" He said: "Sure." He showed it to me. It was bad, very bad. I said: "This isn't the appraisal they told me I'd get. They said I'd exceeded all my standards. They said I'd done a fine job. I don't understand it. I wrote my appraisal and this isn't it."

Well, I was upset. I was pissed off. I went to see my old manager. It's Christmas Eve and the manager was standing there in a Santa Claus suit. So that was not a good time obviously to tell him how I felt. Anyhow he changed his clothes and offered to buy me a drink. But I decided: "Hell, I'll let it go." I'd received the lowest rating you can get without being actually fired. I couldn't see how it happened when they'd told me I'd done a fine job and exceeded all the standards.

That spring I was stationed in Arizona, and I was bored. My wife and I were together. We had had, by the way, our newlywed-type of disagreements. I also started to run into conflicts from working very hard, very late and being so tense. But the conflicts in my marriage weren't too serious.

Anyhow I felt that if I were to be in the service I wanted to be doing something significant, not just wasting my time. I had a platoon down in Arizona that had out-dated equipment. We would travel down into Mexico once in awhile and I had to go hunting down there. Oh, that was beautiful! But if I had to take two years out of my life, I wanted to do something with them that I felt was important. So in March, 1966 I was assigned to a company going overseas.

We flew overseas, landed and I guess I had been with the outfit about ten days when the first platoon was supposed to be deployed. I wasn't familiar with that particular kind of artillery, but the company commander, although I was the newest lieutenant, decided to assign me to the first platoon; quite a compliment, really. I was going to take the first platoon out and join with the first infantry division to provide support.

We were going to provide signal support out of the base camp while elements of the platoon would provide forward artillery support as needed back to head-quarters. We had been building sandbags, putting up tents and a lot of other stuff. I was down at the officers' mess tent one night, not paying a hell of a lot of attention, when suddenly we heard an outbreak of shooting damn close—an attack. Everybody leaped and grabbed their weapons. Mine wasn't exactly Army issue—it's funny but I used to carry a six-inch barrel 35 magnum under my armpit. I guess that's part of my male image or maybe a phallic symbol—I don't know.

I ran down the dirt road. My platoon was located about 400 yards from where we were—some 200 yards to a corner and about 200 yards to the platoon. I ran the first 200 yards to the corner and then I could see down the road that my platoon was in the area being hit. I'll never forget that sensation as I turned the corner. It was: "Holy shit, I don't want to go down there!" You could see the explosions and the shrapnel blowing through the tents; you could see the fireballs as the shells were exploding. My troops were running all over the damn place, total chaos. It was the first time they had been under fire, and I was scared shitless. I turned my corner and I didn't break stride, but between lifting one leg and putting the other down, it was like an eternity. A thought went through my mind: "What the hell am I going down there for?" It was like a conversation within me: "Well, that's why you have a bar on your shoulder. . ." I remember leaving Mam and Dad and my wife's mother and her father and my wife at the airport. It was funny. I went to kiss my wife good-bye. She started crying. So I moved on. I went to kiss my mother. She started crying. I went to kiss my mother-in-law. She started crying. It was getting messy. I shook hands with my father-in-law and my father, who said something to the effect of: "Be a good officer. Do what you have to do but don't be a fool." I said: "Don't worry about it. I'll do exactly that." In essence I guess it was: "If I can't come back with pride, don't come back."

So I ran to this corner and I said: "You can get hurt down there." I answered: "Yes, that's why you got to go on. Well, you got a wife. Yeah but you got in-surance. But you got a job to do. Well what about the guys down there? I don't want to go down there. Then you get right down. . . Yeah, but what about your pride and your self-respect?" I guess the conclusion was: "What the hell, here we go." My platoon sergeant had his shoulder blown off. He was a young guy, and here he was on his knees and with his right hand he was trying to direct the troops. There were others who were lying around—hurt in various degrees, and some dead. I was practically shaking in my boots, but I took over and started to give orders: "You do such and such. Get the sergeant under cover, blah. . . blah. . . blah. . . Get it done."

It was almost night when the evac choppers came in. We had a couple of dead, a few wounded—maybe seven or eight casualties altogether. One guy I remem-ber who came from Massachusetts, an only son, and his wife and he had a little boy, six weeks old, an only son also. I had seen his mother and father, his wife and his son when they came to say goodbye, lingering around that day, shaking hands. They had to pick up his guts now and put him in a green bag. Then finally after everything had calmed down, I called the company commander. Being in the signal corps, I had very businesslike ways of communicating; so many casualties and so forth. I told him I was turning the platoon over to the next ranking person, by this time an NCO, and was going to accompany my sergeant in an evac chopper. The other guys weren't hurt so seriously, puncture wounds and things like that. But this guy's shoulder was open—it was just blown off—and I was sick, I was sick.

It's not like in the movies where a guy gets shot. There's guts and gore all over the place. It was my first time under fire, and if you ever see shells hitting around you, I'll tell you it's upsetting. In the movies you see them bursting and that's it. But you see jagged pieces of steel, ten or fifteen ounces, go flying through, and that's reality, but you don't understand that until you get into it. It's ugly, it's dirty, it's disgusting, and these are young troops.

That night at the evac hospital, the company commander, the sergeant and I were all there because we were the first platoon to be deployed. We were upset, so after leaving the hospital, I went back to the company headquarters that night, and tried to get bombed. I drank and I drank and I drank—gin and tonic, gin and tonic—but I could not get drunk. The next morning—I had sat there all night—I was sober as a judge. So I said: "What the hell, it's time to get back to work," so I took another chopper back. I was nervous and upset and all the rest of it, and my platoon needed direction. I had lost my platoon sergeant, so I vacillated between being a platoon leader and a commanding officer since we were detached from the company. I did such things as direct the work on the sandbags and so forth. They were going too slowly—the troops were shook and they were not reacting properly—so I would get in the middle of a sandbag line and double the pace. It was an open challenge—you follow me; I'm doing it; you get it done. This was my style—challenging to a point. By the way, I would even accept a challenge from the NCOs for a little boxing match. I was known also as an arm wrestler and I'd challenge any NCO or any officer for that matter to try to put me down.

There is one thing I left out and I think perhaps it had something to do with my assignment there. I had been in the country a couple of days when we landed at what was to become the biggest supply base in Vietnam before the war was over. At that time there was nothing there but a little piece of barbed wire and a couple of command tents behind it. We had to set up in tents on ground that had to be cleared of shell casings, and out beyond it was the jungle. They had the barbed wire, the searchlights and the machine guns behind us. I was real jumpy thinking something would start and there we were between the shooters and the shootees.

One night we had gone down to Saigon when a series of three warnings went off. There were three mortar shells and boy we really moved out in that jeep. Coming back that night we were really moving, especially after what had happened coming in, and this flat-bed trailer backed across the road—the worst driver I ever saw. Our driver down-shifted, hit the brake, cut the steering wheel to the left and we went flying off into the air. I was sitting in the shotgun seat next to the driver where there's a metal windshield coming over. The jeep wound up turned over. I was trapped underneath. My foot was pinned by the jeep. I felt fine. "I'm in one piece," that was the first thought. The second thought was to reach for my rifle. Then I saw gasoline. The gas tank was dripping. Two lieutenants, who had been riding in the back with us, were seriously hurt. They'd been thrown out. One of them had his pelvis broken. Both had to be evacuated stateside. I was very lucky. There has to be a God up there Who says when. I got a big scar on the side of my face, but the top of that jeep was sheered off and my seat was twisted around backward. When that windshield came over, it seemed to me I should have been decapitated. Don't ask me how I survived. I don't know. Anyhow I found myself pinned there and my first words were: "Is there anyone around?" I heard an American voice, and my next words were: "Well, get this fucking jeep off me." I took charge of getting the guys to the hospital and that may have been what got me my assignment to the first platoon—I don't know.

Shortly thereafter, the colonel called me back and for the last half of my tour he had me put in charge of all circuits from the big camp south to the Delta. My job was to make sure the circuits were working, that the messages got through somehow. It was a compliment but it wasn't my kind of assignment. I liked much better getting into a chopper to go over the countryside—crazy things like that. Absolutely crazy. So one thing Vietnam did for me: it made me tough. It reinforced my need, my ability to accept a challenge, to accept any challenge no matter how tough or dirty it was. Of course, after seeing Vietnam, Japan and Thailand, I knew a little more about people and life in general.

I came back from the service and went back to the corporation to work. I found out in later years that the company didn't expect me to come back. Before I'd read the new appraisal, I'd thought I'd done a tremendous job, but in later years I found they really thought they were rid of me. I was on a new assignment with a representative in a territory in the city. This continued six weeks just to get me broken in again, and there were no problems whatever. So I was promoted to representative and assigned to a very difficult territory. It was rough. I went to meet my new boss, the territory manager. I was now the equivalent of the guy who had given me that bad appraisal after telling me how great I was. I said: "I'm Joe Hardy. Hi—I'm very pleased to meet you."

He was a heavy set man, cordial but very cool. He sat me down and said: "Now, Joe, I think you are going to fall flat on your face. It's my job, when you do, I take my foot and kick it so far up your ass, they'll have to take us both to the hospital to get it out."

I couldn't believe this. First of all, this is supposed to be a high class company and this guy, while middle-aged, was clean-cut. Now my nature is that when you give me a physical challenge like that—after all I'm six foot five and weight 240 pounds—I'm going to stand up and say: "You're not man enough to do it!" But anyhow I bit my tongue and I just said: "Sure." I was shocked. I couldn't believe I was getting this kind of greeting from a man I'd never met before in my life. Then it started to dawn on me—I had seen the bad appraisal. I was starting off with two strikes against me.

This guy had a new boss who had come in about the time I did. This territory was not doing well—it had problems with accounts where collections were going to hell. Company standards were not being met anywhere. I came up with plans and I was going to do my thing with my accounts. I had a certain approach I'd been trained in, and I asked our territory manager if he had any objections if I used my approach on these accounts. There were no objections, I could run my accounts the way I wanted to.

I went around to each customer's offices and worked out new schedules, new service routines, new billings, everything. I got to know the men in charge and to study what they were using our stuff for, what they needed and I showed some of them how they could do what they wanted to do more economically, faster or better. I gave it a lot of time and effort. I got our guys going on these problems and in a few months they were really operating.

Then my manager's new boss came down. He started to review the accounts and he found my new approach had really taken hold, that it incorporated the best elements of the approach used in other territories and was like the operating systems used in the district he had come from. So he said to my boss. "I want complete reorganization of our accounts here. I want you to use the approach Hardy's instituted in his accounts. We've got to get some service here. We've got to tighten up."

So through no fault of my own, I found myself in a squeeze between my boss and his boss. There was resentment and I was persona non grata again because of this. It was very tense, but a few months later a young up-coming star was put in charge of our territory. He replaced my boss who had been relieved because he hadn't initiated my approach and our accounts were not picking up fast enough. After we had talked the new manager said: "Joe, I'm going to work with you. I'm going to see if we can't make it here. I've just been shown your new appraisal but don't worry about it. Do you want to look at it?" That appraisal told me everything. Every time anyone had said anything about me, my impatience, my driving to get things done, my former boss had collected the remarks and put them down. It was murder!

After about three weeks, my new boss called me in. He's very glib, a very personable man. I'd learned a lot of that from him. "Well," he said, "Joe, I hear you're working hard. Your accounts are getting squared away and I sure hope you make it. But tell me this, if you don't make it, what are you going to do?" It was like the stroke of eleven on my clock of life. I sat there. I looked at him. I started to twist my tie right and left—it was the first time I had really let myself go. I said: "Why the hell do you care?" and he said: "I care." I said: "It's not your job to care. Your job is to look at my results, my performance on a very objective basis." He answered: "Well, I care." I said: "Well, since you've asked, I'll tell you, but I don't think it's any of your business. I've got a mortgage, a wife and responsibilities." He said: "Obviously you have a problem." I said: "That's my problem, not your problem. You evaluate it the way you see it. You call it. And when you've made your decision, I'll make mine." There was no smile on my face and my voice was hard. I got up and walked out.

Well, let me tell you, we continued to volley back and forth, but in a working sense. I wasn't doing the things exactly the way he wanted me to do them. But finally about a month later, he said: "Joe, I think you're going to make it." I liked that guy. He had changed that appraisal to satisfactory; not really a great appraisal, but satisfactory.

I was gradually picking my pace up, till it came to the point where one day he said: "Hey, Joe, I've looked at this and this and I think this account is going to be a problem. So why don't you do such-and-such?" and I'd reach behind my back and give him a report on it. He was shocked. He sort of smiled, sat down in his chair, and reads: "This is what is going to be done by such-and-such a person and we are going to do such-and-such . . ." and then he's almost to the end of it and he's got this very contagious laugh. I said: "What the hell is wrong with you?" and he said: "Jesus, I've created a Frankenstein. I hope like hell I can control it!"

Our relationship became one of mutual respect, because it got to a point where I could anticipate. He would say two words, and I would know what he was thinking, and I would give him a two-word response. We would have a thirty-minute conversation in less than two minutes. I got a feel for where he wanted to be and I did what I could to keep him there; to a point where he never even looked at the territory I was responsible for, because he knew I had it organized and operating. That was the greatest time I had at the company. There were three men besides me who got top-rated. Then he moved in two other top-rated guys, so now we are sort of all in competition. Let me tell you, it was vicious.

In those days we started to develop a real dinner gang, sort of like in college but with the difference that this is in business and all of us were friends because there was mutual respect. One of my philosophies is that you can get friends so long as you are all doing a job, but if someone is working for you and is not performing then the friendship ends. But this was great because it was sort of a dynamic tension situation. We all liked each other; we were all competing at the same time. In those days they coined such phrases as "a Hardy." A Hardy was being talked out of your socks without realizing it—like standing there and not knowing what's happened. You're supposed to get twenty dollars and you find you've got two dollars and you're standing there scratching your head—that's a Hardy. That's how we kidded each other. It was a compliment to be part of it all. This was a vintage year—we'd worked together for a year, and we were a great team. We had developed new accounts. We had built a great territory. We went out for lunch; we had a ball. We even got together at this guy's house in the evening, and I never laughed so hard in my life. My sides were literally aching. We had the wives there, and we had drinks, and it was one of the greatest evenings I ever had. It was quick, cutting remarks, joking back and forth, and it never ended. It was great.

I was promoted and made manager of another territory. I went in and gave it everything I had. I worked out a training program. I kept role-playing tapes. I pulled out everything I could think of. This territory was floundering and my approach pulled it all together. We went from one of the worst territories in the district to the number two spot, but once again I was in conflict with my district boss and once again things were getting very tight for me. I guess I was tactless but I was a guy who liked to get things done. Just as it was all coming to a crisis situation, my old boss, the one who'd sent me down there, was promoted to assistant vice president of a division. He sent for me and asked me to take over the worst territory in that division—a territory so bad it had become notorious all over the country.

While I was not particularly flattered at being sent there, I realized it had gotten me out of a bad spot and that I was starting to get a reputation at least by some people of being the man they sent for to clean up a mess. I went into this territory and it was like hitting the beach. Our deliveries were as much as a year behind schedule; we had all kinds of cancellations. Our equipment was breaking down and our customers were looking around for other suppliers. The first thing I needed was some guarantees of complete support not only from my district but from my division and area. I went up to my district director and we sat down for an hour of hard straight-from-the-shoulder talk. Then we both went to the division and back to my old boss and I got guarantees from them both on deliveries, service, everything.

I went out to reorganize and train, to see our reps and to go with them to every single customer. We worked out a Hardy schedule. This means study the customer's situation and do a real basic design of his needs. If he's got too much equipment or the wrong equipment, get it out of there even if we lose money on it. Get him what he really needs and see that we keep it up as his business grows or changes. Get ourselves on a sound basis with our customer. When he grows, we'll grow. Every representative had to have this approach. I'd learned something of team-building too. We had to get some morale going in our own ranks, and we started to do that by meeting and setting standards and giving responsibilities that had to be lived up to. We were beginning to learn the right operating procedures and get our paperwork and record flow in good order. We set standards, reinforced them, encouraged our people, and within a year this territory had begun to turn around.

At that time, the vice president who headed the whole area—I got this from the grapevine—looked over the records of his divisions and districts. He came to my territory, saw my appraisals and he said: "By God, that Joe Hardy may be a pain in the ass but he knows how to get things done." To me that was like walking on water—it was like that great vintage year I'd had when I was learning. It was good, it was fun, but it was such hard work you were consuming yourself with the intensity of it. We were working nights and weekends because I couldn't only give training then. I had to write the presentations and tape them. It was total involvement all over again. We were known as Hardy's Hellions and it was like the other managers' prides were pricked; the whole district began to pick up.

My district director, Art Gilmore, was ecstatic. He told me: "Joe, when you walked in that door the first time, sent down by our division boss, there were a lot of managers I would have preferred. But tough as you are I wouldn't take another manager over you now for anything in the world!" which was quite a compliment. When I left his assignment, he had put me up for promotion to the district level.

About the end of April, I had a call again from the assistant vp, Art Gilmore. He said: "Hey, Joe, would you like to compete to go to. . ." and he named a famous school of business administration. . . "on the company's new executive training program for higher management?" It was a two-year program leading to an MBA. I said: "Are you shitting me?" He said: "No, why don't you call so-and-so—I've recommended you." I had to take the entrance tests that go to all the schools, and I came up with a very decent score. It was right in the middle of the people who were being accepted. Even so I didn't think I had a snowball's chance in hell of being accepted. Well, as I said, I'm not a genius or a mule and I was competing against three or four others in the corporation in this program, another of them a black guy. Well, I made it and that fall I was accepted at the graduate school along with a couple of others. So then the company tried to decide which of us was going to go. I had been with the company longer and I guess that's the reason I was chosen.

So the day came I was to go to this graduate school. No one had been sent from our company before for the two-year course, so I had to make my own arrangements, get an apartment, and everything was very hectic. I was going without my wife because by the time I was told I was finally accepted, it was August and Irene was working. We didn't have an apartment up there; she didn't know anyone in that town. I thought maybe she could go to school there too if she couldn't get a job, but there was no chance for her to get in. There were a lot of graduates, women with Ph.D.s and masters, working while their husbands were in school and also those who were husband-hunting; lots of secretaries, very educated women, who were just waiting for the guys to come out of graduate school so they could snatch them up.

Now before we start at the business school, I flash back and just try to put in perspective the impact of all this on my wife, Irene. It was pretty rough. Obviously, I was ill at ease; I was tense; I was argumentative. I am by nature sometimes hard to get along with—I have some of my father's traits in keeping people at arm's length, depending on how I am approached. Unfortunately, from my point of view my mother-in-law is a very strong-minded woman, and like mother, like daughter. I had a great father-in-law but some of his best friends said that he'd given in too often and lost too many battles. So he would rather switch than fight, but I wasn't going to switch; I was going to fight.

So Irene and I were cutting from two totally opposite poles. I'm coming from a very masculine-oriented family and she is coming from a very feminine-oriented family—or if it wasn't completely female-oriented, it was more female oriented than mine, that's for damn sure. So I got to the point where I was working long hours in order to get ahead, while Irene was looking for me to be more like her dad in some ways. But in all fairness, I think it was very difficult for Irene, because while I can sacrifice myself or take years off my life with the tension, the frustration, the agony, the worry and the rest of it, I'm not so sure it's fair to expect that of a wife. But I don't know either how it's humanly possible not to reflect that. Obviously she had to suffer when I was working those long nights and long hours. Eight in the morning till eight or ten or eleven at night became routine. Now don't forget there was a time when I was away in Vietnam. Irene would have loved to have kids and at that time we didn't have any, so all in all she had to put up with a lot from me.

She didn't go with me to business school. She would come up weekends every other week and allow me to study, and that's one of the reasons I became a good scholar. I had full time to dedicate to it.

When I got to this fancy campus I was scared, because once I was accepted there I didn't dare flunk out. I'd have blown my career, everything. The other guys would go to class dressed informally; I went to class like I was going to work. I considered this an extension of the job. I had on my tie and shirt and all the rest of it—my attaché case. I had expense account privileges and I used them when necessary. I drove a large car and I didn't act poor. When I was challenged in class, I cut the nuts off the challenger. I played to win.

Some of the guys up there, both Blacks and Whites, resented me. The Blacks resented me because by the end of that first year I came out in the top 15 per cent and made honors. They have a joke up there: Black honors is an average grade. They grade you on a sliding scale. It's vying for scarce resources, so to speak. Only so many people can be in the top 15 per cent, the honors grade, or in the top five per cent, highest honors. They'd never had a Black as a top-honor scholar. I think two per cent of the entire class doesn't finish, but something like 20 to 30 per cent of Blacks flunked out. It says a lot about selection and preparation but it is also a reflection of the business world. . . . There's leeway for professors to give you grades. There's subjectivity that does enter into it. You know generally where you stand but sometimes there's a borderline decision that has to be made. I had to confront one professor while I was there. In essence, I had to challenge him in his grade. I had to fight for every point along the way.

When my grades came in, I talked to the company; I tried to keep in touch. They'd just got a new vice president in personnel. I called him and he said: "How's it going?" and I said: "It's the roughest thing I've ever done." He said: "Well, at least you didn't flunk out." My ego was really hurting then. I was indignant. Just because I'd said it was the roughest thing I'd ever done didn't mean I was going to flunk out of the damn thing. So I said: "No, as a matter of fact, I landed on the honor list," nice and subtle, you know—like an elephant. He said: "You did? Can you prove it?" So then I had to get the letter from the dean and I sent a copy to him. They were amazed. They acted as if they couldn't believe it.

Now the game had escalated a bit. My impression was that some people had intended to send a nice black boy to school, to give him some credentials so that he would be acceptable by the Whites who wouldn't like him. You've got to have a reason to move him ahead, you know. But they didn't expect that this black guy would try to come out with the brass ring. The second year, I was hell bent for leather. I had two objectives. One was to ace every course and the other was to know myself better when I came out of it. I had several courses in organizational design and organizational behavior, and those courses plus some interpersonal behavior courses started me to think about questions of control. The other course, the ultimate in behavioral science, made me think about some of the things I had done and put them in a different framework. That led to a crude effort to try to organize some of the factors in the environment that caused me to be what I was and to have the problems I had and to separate and examine myself as a Black and as a manager.

But then I was challenged to go for the best. They had never had a black honor scholar before and they haven't had any since. I was one of three people who aced every course they had that second year. I had thirteen courses; I got thirteen excellents.

When I got the official honors letter, I sent it back to the company. I understand it was acknowledged at the president's meeting with his top company officers.

Upon.my return to the company, I got the letter inviting me to consider being a White House Fellow. I gave it to my boss, and he in turn was told by his boss, the vice president, basically what the company's attitude was at that time: "Hey, get back in your place now! You've been away. Come back here, fellow. Don't let this go to your head! Don't get carried away with yourself. An honor scholar has to be forgotten once in awhile. You came here to do a job. We've heard enough about Joe Hardy for now. Shut up. Be quiet. Sit down."

Now I want to flash back for a minute to an interesting experience I had when they were trying to tame me in the company. I had just had a lousy appraisal and since I didn't seem to be getting along with people they decided to send me to a sensitivity training and awareness group. Now at that time, my receiver, as I call it, was telling me my boss was not too pleased with me. So I went to this five-day course and I knew I had to excel. By this time I was starting to be shaped by a hostile environment; I started to learn from being exposed to these corporate norms and these levels of sensitivity and awareness, which were beginning to be reflected in my behavior. I went into this group with a few other administrative and territory execs. I manipulated and maneuvered until at the end of the session they voted me the most outstanding contributor. In that T-group, you are not supposed to send back an appraisal, but damn if they didn't. I finally got unnaived there. I knew they weren't supposed to send back an appraisal but I also knew my bastard of a boss wouldn't have sent me there unless he would get some kind of report, which he figured would be a negative one. I asked him if he had received it when I got back and again a couple of weeks later, but the bastard had thrown it away because it had been so good.

In that T-group there was one very sharp participant who was the only one astute enough to figure out what the hell I was doing. It got to be a confrontation. This person was able to show the group and Joseph Hardy that he shouldn't manipulate and maneuver. On one part of the exercise on about the third day they asked for volunteers and observers, and this person volunteered to observe my group. When feedback was given, I was really reamed but after a lot of smoke and a little dust, I made it seem like the point had been missed. When I was nominated as the one who had contributed the most to this session, this person burst out, "But he hasn't been honest with any of you people this whole session!"

I pretended to be hurt and I said: "I don't see why you are so upset." The rest of the group then came to my defense. Now I'm saying to myself I have a hell of a mess on my hands. Of course, I didn't mean to hurt anyone or be dishonest. I was just trying to manipulate and maneuver this group to get a damned good appraisal, because I'm starting to suspect that my butt is on the line. So it was I who was being manipulated and maneuvered openly at the door and then starting to manipulate and maneuver in as ridiculous a place as a T-group.

I also set out to set the stage here at the graduate school, but I came close to getting into trouble that time. In other words, I was almost directing my whole being, my whole existence toward making good, toward showing what I could do. I was accepting the challenge I had made. On the whole, though, those two years were a good experience for me.

I finally came back to the company to another level as an assistant to my old boss and mentor, Art Gilmore, the assistant vp of a division. There was resentment toward me for being promoted to the regional manager level. My new boss and I knew each other well. We didn't have to develop trust and all the rest of it. He told me he expected basically to get all the territories on a level of performance of that of the best. I told him what I expected. I said: "I would like to get a region of my own." He said: "But you're a newly promoted guy. You're not proven." I said: "Do you want to give me a rating based on experience or on performance?" He agreed that if I did certain things, he would recommend me. We could be that candid. We knew each other and he had confidence in me.

I went out into the new job and it was as if my reputation had already gone before me. I was the hatchet man. Everyone expected the black wrath of God to fall upon their heads. They were sitting hunched over, afraid to stick their heads out. When I went in there, I recognized the tension right away. The managers were trying to be casual but I knew they were tense, and I debated which style would be best in this situation. I had determined while still at graduate school that I would go in there like any other person of my level and wouldn't make anything special of it. But then as I saw the tension continue to build that first week or so, I knew I was not going to be able to do that. I had to call it for what it was and bring it out in the open.

I had my first territory managers' meeting, which I had held off for a week and swore I wasn't going to call. There were four white guys, college graduates, one of whom I'd worked with briefly, another who had been in training with me, a third, an old-timer around 40 and a young fellow who had just graduated. I said: "Now look, if I were in your situation, working for the only black territory director who had just got out of business school, who is supposed to be a superstar and a hatchet man, I would have some serious questions in my mind. I will lay those to rest right now. We all put on our pants the same way. I expect the same thing of you that any boss would, and one of these things is honesty, because if you and I can't be honest with one another, then you and I will not be addressing the same problems and we are not going to be working toward the best interests of the territory. So I insist on that.

"Number two, I expect everyone to shape his part of the territory to maximum service. Some of you guys were with me in training, so you may resent the fact that I am here. But quite frankly, I'll take my record out and compare it with anyone of yours, territory for territory, assignment for assignment. If you can match me, perhaps you should be in this chair. Let's get that out of the way now. So this is no time to have hidden agendas and hidden resentments." I started very gradually to rule out the managers between me and them. It was a calculated sort of thing. After five months all the results were beginning to improve. I was monitoring and directing very closely. Then we got to a critical point: the rubber was starting to hit the road; serious problems were cropping up, and I then broke into my old style—and that was one-to-one with the representatives and going directly to customers in the territories. I called the representatives in and skipped the managers. I had the managers sit at the back and the supervisors up front in the meeting. And I ran the meeting from soup to nuts: Here is where our problem is; here is where we've got to go; here is why and all the rest of it. I am fairly articulate, flexible and fast on my feet. Some of the representatives were astounded that I could be so quick and analytical and "Hey he is a pretty smart guy!" So gradually I started to develop individual relationships with the representatives some of whom were never close and never would be close, but were as close as necessary to do the job. I never needed to be loved, just effective. But I was always fair. This is important.

Back when I was a territory manager, we had an opening for a woman office supervisor in our district. I had an Irish girl in my office working for me who was very well thought of and she was a candidate. One of my peers had a black girl working for him, on the same level; and she was his candidate. We were told to make recommendations for the promotion. Our regional director was going to be the judge and jury, so you have to make a convincing case for your girl. You have to go on stage, so to speak, and out-perform the other. So there's a white territory manager representing a black girl for the promotion and a black territory manager representing a white girl. As a person, as a Black, you want to see a Black get ahead you want to give them the benefit because there's been enough injustice; this country hasn't been fair. By the way, while we have a lot of problems, my philosophy is we have a lot less than other countries. But there are other principles involved. My responsibility is to the people who have done the job. This Irish girl had done the job and I felt she was more qualified. It would have been inconsistent for me as a person to say that I was going to reward someone who does a job for me and then, when this other manager has a black girl he is trying to get promoted, not support the person working for me whether she is black, white or polka dotted. Well, I pulled a Hardy and the Irish girl got the promotion. It put me in an interesting situation with my fellow Blacks as a traitor to my race.

In another incident, my boss had asked me to talk to a young Italian representative about his hair style. This was a young man working for me and my boss thought it would be more businesslike if he didn't have such long hair and did something about his choice of clothes. He didn't look like an executive. I pointed out that if all of us had to fall into a mold, my ass would be grass, because as a Black, there was no mold I was going to be consistent with and certainly didn't look like the other executives. He thought about that and he said: "I believe you're right." I said: "OK, so he looks Italian. Well, I got a problem because I look black, so if it's going to get down to a question of a guy getting ahead who looks more like his boss or like the corporate norm, I can't back that because I'd be cutting my own throat." That's the type of thing that came up from time to time.

I remember one other situation when a cop came into the office because we had a typewriter stolen. I was outside talking to one of the managers reporting to me and my regional secretary took the police officer in. He removed his crash helmet and, with his walkie-talkie blaring, walked into my inner office. He was sitting there while my secretary gave him the information when I walked in. He looked at me—this guy was about 22, 23 years old—and said: "Hello there, young fellow, how are you?" I didn't answer right away. I went around, sat down in my chair, looked at him and said: "It's very complimentary of you to call me young fellow—do I look that young? What information do you need of me?" I said: "Sue, would you take this gentleman outside, sit him by your desk and give him the information he needs. Give him the additional folders—I'm busy right now."

Somehow this cop had to assert his superiority over me, whether it was in age or whatever. I was obviously older than him. A regional director of a company of this size and importance, with four territory managers reporting to him, responsible for some 25 million dollars in accounts, does have a little authority, a little respect—he is an executive. I could not conceive any cop calling any regional director "young fellow" when the cop is 22 years old and obviously 10 years younger.

Here is another incident of what I call status shots. I got that young Italian representative a promotion to administration office manager. Hugh went with me to a business association meeting at which one of my former administration managers had been the official company delegate. Hugh was to be his replacement so it was only fitting that I go along the first time. We were talking to different groups as we were drinking. Finally, I was walking toward a group that Hugh was talking to and Hugh introduced me: "Hi, this is Joe Hardy—he and I work together." I was taken aback. I'd never heard anyone introduce his boss that way before. It made me mad. Later in the conversation I said: "Yes, you fellows all know Burns. Well, Hugh is the manager I'm having replace Burns here to represent the company." That put things into perspective, but I've never introduced a boss of mine by saying: "He works with me."

Those are the little things you take when you're black. You're often introduced by your subordinates only by your first name, when in our corporation a superior is usually introduced by "Mr." It's as if they're ashamed to be working under a Black. I can be a devil at times too with customers. I don't sound black over the phone—that's perhaps one of my assets. I've been told over the phone:

"The trouble with the goddam company now is you're getting in all these Blacks and Puerto Ricans—that's why we can't get deliveries on time." My response is: "Well, after all, sir, we are an equal opportunity employer." Or there's another game I play. I make an appointment with a customer and the representative of that territory goes out with me to the appointment. The representative is this white guy with this nice white shirt and dark tie, and invariably the customer goes up to him and says: "It's a pleasure to meet you, Mr. Hardy." The white guy must be the boss—the white guy is always the boss. Another thing is that I'm aggressive and people don't like that in a Black. In a White, it's called competitive and it's highly thought of; in a Black, you're a bad nigger, and even in the eyes of Blacks it doesn't go over too well. The aggressive or competitive Black is the guy I saw in chains in *Life* magazine back in the 1950s. The bad nigger is that lieutenant colonel who was killed coming back from the march on Washington. It's interesting that in a study Blacks ranked aggressiveness toward the bottom. It's a tremendous conflict because in Whites competitiveness is the key to getting ahead, and here we have Blacks looking down on the very quality they need to get ahead. But I say screw it all. I'm aggressive or competitive and if I'm acting out of context, that's the way it has to be, because I'm going to get ahead.

Now let me turn to something that about brought me down, that really about ended it all for me. I was now a territory director, as I told you, with these four white managers, two more added later on my staff and a really big territory. I had come to the period in my career where my boss had recommended that I be promoted into higher management but that first I take over a production operation or get broader administrative experience in other areas of the corporation. So I was poised and ready to get into the big time, when one of my managers, who I guess now must have resented me, asked that my territory director's expense and time code assigned to his group be transferred out of his territory and into another area which had taken over two of the big customers of that territory. My secretary, assuming this was standard operating procedure, proceeded to put through the transfer. That went right through to the assistant vp who headed up that division. He called my boss and asked what was going on; some of my expense records were being charged to his territories. My boss said: "I don't believe it. Why would he do that?"

He called me and I said: "Well, I don't know anything about it, but I'll check." So I called my secretary and she said: "Your territory manager, Jack Dale, of such and such a territory had given me certain information and said I was to transfer your expenses assigned to these customers to the new territory taking them over." So Joseph Hardy had nothing to do with it.

Then I called in Jack Dale and he says: "What's the big deal?" and I said: "Please explain this to Art Gilmore, our assistant vp heading the division, he's got a beef on it from another division, and it seems to me you might have consulted me on it. It looks as if I'm trying to lay off some of my expenses onto another division."

Well, would you believe it, Jack Dale implies to my boss that that's the way I wanted it. He tells me one thing and he's telling my boss another. So my boss says: "Well, Joe, let it drop." Well, that tore. I tried to get this manager to admit he'd done it without consulting me but he'd admit it only to me, not to my boss. So I felt helpless. I felt my honesty was in question and if someone can question your honesty, your character, your integrity, how can you address that? Once the question is raised, how can you ever remove the doubt? If there's one thing that can bring your career to an end in management, that's it.

Now from this and from the pressures of the job I felt I had come to the end of my line. I felt this was it and someone of all those who resented me would finally get me. That was in the summer and I got on a boat and went fishing and tried to think things over. I asked myself: "Hadn't I better give up these ten years of sweat and strain with the corporation and start over some place else?" This was my dark moment we've talked about—the dark moment that comes in everybody's life and this was mine. I felt my career was over. Well, to get back, I sat around trying to get up guts enough to quit and then I thought: No, this is where I want to make my life. The corporation is where I'm going to make it. And then it happened—the kind of thing you see in the movies, the Marines landing just in time. It happened to me.

This was now September and I was about ready to go in and say goodbye and then the phone rings and there's this voice on the phone. It's an executive vice president, a man named Bill Coburn, and he said: "I wonder whether you could have lunch with me, Joe?"

And that was it. When I arrived at the dining place, there were three of them, two other vps besides Bill Coburn. We sat down and after a little fencing around—they had a few questions they wanted to address about my work and my ambitions and then Bill Coburn said: "You know, Joe, you're really an interesting guy. Now we wanted to ask you something. Hal Bryer, our president, has been selected as chairman of a big fund raising association and this association has been working for some kind of environmental changes and their efforts haven't jelled, the whole thing isn't working. Now Hal Bryer wants to get it going, make it effective and we understand from your record you're a good organizer and know how to get things done, and we want to know if you'd consider going as Hal's assistant on this assignment for a year and whether you can't help him pull this together. It's not just a show case job; it's the hardest kind of work and will reflect on our president and the company.

I said: "Is it possible to effect any change with a program like that?" And Bill Coburn answered: "Well, Hal wouldn't have taken it on if he didn't think it could be done." So I said: "Well, then, I'll try it." And Bill added: "It'll be for about a year."

Now this was the first time I had had other than on-the-line kind of jobs. What they didn't tell me was that there was a promotion involved, the man who had been doing the job they were turning over to me having been at the assistant vice presidential level. OK, not knowing any of that, I agreed to take the job, and then a week later they told me there would be a promotion involved and I was going to be working directly for Mr. Bryer, our president.

Well, it's been one hell of a year and I'd not want to go through it again. But I got to know some top people, top people not just in my company but in a lot of major corporations all over the country and I learned a lot about setting things up and organizing and getting along with top personalities. Whether I did the job Mr. Bryer hoped I'd do I don't know but I think so.

So now the year is almost up and I'm ready to come back into the company, and the new challenges will be starting. I'm fairly senior now, and there are a lot of top brass who know me, know what I can do, and are for me—and not just because I'm black. On the other hand there are people who resent me for the same reasons. There're other Blacks in the company—one who didn't want to be associated with me until I began to go up. He didn't even want to be black until black got to be beautiful; then he became a professional black, because black was so beautiful and the in-thing. He got on the bandwagon and he made black too beautiful. Of course, in a way I understand this. Jealousy and intense ambition exist in all ethnic groups but it's more intense in Blacks, because they've achieved less; they've been less assimilated. Therefore it's more important to them to have the symbols, the trappings of what has been achieved. For example, it's interesting to see well-to-do guys in soiled sneakers down by the boats in summer; they look like old rummy Hardy, but you get a black guy on 121st street and did you ever see the fancy outfit on one of those hustlers?

Yes, this does exist strongly and more intensely among Blacks because there's one little problem we have: No matter how much you achieve in a white dominated world, no matter how far you go, when you walk in the door, the first impression still is: he's black. Was it Martin Luther King who said: "You can become a Ph.D.; you can become a Nobel Prize-winning scientist, you can be Ralph Bunch, but when you go through that door, the first thing they notice is: he's black. On the other hand you can be Irish or Jewish and yet when you go through the door the first impression they get of you is what you want them to have. So with Blacks, they all have to start out with an impression that's hard to undo, as opposed to the Irishman who often doesn't come off as Irish until they see the name O'Shaugnessy. . . .

Well, we have come a long way in a short period but there's still a long way to go, and you see, unlike the Irish, who after awhile sort of melted into the non-Irish world, until we actually get to the stage maybe 200 years or so from now, where we're all coffee-colored or mulatoes, I think we blacks are going to have that problem. But there's still hope for our kids, because I think that the beauty that came out of the sixties generation's questioning of statements and behavior by our institutions and individuals which had built-up conflicts and hypocracies will make our world better. Our older generations were being hypocritical. We were saying one thing and doing another. We talked about being honest as parents; we talked about peace, about not cheating on income tax, and that was accepted for years. Then students and kids started to challenge these things we were saying and not doing, things like this Nixon thing, and they are demanding a new morality, a new set of norms. So there is hope. . . .

Anyhow, here I am and my year is up. And I'm coming back into the company, and I'm coming in at a higher level. I'm known. I have great contacts. I've dealt with top executives of my own and other corporations. I've walked and talked and politicked with them. But most important of all, I've learned to know myself. I've learned how to live at a higher level and I expect to go on. I ask myself sometimes whether I am not paying too high a price for it, for the price in energy, in anxiety, in sweat in pressure is very very high. And perhaps the greatest price of all is the time I can't spend with my family and the tensions they are exposed to when I get home. I am trying to make adjustments in this area because in the final analysis my family is the most important thing that I have on earth. I am trying to make adjustments so that we can be a happy family but without abdicating my career opportunities.

Yet in spite of all these considerations, I'm with the corporation and this is where I want to be. I'm going to make the try. I'm going to try to go the whole route. . . .

*   *   *   *

Getting there . . . Yes, Joseph Hardy has had his vintage years in the corporation as well as a lot of grief from culture shock, but now he's committed. He's on his way to higher management. He's a comer. He may end up the first black president of a multibillion dollar white company. . . . It's possible. He has a chance. . . .

Our next executive, who also spent years getting there in the corporation and found satisfaction and fulfillment doing so, is not a comer, however. He is a man whose career has peaked. He will never reach the top. He will never go any farther but he yet found challenge and pleasure in his career going as far as he went. Getting there . . . that is how he spent those years. He made it to his capacities and he is satisfied. David Danbury considers himself quintessentially a corporation man. . . .

6

"If You Have to Make a Living, a Big Corporation Is the Place to Make It. . . ."

An executive finds fulfillment in the corporate life

David Danbury is a quiet, composed man who speaks in low, matter-of-fact tones. One would not take him for a man who had been an officer under fire in World War II, had very narrowly excaped death at least three times in his life and who had been in a peripatetic, rather high-pressure job up until about five years ago. After 30 years with the company he reached the position of controller just below the vice presidential level in a multibillion-dollar corporation. His life, he feels, has been the corporation. He views himself rather objectively and unemotionally on several planes, but he seems to consider himself without any regrets truly a company man.

When I began in the great corporation where I've worked for more than 30 years, the company had about 2,500 people and sales of about 15 million dollars. Today, it has over 50,000 people working in plants and offices in 30 countries of the world and sales of over 3 billion dollars, and yet I would say in terms of its objectives, its flavor, what you call "its life style," it has hardly changed at all. It is a people-oriented company in mid-America with the goal of producing for a world market, and people were and always have been important to it. I speak from experience. My father worked here before me. He retired in the 1950s and died soon after retirement from a heart attack. He dropped dead on the street. I started work here just before World War II—and I expect to retire from here five or six years from now. I liked the company then. I was offered two other jobs that paid more at the time and I came here. I like the company now. I am quite willing to tell my story. I don't consider myself an outstanding success, but I was fairly treated, I made many good friends and live a good and interesting life here. I do not think this untypical. I do not think my life could have been necessarily richer elsewhere or even as rich. I did not find complete conformity. I found variety, challenge and excitement. I was often under pressure. From time to time, I have been frustrated. From time to time, I did not move as fast as I wanted to. Sometimes my projects were overlooked or stymied. I never reached the top, but I feel my talents and capacities were used wisely and I feel that I reached the level I earned and have been given my just dues. I am a company man.

I guess I can divide my life into three parts: my youth where I did all kinds of odd jobs and tried to scrabble together an education, the years in the army during World War II and the biggest chunk of my life, that as a corporation man.

My parents were people of modest means, and I suppose if they had a goal in life, it was to see that their children, my sister and I, had more opportunity than they had had. My grandmother "hired out" as a housekeeper for a year in exchange for her passage from Germany to the U.S. My father completed high school in the evenings. I never graduated from a university, though I completed a year of business school, but my three daughters all have degrees. So for each generation, the opportunities were increased.

I suppose the greatest triumph of my youth was when I became an Eagle Scout. Scouting was important to me. This was during the depression and my dad had had a 30-percent reduction in pay. From the day I left high school I was never without some kind of job. Most of them were temporary: typing or taking inventory in a local firm. I studied accounting and business at night, and also took correspondence courses in accounting, law, management and taxes over a fourteen-year period; interrupted by the five years I spent in the service during World War II. But after high school, the jobs usually lasted only a short time. One of those jobs I remember was working a night shift. A friend and I would drive back and forth in his Model T, leaving work at two in the morning.

Later the jobs got steadier, but we were still hit pretty hard by the depression. I remember holding the seat of my trousers to the light each evening to be sure they hadn't worn through so I could wear them to work in the morning. Finally I got a job in the company I'm with now in the accounting department. I liked this company from the beginning. Now it was getting toward wartime, World War II, and the draft had started. They began the ceremony by drawing the first draft numbers out of a fishbowl, and I realized soon my number would come up. I looked around and there were three of us in accounting with pretty well the same type of seniority. I got the bright idea that our numbers would be pretty close together and we might all be leaving at the same time.

I don't think the corporation would have closed down, but I went in and told my boss: "It looks to me as if three of us will be called up about the same time and you'll be in kind of a bind. What would you think if I volunteered now and got my year over with?" He answered: "I think that would be very commendable. Why don't you go in and talk to Jim Keller about it." Jim Keller was the vice president of finance and this company, as it always has been, was a first-name, family type of place. So I went in and talked to Jim. He was a World War I aviator when they were flying these little box kites, and he thought it was very patriotic of me and approved. I knew if I left first, I'd be back first. I was single at the time and would be going anyway eventually.

So I went in in December of 1940—you remember how it was: 21 dollars a month, poker on payday and you'd win 30 bucks. Then just as my year was up, bang, Pearl Harbor, and I was in for the duration. At this time I had climbed to the rank of staff sergeant and a group of us found ourselves on board ship headed for, believe it or not, Alaska, the Aleutian Islands. Now we move to the second phase of my life.

We arrived at the islands on board ship, and you never saw anything so desolate, so absolutely without anything to sustain life in all the world. For the first month we lived on board ship, and our first job was unloading the ship to set up this outpost. What we knew about unloading a ship you could put in your ear. I've been under fire a couple of time since, but for sheer danger the way we tried to unload that ship equaled anything you could get from the enemy. We'd unload the material into a barge, take the barges ashore, wait until the tide changed, empty the barges, and then refloat them when the tide came in.

It was kind of slow work, but that wasn't where most of the danger lay. It was on deck. The way we were unloading things, you never knew where the next casualty would be. There were oil drums rolling around, winches falling free. Everybody would get in the corner of the barge as they were loading, and then something would fall and bounce near your head. I remember I got a call to unload some girders. They got one of them on a winch down to a foot and a half above the barge and there was only one place for that girder to go—the place where we were. We were easing it down and then the guy dropped it. It ripped the sole of my shoe off but didn't even scratch my foot. It was all in the line of duty, of course.

So finally we got on shore, pitched tents and the first night the wind blew our tents away. Our weather was known as the world's worst, and I can believe it. It wasn't just that the wind was always blowing; it was its extreme variability. When it was blowing from the north, it was bitter cold with very heavy snows. We would lose some of the men who had been posted at our perimeters, because they became confused and froze to death trying to return. Then the wind would shift and come from the south and you could stand there and literally watch the snow melt. The differences in temperature were so extreme that you could have parkas and everything else on and an hour later you would be in shirtsleeves.

We had been sent there to map the area and to prevent a Japanese invasion. We were situated on Cole Bay at the extreme end of the Alaskan peninsula, three miles from the Bering Sea and the Pacific Ocean. The Japanese were on Attu and Kiska some fifty or sixty miles away along the channel, where they had established outposts. We dropped bombs on the Japanese outposts and then we sent reconnaissance planes over and took photos of the bomb craters and found that the Japs were living in the bomb craters. We'd done all that work for them. A bomb crater hasn't any other use but to put your tent in it.

So that went on for a year and a half. There were no geodetic surveys, no maps of Cole Bay area, so every day I would go out with two or three guys and we would map the area—a tremendous job. The Aleutians were originally volcanic and magnetic fields made compasses practically worthless. So we'd just try to triangulate and say: "OK, this is where I am and I'm guessing I'm about 100 feet above sea level," and that's the way we'd draw it on a map the size of a wall. This job took us over a year and a half and we got fairly sophisticated at it. We also had got some 37-mm antitank guns on an outer perimeter of defense in case the Japs invaded, but of course they never did, fortunately.

Periodically, the first 200 of us were augmented by new troops, and oddly enough, despite the fact that we got soaked and frozen and dried off two or three times a day while running around the tundra and muskeg, there was not a hospital case among those first 200 men, not even respiratory disease, until the new troops began coming in. While we were working from seven in the morning till around midnight seven days a week, we did have breaks once in awhile. On one of them, I helped kill my first bear. There were four of us mapping in an area 5,200 feet above sea level. Everything else peeled down to sea level within a very short space, so we were climbing the side of this mountain. This area had a lot of Kodiak bears, which are of tremendous size, and one of them was coming toward us. We were struggling up a canyon about 100 yards wide. We dodged behind some rocks and the bear kept coming—he didn't know we were there. Then one guy got jumpy and began firing and we all began firing. We hit that bear with about thirty shots and the only thing that pierced its hide was the armor-piercing ammunition. That bear was 16 feet tall. It weighed over a thousand pounds and the skin alone weighed 350 pounds.

At this time, I had about a dozen native Aleuts in my section, people who lived by trapping and fishing. They would trap foxes and come for the salmon run and worked on fishing boats. I don't think that but one of these guys had ever been out of that part of the world, but they were naturals for my group since we were out in all terrain. Now one of these natives wanted to see that bear and the colonel decided he wanted the hide. So we took our native up to see our bear and he said that was no way to kill a bear. He said a bear always stands on his hind legs and roars before he makes his rush, and at that point you shoot him through the throat. I replied we hadn't been worried about shooting the bear through the open mouth, only about hitting him any way we could.

After a year and a half we finally got all the mapping done and all these heavy guns out there in the swamp. To all intents and purposes my job was now done, so the colonel called me in and said: "Now that you've finished our primary job, you are going to officers' candidates' school." I said: "I don't think I want to go to officers' candidates' school." He said: "Well, you're going." I answered: "I don't know whether you're aware of it or not but the quota for officers' candidates is about three per month and there's a roster of probably 150 names that have passed the exams up here, and at three a month if I can get on that list, the war will be over before I get to officers' candidates' school." He said: "You are going to go before the reviewing board next Tuesday."

There is a certain amount of politics even in the army. So I got on my best bib and tucker and appeared before the reviewing board, which consisted of four colonels and a general, who was the base commander—all of whom I knew and had worked with. I went in, saluted and stood at attention. They were very formal. They asked me my name—hell, they knew it—and they said: "Who is your superior officer?" I answered: "Colonel Grebner." They said: "No, no, who is your immediate superior?" and I answered: "Colonel Grebner." Then they all looked at the papers they had and said: "That will be all, sergeant."

The next month I went to officers' candidates' school. Now the first thing everybody does there is take this test. I'm good at taking tests like this. I have an analytical mind, and they come easy. I took the test and about two days later I had a call from headquarters and they said: "Would you mind taking that test again?" and I said: "Not at all." I took the test again. They said: "OK, you just merely confirmed it." and I said: "Confirmed what?" They answered: "This is the highest score that has ever been made in this test."

So I got into the last class of the 90-day wonders, as they called them. I finished second in a class of 300 and was assigned as a combat instructor at the school and given ten days' travel time to report. Since it only would take me half an hour to get to my new assignment, I had ten days free and they turned out to be among the most significant days of my life. I came back to the city and went over to the company. I was a second lieutenant now. In the office, the wife of my friend, Harry, the guy with whom I used to go back and forth to work in his Model T, said: "You've got to go out with Harry and me tonight." I answered: "I don't know any girls anymore. They're all engaged or tied up with somebody," and she said: "Take your pick." I was standing at her desk and I looked around and saw this good-looking blonde and I said: "I'll take that one." The introductions were made, and the four of us went out Saturday night, and that's how I met the girl who was to become my wife.

Everything moved fast after that. I had two more dates with her before my leave was up. We wrote to each other, and later on her way to Miami, she stopped where I was stationed and stayed over the weekend at the bachelor officers' quarters, and I gave her a ring the first night she was there.

Two months later, the colonel of my regiment interviewed the young officers. He got to me and said: "Lieutenant, I see you're not married." I answered: "If the colonel will permit, I will rectify this at the first opportunity." He answered: "When do you want leave?" So Josie and I were married. After the wedding, we were driving back to my station when a truck coming the other way barreled toward us. I pulled the wheel to avoid it; the car started to zigzag and over we went into a ditch, the car turning over three times. It was a miracle. The running boards were smashed; you couldn't get out through the doors, the windows were broken, but somehow we both escaped with only a few scratches. I squirmed out through the back window. A farmer was standing there. "Are you hurt?" he asked. We both answered: "No." I had to jump up and down on the running board on Josie's side to get the door open. The accident had knocked her shoes off. "I think I'd like to have my wife looked at," I said after the farmer had taken us back to his house and his daughters had come out to ask if they could help. We then drove into the nearest town and called my sister and she came out and picked us up.

On the way back to my station we passed the scene of the accident and the car was gone. We continued about a mile down the road and there was a garage with our wrecked car in it. The garage man said: "I thought you'd want your car towed in? Now what do you want to do about it?" I said: "That's great. Thanks. Just sell it for junk." We had to get a blow torch to get our steamer trunk out of the back. Later the man sent me a check for the junked car to where I was stationed with a note saying: "I took out $10.00 for my effort—is that OK?" I'd never seen that man before in my life—there're fine people in the world.

Josie and I had three months together before my regiment was broken up for D-Day replacements. I was now a first lieutenant and was put in charge of some ten second lieutenants and 300 men to wet nurse across the ocean on our troop ship. When we arrived at Liverpool, we had to move from camp to camp all across England to get to the jumping-off place for France. The men weren't used to walking that much and they had ill-fitting shoes causing blisters, so every night we'd line them up and inspect their feet and swap shoes where somebody had a pair too big or too small. Every camp we were in I had to argue like hell with the quartermaster to get any decent equipment for these men. But finally we reached the jumping-off point as ready as we could get and boarded all these small boats. It was a few days after D-Day and everything was still pretty messy. When we arrived, I was assigned to the Eighth Corp as a liaison officer. My job was to move between corps headquarters, normally 20 miles behind the lines, up to divisions on the front lines and find out exactly what the problems were and report them to corps headquarters, also placing the positions on a large map.

So it went until the big breakthrough. I guess you've heard of the big breakthrough—the Battle of the Bulge. Just when we thought we had it made and the war almost won, bang—it was the Germans' last gasp and it almost destroyed us. Our corps was headquartered at Bastogne when it happened. It was the first time I saw U.S. troops disorganized. There were our guys helter skelter re-treating. Someone grabbed me and said, "You're an officer in the United States' Army. O.K., you're in charge. Send all the boys you can over the hill. . . ." That's how it all started for me. Thirty-eight hours later I finally got back to headquarters. "Where the hell were you!" my commanding officer said. I told him. The jeep I'd gotten back to headquarters in had 48 bullet holes in it. You get a bit fatalistic about being under fire, though. While some had a better chance than others, there were 20,000 rounds of ammunition fired for every casualty in World War II, so the odds were there. Anyhow, that was the third time I'd say death decided to pass me up. The shooting war was finally ended.

I now had the points to get out, but I was declared essential and spent two more years in the army after the war was over. I served in the occupying forces and then as a special services officer, first promoted to captain and then to major. Finally my hitch ended, I decided to go back with the company, and the third part of my life, my life as a corporation man, began.

The day I had gotten back from Arizona where we'd gone to visit my sister, we were in the old familiar city and in the company's headquarters, and I had gone in to see personnel. "No point in my talking to you," the personnel man had said, "Go on up and see Jim Keller."

Jim Keller was the vice president who had thought it patriotic of me to volun-teer and when I entered he got up and came around and shook hands. He was glad to see me. "Dave," he said, "we've got just the job for you. You're going to be an auditor." I answered: "Fine, anything you say, Jim." That's how this main part of my career with the company began.

Most people don't know what an internal auditor in a company does, but there's no better way to get to know a company than in this job. You're sent out to different locations to make examinations of their operations, accounts and other prescribed areas and to report on them to the general auditor after discussing your findings with the manager or executive in charge of that loca-tion. So you get to know what's really going on, you get to know people, and you get to know how to deal with people, your superiors and others—or you don't last very long. When I started, there were only three of us in this area, the general auditor, a real son of a bitch, another accountant and me. You have to remember, although I'd gotten up pretty high in the army, I'd never graduated from college and didn't have a degree, not so uncommon in those days. We were homegrown, so to speak.

I was started out under a tough old-fashioned, backward man. Everything had to be done a certain way, whether it made any sense or not. Nothing pleased this man, and when you're up against this kind of thing, especially as a young fellow, it's tough—you go home at night tired and tense. I don't think this man liked his life here or even himself. We have a practice here of giving an award and a gift of stock in the company for every five years of service. This guy was with the company 40 years and every share of stock he ever got on one of these anniversaries he sold the next day. He finally had a heart attack and was gone for about a month and a half. While he was gone, I made a few decisions that had to be made—all for the good, and when he gets back he finds I've done certain things and he says: "What are you trying to do—take my job?" I said: "No, you were gone. I'm the number two man. I made the decisions in your absence." He answered "I don't take a very good view of that." Two weeks later, he was made disbursements auditor and I was given the division to run. At that point he suggested he would have another heart attack. He was a very difficult man.

To get back to the job, you are sent out to a plant. You check in. You are just a kid from headquarters and the plant manager has been a plant manager for twenty years. If you're smart, you ask to see the plant manager and you tell him what you've been sent out to do, and if there're any problem areas he'd like you to get into directly, you'll be happy to do so. So I had enough savvy to know I had to get to know these people I'd never met before. I always played a very soft sell. I am not going to tell the plant manager how to run his business. I tried to do my job and I didn't push.

I recall one incident that began with a rather cool reception. This was a southern plant and the first trip I made down there, I introduced myself to the manager, an old-timer, a very fine aloof gentleman. He acknowledged the introduction and that was about all. I sat at a desk outside his office for two weeks. "Good morning, Mr. Griffin." "Good morning, Dave." "Good evening, Mr. Griffin." "Good evening, Dave." I guess it was the last Friday I was there, he said: "Would you like to go to a Rotary luncheon with me?" I answered: "Yes, sir, I would be happy to." We went to the Rotary luncheon together. We chatted. He had the decency after the lunch on the way back to say: "I'm sorry I've ignored you these two weeks, Dave. I should have gotten together with you for lunch the very first day!" This man has been retired for some five years now; yet I get a birthday gift from him every year. Nothing big but I made a real friend. Now I don't think we have a single auditor on our staff—and we have some 30 of them now—who hasn't some kind of friendly relationship with every manager he audits.

But of course not everything goes as easily as that. Once in a rare while you run into something. In one case it was a foreman out in one of the plants selling some of the company's products on the side. I had to sit down with him and say: "OK, here's what we know. Here is where the records have been changed. You're responsible. You're the only guy who could have changed them. These dealers admitted they purchased the product at a discounted price over the dock without any billings. What do you think?" Normally the guy will say, as this one did: "OK. I did it. I confess." Then they fire him. It's usually a couple-of-thousand-dollars kind of thing.

A much more painful thing for me was when I had to make a judgment in another area. One of the fellows above me who had been in our office was transferred out to a plant and we were close friends. The following year I was sent out to audit the plant and it became my painful duty after careful investigation to advise the manager that my friend was not doing the job. It led to a parting of the ways, but that's one of the bad things that can happen in this kind of work.

But mostly our investigations are careful and helpful and we get together with the manager afterwards and report our findings and make our recommendations, discussing them thoroughly with him in a meeting that may last for four or five hours. He brings in anyone he wants involved in the examination or affected by the recommendations so that it has all been thoroughly discussed before our report goes to the chief auditor. The company has good internal control, and I can't remember any frauds or irregularities involving anyone above the level of a foreman in all the years I've been here. As for disagreements and differences of opinion on our findings or recommendations, we try to work those out in our final meetings, and if they can show us we're wrong, we admit it; if we can show them we're right, they'll almost always cooperate. In the end a report is written, and it goes to the manager and to his superior and to various others who are interested in certain phases of it, like creditor accounting stock control or whatever. The manager is expected to reply in detail to that audit report, indicating every action he has taken.

When I look back, there're a lot of things I remember about my career, most of them good. Of course, this kind of life has its frustrations. I started out with one of them, having this first boss. When I got back from World War II, I'd gone up pretty high in rank, and it was usually company policy in those days to place you roughly at the station you were in when you left and pay an equivalent salary. This changed. The vice president in charge of my department called me in six months after I returned. His question was: "What do the veterans think about the company now that they are back home?" My reply was along the line that they were not uniformly all that happy. Some who had been officers were actually making less money. Some who had been away as long as five years felt they should be paid at the same level as those doing similar work who had not served. I don't know what happened to anyone else but I received three increases in the next twelve months.

I suppose one's progress through the corporate strata can probably be measured by bench marks. There are perks at all levels. I recall being granted an additional week vacation before I had been there the required number of years. Making the discretionary bonus list was a milestone. My first stock option was another.

Some of the practices of big corporations could well be categorized as status symbols and in a sense are carried to extremes. Our company is no exception.

We have four sizes of offices, ranging from those provided the four highest ranking officers to those for supervisors and department managers. There is actually a manual which designates the dimensions of each office and lists the furnishings. Expansion often means creating positions and building new offices. There have been occasions when changing a title without a change of responsibilities has resulted in a change of office size. To many this is important. There are really some people who are quite proud of the fact that they have an artificial tree in their office. Others who don't rate a tree think this is rather ridiculous. But in the end, it's the job that counts, and it's the work itself I valued and remember best.

An auditor's job involves traveling, and for those who envy us seeing the world, let me say this is not the most satisfying part of the work. One accepts the loss of luggage, missing a connection, arriving so late your confirmed reservation is no longer valid, or the weathering in of an airport that may mean staying overnight in another city. Sleeping in a house of ill repute, however, goes beyond the call of duty.

This particular trip involved the audit of one of our major plants in conjunction with a visit to a satellite plant. My reservation at the second location was made by a secretary at the major plant, who said I'd have no trouble. I arrived in a small upstate New York town, off the beaten path, with not much commercial traffic. The only transportation serving the town was the bus. I arrived just before midnight, took a cab to the hotel—no room. The annual graduation of the small college nearby had filled the place with proud parents. I went back out to the cab. We tried a motel, two rooming houses—no room. "There's only one other place," the cabdriver said. "You want to try it?"

At one in the morning after four hours on the bus, I'd try anything. It turned out to be a tavern, going full blast. The sweat-shirted bartender was surprised when I said I wanted the room alone. Nevertheless, he took a key from the cigar box and pointed to the stairs. I found the room, pulled the string hanging from the bare light bulb, pried open the window and slept on the sway-backed bed. Early the next morning, I found running water in the little room down the hall, did a perfunctory job of washing my face, picked up my bag and went down the stairs. A different bartender was surprised at my question as to what I owed: "Didn't you pay when you came in?" When I answered no, he mumbled: "Make it a buck." It turned out our local manager was on a citizens committee having as one of its objectives the closing down of this establishment.

But as I went up, the traveling was not confined to one country. We were in some 30 countries of the world and the corporation was expanding rapidly. My division was expanding with it, and I guess I am proudest of having been mainly responsible for building this division up. Eventually there were about 30 of us trying to audit some 280 locations throughout the world, and, as I advanced into higher management, I was involved more and more in negotiations for acquisitions or divestments. So in the course of auditing and this kind of work, you find yourself in a lot of out-of-the-way places. I can remember sitting in Corretro, a town a hundred kilometers from Mexico City, and one train a day gets you down to Mexico City. You get down to catch that train. They post a sign: one hour late, two hours late, three hours late . . . discontinued today.

One evening I went from Guatemala, destination Mexico City, which is noted for dust storms. We circled Mexico City for two hours, never landed, and finally came up to Houston. I was the only North American on the plane. The rest were South Americans, either Mexicans or Guatemalans, going to Mexico City. In Houston do you know they lined up 150 people and gave them shots, because they were in the U.S. without health certificates, before they let them go to a motel and stay overnight? These are some of the joys of traveling. It's not fun —really it isn't. But you do learn about people in different countries with different customs and you find yourself facing tough situations. You learn patience and to accommodate yourself.

I remember representing my company in Japan at a conference with the people from one of the great Japanese corporations. We were talking about getting into Japan on a business deal. There we were, an attorney and myself, having dinner with one of the corporation's head men at their club. The head man sat at the head of the table. I sat at his right. The attorney at his left. His number two man sat at the foot of the table. This guy didn't say one word unless it was in reply to a question from his boss. That's the way they do business in Japan. They bow to each other on all the street corners, you know, and nothing gets dones quickly.

In business, I found Italy the world's worst. In Italy everything starts with drinks. You drink for an hour before you even start to talk about the matter at hand. A good meeting in Italy results in determining when you are going to meet again. We were affiliated with a big company in a joint venture in Italy, Germany and Holland. We decided this wasn't working out, so it came to: "You buy us out or we buy you out." We agreed to buy them out. I was sent to Europe to work out the deal, at this big fat meeting in Brussels. There were the representatives of their company from Great Britain, Italy, Germany and Holland. The British guy was really British—handle-bar moustache and the works. Then they had their head guy from Germany in with his attorneys, their head guy from Italy with his attorneys and their head guy from Holland with his back-up people, and me alone.

We were sitting around this big board table in our company's offices in Brussels, and the British executive says: "Well, Dave, I think this is your meeting," and that's the way we started this meeting. Now there was a sum of about half a million dollars that was in controversy, and I began: "Before we go any further, that $500,000 stays in the corporation." "Oh, that's not quite our understanding," they answered. "Well, I'm going home." "Wait a minute," they said.

They couldn't make a decision. They had to call their various offices because they had no authority on their own.

But we got all that worked out. Then I went to the various locations in each country and I told these people what records we needed—all the documents, the contracts, the pension programs, all translated into English. Then I returned to the states while this material was being gathered. After three weeks I went back. Germany was typical: stacks of papers this high—copy of the German pension plan, copy of the English translation, copy of all the contracts with their translations, everything in great shape. I get down to Italy. Here is this clown who had been up there in Brussels three weeks ago, and I went with our Italian manager to his apartment to work out these negotiations.

We get to this apartment house. A maid lets us in. Here's our guy stretched out on a sofa in the living room in bathrobe and slippers. What happened? He slipped a disk on his way back to Italy from the Brussels meeting and was flat on his back ever since. In come the flunkies with all the booze and what have you. We have a few drinks and we talk about the controversial items. Every time something came up that he didn't see eye to eye with, he got his backache. He closed his eyes; we waited till the spasm passed, and then we would get on with it. It was a dull, gloomy day and the room was dark. At three o'clock the lights went out. We just sat there squinting and nobody mentioned it, as if that happens every day. That's Italy.

They didn't have half the stuff ready. Back to the states. A month later I get back over there and down to Italy. This guy is well by now and most of the papers are ready. There are still a few odd points that we do not exactly see eye to eye on. One of them is a 120-year-old plant which wasn't even built for the purpose we're using it for. It's very archaic, but they want to sell us this plant as part of the whole package. I said: "We wouldn't touch that thing with a ten foot pole. Have you been down there recently?" He answered: "No." I replied: "I have. Do you realize that three months ago, the roof slid off?" He answered: "I believe I did hear rumors of that." I said humorously: "I can see why you didn't want to go down to see it—you were afraid of being hit by falling slates." He thought a moment, then laughed. He had to make up his mind whether that was funny or not. But that's the way they do it—no two countries alike.

Then we get back to Holland. Our vice president meets me there to sign the official documents. We are working over the final documents and we suddenly realize we are buying a corporation in Italy, we can't use its former name, and we don't know what to call it. So I made a suggestion, and that's how I named our corporation in Italy. So finally there are 120 pages of documents, four copies of everything, and this guy calls his secretary in and, would you believe it, she licked a stamp for every page of those four copies of 120-page document. We sat there and watched her lick 480 stamps. Then this guy hands the four copies of the documents to our vp and says: "Sign through the stamp. It's the law. Every official document has to have the signature over the sales tax stamps." I leaned back and watched him go to work.

You've asked me whether big corporations like ours moving into other countries don't create problems. Maybe they do. All I can tell you is what I know from experience. We're one of the biggest grain and food companies in the world. We create products to feed the world. From the day our founder shoveled the first shovelful of feed, that's been the objective of this company. It's still the objective. Now you look at what we do when we go in, say, South America or Mexico. I remember when our first international operation was established in a little town in Mexico. I went down to work out an accounting system for them. As part of the original plant we established a very small research farm on the plant grounds. We started to put in a few chickens and what have you and I was down there when the first egg became available. The plant manager made one big mistake. He took a dozen eggs down to that office and he says: "OK, what am I bid?" Those people bid those eggs up so high they couldn't afford them.

When our company went into Mexico, a working man's family had one egg a week, and the head of the household ate that egg on Saturday night and the rest of the family watched him. There weren't any concepts of selling eggs by the dozen or by the kilo. You bought an egg and it was expensive. Now you can walk into the markets in Mexico and you can see chickens and eggs just like here in the supermarkets. Now what's that—sixteen years ago? This has happened in every country we have gone into.

Take Guatemala; there were no chickens in Guatemala when we went into it. You couldn't buy a chicken. Well, Guatemala is a country of two things: Guatemala City and the rest of the country. Guatemala City is where the dictator lives and a few wealthy families. You go 40 miles out of Guatemala City and the people are still dressed the way they were 300 years ago. You can tell what region a family is from by their dress. They either wear a red blouse, a blue skirt or a bandana with distinctive coloring, and these people see five dollars a year in cash money. The biggest thing that anyone ever did for Guatemala was the Rockefellers, and you know what they did? They put a pump in every town and it pumps water up the mountainous terrain into what looks like a swimming pool in a backyard above ground. Women are there washing their babies, washing their hair, getting pails out of there for drinking water. That's it. Do you know what the men do all day? They go up in the hills with their little burros to get firewood, and now it takes them all day to get a load because there're no trees any more close to town. They grow a few beans. That's what they live on. There are many, many people like that all over the world.

You may go to Mexico and you'll go to Mexico City or Acapulco or Tasco, but you don't get out to see these little towns. When we first went into the little town we picked to set up our plant, we were the first piece of industry there. These people were living in mud huts. That's what we do when we go into a lot of countries. We are in India and Korea and African places and all kinds of countries and even exploring possibilities in Russia and China. Nobody is going to love us for it and nor do we expect them to. It's business, but our objective as a company is to feed the world. I think that's an objective worth struggling for. . . .

I suppose when you think about it, my life in the corporation seems to go against all the conventions about conformity, ruthlessness, the coldness and impersonality of the big company, its insatiable need for profit that colors everything it does. To some extent my experience during these thirty-five years does belie that picture—not completely, of course, but for the most part.

First of all, though, we worked hard. This was in no sense a charitable organization. We had to make profits to survive and we knew it. You can't sit in any of the year-end reviews of our top people, as I do, and not realize this. The heads of our major divisions pretty well run their own shows up to a point. They do their own research and look to their own products, but when the yearly review comes each head makes his presentation personally to the top officers and his peers. He listens to them and then he has his turn and he answers some hard questions about his division's performance and about his budget for the next year and capital expenditures for the next three years. He has to justify everything. "Why are your costs so much greater this year?" or "What are you going to do with eight more people?" or "How can you justify a return on investment of this order?" or "Should you continue to support this product?" So while this is a company that cares about people, it's a company that cares about performance and profit also.

But, as I said, it's in no sense blind or insensitive to the human factor. When young people talk about the corporate jungle, they imply that it's different than any other part of society or in life itself. That's ridiculous. Whether you're in the academic world or the Peace Corps or in science or the professions or the UN, you're going to find that it's sometimes a jungle, that sometimes human factors go by the board. In corporate life, we've not always done the right thing, but here we're definitely people-oriented, and we recognize there are all kinds of people. Now I'm sort of ambitious and I've always been competitive so I'd come in early and stay late and I could never understand people who got in at nine and quit promptly at five and were perfectly happy staying in the same niche for twenty years, doing the same thing. We have people like that. They do their job and get home for supper and that's the way it is. I suppose they look at guys like me and a lot of us in management and they say: "What're you killing yourself for? What's the big deal?" and they think we're crazy. Still here people do their job and the general tenor of this place is one of a family feeling. People care about each other.

I remember the vice president who got me started, and I remember on the walls of his office he had the pictures of the men in his group who were away at war. He cared about them and admired them, so it's no wonder a lot of us came back to the company. I guess I'm proudest of the fact that I'm responsible for many men who have risen in the management of this company.

But of course you have to serve the company's purposes. If you're in the area I was in, it's put something of a burden on your family. You're traveling a lot; your hours are long; pressures are heavy. My wife and daughters took it all in stride. They knew that's the way I had to make my living. We were a close family and we were lucky. Although I was away from home a lot, I made the decisions and though my daughters grew up at a time when some youngsters were anti-establishment, they came through well. Yes, we were lucky.

Now to conclude: A few years ago I was called in and told the other assistant controller and I were to swap jobs. I had been running a division of some 300 people, encompassing the auditing, budgeting, general and international accounting functions and he had been running the data processing and systems operating functions. So one morning, I came down and took his office and he came over and took mine. Well, it was rough. I knew a little about data processing, but I tell you I never worked so hard in my life. I went to IBM schools and Honeywell schools; I read all the literature; I probed into all the processes, and I finally got a handle on it. Then four years ago, the company made another reorganization. We were getting involved in a number of major programs. The financial vice president called me again and said: "Dave, we need somebody to make analyses of these programs and get some of these damn things under control. So we're setting up a financial analysis division and we'd like to have you take it over."

I said: "Fine." But there's more to the story. What happened is that the guy I swapped jobs with is now my boss. He was made vice president-controller, and deservedly so. All this cross-training was important and in retrospect we were really vying for this top job when it opened. It opened a bit too late as far as I was concerned.

Rivalry—yes, but Paul and I are still great buddies. We play golf together. We knew what was happening. We knew it was going to be one or the other of us, depending on when it happened. If it had happened sooner, they told me, I probably would have gotten the top job, but I was too near retirement. I remember they were a little dismayed to have to tell me that, but I said: "That's all right. It's the way it should be. It's the decision I would have made, if I were in your shoes. In fact, I have been thinking about this and I'm not sure I would have accepted the job, if it had been offered to me." For the truth was I had come to the time when I don't think I really wanted any more responsibility. I had the biggest house I'd ever want, the latest model car, my girls were through school and sooner or later you come to the stage where five or ten thousand more a year isn't worth the additional effort. I had come to that time.

Today I am in a job where I am off the intensive travel schedule. I can plan my vacations. I no longer have to sustain the heavy pressure of constant brush fires and alarms. I no longer have to hold hands with 300 people and I realize now how much of my time was taken up in administrative pressures, in listening to people's troubles, in trying to help straighten out problem areas. I suppose I've been influenced somewhat by the fact that my father fell dead at 63 and I would like to last a little longer. I'll be doing my best for the company for the next three or four years to retirement, but I've reached the summit of my struggles.

So let me sum up briefly how it seems to me. I guess you could call me a representative corporation man, if there is such a thing. I've liked the company. I haven't been fazed by it. I've had some tough and interesting jobs. I've traveled a lot and given a lot of myself. I've seen something of the world. I've been under heavy pressures. But I've felt by and large the company's treated me fairly and used my talents. I've felt I've been treated with respect and my programs and recommendations carefully considered and more often then not adopted. I feel I've made a contribution and had some influence, and I've made a good living here and some good friends.

If I were talking to a young man who liked people and who wasn't afraid of challenge, variety and stimulation, I'd say to him: "If you have to make a living, a big corporation is the place to make it."

*   *   *   *

And now we turn to higher management and watch the pressures increase. . . .

PART III

The pressures grow. . . .
These men are nearing the top.
Again one runs off the
rails. . . .

A few years ago, a chief executive officer arrived at his office at nine in the morning, walked to the window, smashed the glass with his briefcase and threw himself out, falling 44 stories to his death. Pressure . . . Pressure increases everywhere as one goes up—it increases in the longer hours, the heavier loads, the political maneuvering, the dangers of misjudgments that might cost the corporate empire hundreds of thousands or millions of dollars. It affects the higher executive in all aspects of his life. We see now Ken Burdett, who lost two wives to his job; we see a senior vp remembering fondly the old days in the field when everything was more fun. And finally we see a rising star taking the wrong road of women and the bottle and the conflict of interest to keep it all going.

7

"People Have No Idea of the Pressures You Face. . . ."

A top executive relates how he lost two wives to his job

Ken Burdett is a pleasant, personable, serious man in his late fifties, who as vice predident heads up all the industrial relations and personnel activities of a huge, multibillion-dollar chemical and processing corporation, one of the world's largest with offices, lands and plants in 40 countries. During most of his working life, even though he has been an operating manager, he has dealt with tumultuous labor unions, people in and out of trouble and great administrative systems for ordering the human resources of his company; and he has faced the long hours and incredible pressures this kind of executive must sustain. Yet when you see him and talk to him, he seems relaxed, warm, highly intelligent and unhurried. He lives alone in a very attractive house on beautifully landscaped grounds in a rather wealthy suburb of a southwestern city. He has been with this worldwide corporation for fifteen years and, as he will tell you, lost two wives to the job and the corporation. He is a man who has found what to do with his life. As he suggests, he has, in the words of the old song, "sold his soul to the company store."

The corporation, the job has dominated my whole life. Everything else has been secondary, and I know I've paid a price for it. I've had some fun and some successes, but I've paid a price—there's no question about that, but I'd probably pay that price again.

For instance, I lost two wives to my job and I've reached a conclusion that there's no way to be happily married and successful in business at the same time. I believe that today. I worked. I didn't get home enough. Work came first. If something had to give, it was never business. I feel guilty about this. My first wife really suffered from it. I tried to compromise on it but I couldn't. Then I married my secretary. I thought surely she'd understand the importance and pressures of the job. Now she's left me and I'm alone, but that's the way it's got to be. I'm not proud of it. I guess you could say I've sold my soul to the company store, but that's the way it is.   Between marriage and the job, between almost anything and the job, the job comes first.

You want to know how I got that way. Well, let's go back to the beginning. I was born in a medium-size city in Indiana and went to public schools there. In high school I was sports editor and editor-in-chief of the paper and sports editor of the yearbook the year I graduated. If I could have gone to the University of Missouri or Columbia, I would have gone into journalism, but fate decreed otherwise.

My grandmother was the dominant force in my early life—a very warm, compassionate person. My dad and mother were divorced when I was 11 years old, and my mother left town. She was in the insurance business, an inside person in the field and considered very good. She left the city and went to a succession of places and we really never saw very much of her, until later on when my second wife and I were married.

My dad was an immensely fat man, about five foot six and weighed some 200 pounds. He was a sort of entrepreneur and gambler; he owned and operated a cigar store, a restaurant and a bar. He stayed in the city and I saw more of him after the divorce than I had before. My dad was a guy who ran from conflict and his way of dealing with the conflict at home had been to go and bury himself some place in a poker game. He was a big poker player for big stakes and he won the town's leading restaurant in a poker game one time. But as I said he was very obese and he died of uremic poisoning at 63. Probably this is the reason I'm not obese. It's a fetish with me. I work very hard at that.

I had one brother of whom I was very fond and to whom I was very close. He was three years younger and was always tagging along when he was young. In high school he became a basketball star and I basically financed him when he went to Indiana University where he was captain of the basketball team in his junior and senior years. I have been a sort of driving force behind him, I guess.

In my own case, since we couldn't afford at that time to send me to Columbia or the University of Missouri to follow a journalism career, I chose not to go to college at all and I first floundered around, starting up with a friend a little car wash business and going to night school and taking some courses in accounting and law. Then my dad arranged for me to get an interview at the tractor works nearby of a huge automotive corporation, and that was my first job in a corporation.

I was started in a fledgling credit union they had just set up in the plant. The basic requirements were that we took in payroll deductions and made loans. It was kind of a savings and loan operation with restrictions on what we could make loans for—mostly personal and auto loans. We couldn't make loans on houses in those days. My boss was a severe taskmaster, and he and I also got into insurance too because we had all these car loans and it was convenient for the employees to get the necessary insurance from us. I worked in that plant in the credit union for some four years. The big automotive company of which this was a division was in those days extremely in-grown with an executive group largely made up of self-made men without a college education and largely people who had come up through the plants. But this was soon to change. The major influence coming up was the scion of two of the founding families of this corporation, a cultivated man who was determined to bring in college graduates and who instituted an executive training program, generally reserved for college graduates. The manager of our works, like many of the other old-timers, was not enthusiastic about the program. He felt the way to make your career in the corporation was to work up from the ranks and that college was a lot of nonsense. So he went to the industrial relations manager, also a noncollege man, and said: "Isn't there some young guy we could put in there, who doesn't have a college degree, to see how well he competes with these guys?" Fortunately I was chosen.

They put me through the program and I did as well as the rest. During the period of training, you worked in all the major departments, including out in the plant on the assembly line, and when you got through, every department had had a chance to evaluate you, so you usually had one or two offers from departments you had worked in. I had such offers from industrial relations and from accounting. I considered both these offers carefully. I decided accounting was so well established in the corporation that it would be a long hard road to the top by that route, while industrial relations was relatively new and labor relations particularly ought to present greater opportunity there, so I selected industrial relations.

Of course, when I started, I got all the dirty jobs nobody else wanted like chasing absentees to find out why they weren't there. It was an awakening experience to find out that very often the wives were responsible for their husbands not showing up. Or even more enlightening we'd get: "What d'you mean he isn't at work? What d'you mean he calls in sick? When he left here this morning, he was all right!" I worked there for about two years and then Pearl Harbor came along, and that was the year I got married. I had met the girl who was to become my first wife through friends. She was working in a nearby town in the advertising department of one of the big department stores. The corporation was declared critical to the war effort, and they set up a plant to manufacture light tanks for the army. I was sent to this new arsenal as the employment manager earlier in the year and then the question of my draft status became of concern. First, I was deferred because I was married, subsequently because I was working in a defense industry and finally, although I had my induction orders, the war ended before I could get into the service.

In the meantime two top spots had opened up in my old works. One of the men who had been in the executive training program and was ten years older than I was given the lead spot in industrial relations and I was given the number two spot as his assistant. The top man was not really interested in industrial relations and knew very little about it, but he was a good organizer. I knew a bit about the field, so we made a good pair and got along well.

Industrial relations in those days was heavily oriented toward dealing with unions and managing employee benefit programs. That period was a period of labor unrest and I got my first taste of union relations at this works. When I went over there, we had a union chartered under the federal government but without an international union affiliation or a national tie-in. The union was very ineffective, so much so that we in fact tried to prop it up to preserve a strong management voice about what went on at the plant.

For example, the industrial relations manager and I used to get together before a grievance meeting and we'd say: "These issues the union ought to win." My role then was to see that the union made a strong case. I would get to the union leadership ahead of time and explain what their strong case was without, of course, actually saying: We're going to concede this to you, but we'd say: "Here's your strong case," and we'd do it by reviewing with them the whole thing, giving these union people our viewpoint but at the same time emphasizing the things they should stress. But even so it was hopeless; they couldn't catch on. Finally the employees threw them out and elected a local of a major international union to represent them.

Two of the people I dealt with in the local union became court cases as to whether they were Communists, and one of them was a guy I dealt with regularly. I remember one incident when I went to one of the union parties, a big dance. I didn't drink much in those days, but this labor leader was feeling no pain and he put his arm around me and said: "Ken, you really ought to join us. You're too smart to be working for them. They're exploiting you."

I answered: "Joe, no thanks," but that seemed to me a real insight into the nature of Communist effort then. Basically their aim at that time—around 1944-46—was to create chaos through strikes or disruption of one sort or another. But to get back. My boss was offered a chance to go back to what he really liked, to be manager of a plant. When they offered him this opportunity, he said: "Who's going to be my successor?" and they answered: "We'll give Ken Burdett a chance; we'll make him acting manager of industrial relations." This was typical in the corporation; they always tested you out under the acting title. My boss said: "Why are you going to make him acting?" and they said: "We want to see if he can do it." My boss said: "How long do you think that will take?" and they said: "Maybe six months." "Well," my boss said: "Ok, then I'll accept the plant job in six months. Unless you make Ken industrial relations manager I'm not going to go for it." So I was made industrial relations manager and he did go. That's the kind of relationship we had.

We had a lot of work stoppages in those years. We were at fault 60 per cent of the time, unfortunately. We made it easy for them. As a management group we had become self-satisfied, sure we were right in everything we did. So we gave a militant union every opportunity to shut us down. We weren't careful. We didn't do our homework. For example, a question of piece work price would come up, and our time study men would set a price and the union would say: "That's too tight." We'd say: "No, our time study men have looked at it," and they'd say: "Why the time study guy hasn't even been out there!" and it would turn out they were right. The study was put together from similar studies, and it may or may not have been right, but the man had never even gone out into the plant to see what was going on, to check on it himself.

Or another situation. Someone would put in for a merit increase and the union would back him, and the chief inspector, who couldn't stand having his authority challenged by a third party, would turn it down. He was the boss and he'd say: "That guy isn't entitled to it." We'd look at the man's record, the record would be good and the man would be entitled to it. We were wrong so much of the time, it made it easy for the union, Communist or no Communist associations.   Today the kind of communist theme that workers are being exploited and "let's overturn the whole system and then we'll have the millennium" seems to have lost its appeal, and whether the trend of the times is causing this or whether people are more sophisticated, all of that kind of agitation has long passed. Of course, we are moving in the direction of what used to be called collectivism, but I don't know what else we can do, given the size and complexity of our institutions.

Of course, I have some reservations about our four-billion-dollar company, the size of our present employer and the company's many areas of bureaucracy, and of course our government is just a bigger bureaucracy. Both the corporation and the government, even though benign, compassionate and understanding from the human viewpoint, have become the huge bureaucracies that we were all warned against. We have now a certain collectivism and a certain standardization that they tell us negates personal growth and a feeling of personal accomplishment. Now this is interesting to me, because, as I think of myself, I am a product of this system and yet my experience for myself and those I know and have seen hasn't been of increased loss of freedom and flexibility through this system but quite the opposite, and yet we're all conscious of the dangers.

For example, one day three other fellows and I were making a presentation on a total compensation program that would bring together a number of fragmented and unrelated approaches and on an integrated manpower planning system we were developing. Our chairman, a truly brilliant man, a genius, said to me: "You fellows strike me as being more interested in systems and form than you are in substance." I said: "Bill, maybe you're right but I'll tell you something. If you run a four-billion-dollar company without systems and forms you won't have any substance; you'll have chaos." He answered: "OK, that's probably right too, but somewhere between where you think I am and where I think you are there's a balance between form and substance, and we haven't found it."

I agree with him. I'm probably too systems-oriented. I probably do want to organize the corporation as a system to a greater extent than necessary. Maybe that's because I am a product of the system. Our chairman, on the other hand, is the product of a wealthy background, always destined to be head of the company. Nobody, however, I'm sure ever visualized it would be the size it is. It's largely he who brought it to this size. In the years when I first came here, sales weren't much greater than just corporate profits were last year. This man is a great leader, a fantastic person. But as I said, I'm a product of the system, and I just think that the size of everything and the economics, the economy of scale, demand that there have to be systems and discipline. Yet I think people are reflecting their individual tastes and desires to a greater extent now than certainly they did when I first started in the corporate world.

I go to work frequently with a sports shirt or a turtle neck. That was unheard of a few years ago even in the southwest. No one at the vice presidential level would ever think of doing anything like that—it would have been considered too undignified. Now also we have unscheduled, flexible work hours in our management and clerical areas. Come when you feel like it as long as you've made the arrangement for your full day's work. Of course, all that means for executives is that you can start earlier and work later. But for people on the staff, they arrive and leave at a time agreed upon that's most suitable to them as long as the work gets done—and this is considered no big deal. So in that sense corporate life is much more flexible and people-oriented. Also I think that people are finding outlets outside of business to a much greater extent than they did before. A lot of people are beginning to accept the fact that business is not an end in itself. But, as I've said, business, the corporation is for me. It's dominated my life, and my values have been shaped to a great degree by it. I've paid some prices for that but I've had some successes out of it also.

I'd been employment manager in the original plant for awhile and had gotten their industrial relations department organized and become industrial relations manager, when I received a truly interesting assignment. The company had decided to put up a new plant somewhere in the southeast and they sent me down to one of the old southeastern cities to evaluate that community and to see whether the corporation should settle the plant within that city. It was an interesting experience because I was wined and dined and entertained for five days. They couldn't do enough for me. I tell you I went to the fanciest club I've ever been in in my life and I was treated to all the social and financial life of that old and heavily traditional society. I went back and we concluded that they really wanted the corporation badly enough to, well, bend one of their less savory traditions. You see, one of the reasons for the thorough study down there was our chairman's commitment to equal opportunity. This was in 1946—

a long time before such a stand was popular or even palatable. Now the city had had an arsenal down there and several defense plants and when the war ended all of them closed down and wham, on V-J Day there were 30,000 people out of work. That was another strong reason for wanting us to set up in that area.

Now this was a nice town; people liked it and wanted to stay there, and we were setting up plants all around the midwest and south and at every one of them, the chairman insisted that they were going to have equal opportunity.

So I was sent down to help organize this plant in this town all by myself six months before any of the rest of the group arrived, to hire the people we were going to need. I'm telling you, because of the employment situation down there, I was interviewing people who should have been interviewing me. I was just fortunate I had been working for this corporation rather than those others that had been closed down.

Now I had explained the company's policy to community leaders and to those we were hiring. We were going to employ people according to their abilities and there were going to be Blacks—the emphasis then was on Blacks, rather than women. Of course, the community leaders looked at me askance as if I were out of my mind, but they realized I was pretty far down the line in the corporation and they figured they'd get that crack-pot notion changed. I reported this to our chairman, so he came down and he went around explaining the policy to them. He had two things going for him, of course: they wanted and needed the plant badly because of the heavy unemployment and two, the editor of the city's big paper was a well-known liberal, really the conscience of the community. So they seemed to accept.

At first things went well, but then we had our first major incident. Of course, we had Blacks on the assembly line, working side by side with Whites and they appeared to get along all right at work, in the cafeteria and in the locker rooms, so we thought we were over the hump. Then we put our first Black in with the skilled mechinists, and all of a sudden after lunch one day, the machining department didn't go back to work. So the works manager comes to me and says: "What do we do now?" I answered: "The thing to do is to go out and talk to them. Find out what their problem is and see where we go from here." So we went out and asked them. Of course, not one of them wanted to come out with it so they made all kinds of excuses: "It was too hot. The machinery wasn't in good repair" and so on.

So finally we said: "Look, we can't see that these things are any different today than they were yesterday. So it's got to be something else." At last one guy came out with it: "This fellow, what's his name," he said, "we don't want him." We answered: "Didn't you see this all around you? Couldn't you see it was going to be like this?" They replied: "We just never thought it would happen around here because this is a skilled thing. We can see how they can learn to do assembly work. . . . " Finally we said: "Look, we have news for you!

This is the policy. This is the way we're going to do it." I looked at my watch, and I said: "Anybody who isn't back on the job in ten minutes can go and get his check."

So they grumbled but they went back to work. Besides all the trouble we had here, though, once our people got a union organized, they started to form Black and White factions within the union. There wasn't a whole lot we could do about that. This was the United Autoworkers Union. Of course, Walter Reuther was firmly committed to no discrimination, but what people wanted at the top and what happened at the bottom were two different things. Other than that, though, things went pretty well and the community began to accept integration to some degree. Actually this was harder on the community later on because once Blacks started to earn the kind of money that enabled them to do some of the things they hadn't been able to do, the community began to feel their impact. But as is usually the case, there are some people strong in the community who rise to the top in a situation like that and bring things under control. I was very lucky, as I have been throughout my career, in the people I worked for.

During this period I worked for a man who later became executive vice president of the corporation. He was just a fantastic guy, strong, decisive and we pioneered some things down in that plant for the whole company. I was down there alone, as I said, for six months, so I got a pretty good feel for the community and I had my biases and prejudices about the community and where the corporation should stand there. Now it was a rule in the corporation that when you were asked to make a public statement of any kind, whether to the press or the Kiwanis Club, you had to write it out and send it to headquarters to New York. There they were supposed to approve it and send it back, and by that time nobody cared anymore. Speeches got lost in New York. You might never hear. As a result the corporation was tongue-tied and had a very low profile in all of its communities. Down in our community, of course, we had a very high profile right off the bat because we were the only plant starting up there and there was all that unemployment. You couldn't stay out of the news. So I had an idea: this was a great chance to take the initiative in community relations. I finally wrote a three-page letter outlining my views on how the corporation ought to approach community relations. I carried the letter in my coat pocket for a week, couldn't make up my mind whether to send it or not. Finally, I sent it to the vice president of public relations whom I knew only slightly, and I sent a copy to my boss. My boss, who got the carbon, called me up and said: "That's a very interesting letter, but it would have been much nicer if you'd sent it to me. Nevertheless, there're some good ideas in there and I'd like to talk to you about them. I've already talked to the vice president of public relations you sent the letter to and so-and-so is very interested. Next time you come up to New York, let's all get together on it."

To make a long story short, out of that grew a community relations program, and later on I was promoted to set up this program for the whole corporation.

That's how I got to headquarters.   Another thing we initiated when I got to corporate headquarters was the beginning of national communications about negotiations with the United Autoworkers and the Farm Equipment Workers unions.   For example, we set up a network so that when we finished a bargaining session at night or whenever, no matter what time it was, a summary of the happenings of that day went out to every plant.   The next morning when the foreman went to work, there was a written summary of what had happened in New York.   So we had a good communications network operating.

Our community program also was very new to the corporation.   It was simple.   It consisted of: "Look, let's take an active role in the community and be a leader and give your works manager, who is your number one guy in the community, and anybody else he designates, the right to speak out.   You are going to make some mistakes, but they're not going to be that serious and the benefits to be gained by doing that are so much greater than the risks that you ought to do that."   They agreed.   Then we said: "Let's tell the community what's going on.   Let's not be silent on labor relations matters.   We're back in that era again where nobody says anything, and all the information comes out of the union.   Nothing comes out of the company."

Those were the basic tenets of our program.   Let management talk.   Don't worry about what our managers are going to say.   Yes, they're going to make mistakes.   But take the initiative.   Communicate at all times.   If you're going to have a strike at the plant, give a statement.   Give your point of view.   The union's going to give theirs.   The reason for not doing so, of course, is that this antagonizes the union.   My reply to that was: "They're antagonized anyway, else they wouldn't be out on strike.   What can you do that's going to make it any worse?"   My experience bears this out.   Union workers aren't any madder when you speak your mind; they know where you stand—if you're honest.   If you tell newspapers one thing and the union something else, that's another problem.   But if they know where you stand, they're not all that upset about it.

So I set up a corporate community relations program and became an instructor in equal opportunity in the company's management school, and that was interesting too, because I found out how deep the prejudices went in people who were not in the same position as those at the plant level, who could not express such prejudice and had no choice but to go along with integration.   In the management school, you had a lot of foremen from plants that didn't have those problems also, and, since I was just an instructor, they made no secret of their views; they could let out all their prejudices.   They had nothing to lose.   "It may be a great thing for the chairman," they'd say, "but he doesn't have to try to get along with these people.   Just where are the Negroes in the executive suite?" they'd say.

So in New York, basically I did two things: I set up an internal communications program inside the corporation and a community relations program for the plants and I became part of the staff of the executive office.   Now again in this first corporation, the chairman had been destined to be top man in the corporation by nature of his background. His family had founded the company, and when he came in he selected a man named Richardson as his number two man, the president, who was his complete opposite. He and Richardson were as different as night and day. Our chairman was a philosopher, and my experience with those two men gave me one of the things that stuck with me: philosophers can rarely run companies. Our chairman could give you more good arguments on both sides of the question than anybody I ever met in my life. The result was he had a very hard time making up his mind. On the other side of the coin, everything was black and white to Richardson. You gave Richardson a set of facts and he could immediately see what was white; there were no gray areas in Richardson's world. So as long as they got along, it was great, because our chairman could philosophize and he could talk to Richardson and Richardson could see what was white and something could get done. Well, our chairman went off to Arizona for a few months and nothing was getting done—Richardson's hands were tied.

So finally Richardson started taking things in his own hands. It was in the middle of a big postwar expansion program and he just went ahead and did them. Then our chairman came back and saw what was going on and tried to get the board to retire Richardson early. Instead, the board went ahead and named Richardson chief executive officer, after which our chairman resigned, feeling very much hurt and betrayed, though he remained on the board. But the fact was a company can't be run the way our chairman had been running it, even though he was a very, very brilliant man. He just wasn't practical.

For example, once he had the whole company in a turmoil because he had come to the conclusion that the kind of institutional size the corporation had become was just not good for society as a whole. So he decided that each plant should not employ more than 500 people, and he put the controller's department to work to figure out what the cost structure would be if you were to build heavy equipment in plants of no more than 500 people. They found we couldn't compete on that basis. But he really, honestly was concerned with large groups of people being congregated in highly specialized tasks in great big installations, and he wanted to do something about it. He was a man before his time.

Now all during this period I was one of five in the executive office concerned with communications and it was an extremely interesting experience. Our chairman believed that the chief executive of the company was automatically the chief public relations officer. There was no way for him to delegate that function—nobody could speak for the corporation as effectively as the chief executive officer. So while we had a vice president of public relations, we didn't have a public relations department; we worked out of the executive office. We five had access to everything in the building. You could walk into the chairman's office, ask his secretary for anything in his files and she was under orders to give it to you. Our chairman had said: "There's no way you fellows can operate if you don't know everything that's going on in the company that you think is important to what you're trying to do. So everything in the company is available to you." So we could walk into any group meeting—not the chairman's personal meeting with the president—but any group meeting in the chairman's office that had a relationship to our public image or was in any way to be communicated in some form and you didn't have to be invited. You were just expected.

So I had a very close contact with the chairman and Richardson, the president, as well as with the vps of public relations and industrial relations. I began to recognize, and am certain about it now, that one of the qualities for success of the line executive is what I call single-mindedness. The line executive is not distracted by all the peripheral things that go on. He has the ability to concentrate on the main thing and not get involved in anything else. That's a quality I see in the chief operating officer in the great corporation I'm with now. He's single-minded just as Richardson was.

I once worked in a small family company in Ohio for the vice president of manufacturing, the dominant force in the company of the older generation, and he had the same characteristic. I'd describe it as the black and white syndrome. There are always shades of gray, depending on the person, but if there are too many grays, he's dead. So I'll have to say that the chief operating officers I know who've been successful, the guys who really make the thing run, are very single-minded and tend to be narrow, driving people.

In that same small company in the next generation of management, my boss was one of the most delightful and bright human beings I've ever known and I count him among my closest friends, but he was a lousy businessman, because he was a great philosopher and humanist. We did a lot of wonderful things but we didn't make any money. Making money was too routine and mundane and not exciting enough. We made that little company a great place to work except we didn't make any money. The objective of the executive is to turn resources into wealth and of course into economic gain, so that a lot of executives are not interested in the human aspects as much. This can be a detriment in some ways. Business isn't yet willing to face the fact that the economic system exists only to serve the social system. We think it's an end in itself, and the single-minded guy believes that very strongly. That's one of the reasons he's successful. How do you make that transition from someone who can make the system run the way it's designed to run and at the same time make him conscious that it's not an end in itself, it's only a means to an end, and the end is life or quality of life or whatever you want to call it. Now that's a trick we haven't yet come to grips with. We don't know how to do that. The corporation I'm with now, a great corporation, is probably more fortunate than many companies of its size because our chairman is not the single-minded guy, he does understand the transition. Whether he can make his line managers understand it or not I don't know—but he does understand it. His number two man does not, the number two man makes the thing go. Our chairman has the grand design—this is where the company is going. He's the risk-taker, the visionary, but our number two man makes it go, and ideally you need both for a successful company. But, you know, if you can only have one of them, the visionary or the doer, you better pick the guy who can make it go, because there's nothing to be visionary about if you don't make it go.

Finally we got all these things running and I looked around and said two things to myself. One was: I've reached the stage in the corporation where the payoff for taking risks and muddying up the waters and pioneering new things isn't worth it. If you just sit still and mind your Ps and Qs in this big bureaucracy, everything will turn out fine. But don't muddy the waters, Ken, and you've got it made. The second thing I decided was that the highest position I could achieve was one level below the vice presidency, because one of the guys I worked with, it seemed to me, was going to be the top guy. He had better credentials than I and was very bright. So I was kind of debating what to do about my situation.

Then a man who was a member of a wealthy family that owned a little 75 million dollar machinery company called me up one day and said: "Will you come and talk to me about a job?" Someone had recommended my boss to him and my boss had turned down the job. But the man had pestered my boss for an industrial relations man so finally my boss gave him my name. At the time I was not aware of all this. So this man, Jay Sterling, of Sterling Inc., called me, and we found out that we had a lot in common and that in a sense we were also complementary to each other. Jay came from modest wealth and had inherited this position as president in the company. He had been in the Marine Corps, had sat in trenches and so on. We had a lot of conversations. He is a philosopher and he could talk all night to guys in the trenches who were either union members or union officers. So he came back with some ideas about labor relations which happened to fit in with some I had developed completely independently coming up through the corporate system.

I finally went to work for him. I remember to this day: I went in to tell my boss that I had this offer and he couldn't have seemed less concerned—and I was just crushed. I had thought I had been doing a great job and that my boss and I had a great relationship. I told Jay Sterling that and he called my boss and said: "You've just got to let me tell Ken, because he was terribly hurt." So my old boss said: "All right, tell him," and that's how I found out.

In this little company I found that the family was terribly divided. Jay Sterling's father was the middle of three brothers. Jay himself had two brothers and there were other descendents of the founders involved, so we had this little

75 million dollar company with five owning monsters. The seniors were in their late sixties fighting for control of the company for their kids and everybody falling into the hierarchical structure in relationship to his parent. That combined with Jay's desire to do the right thing and not always the economic thing just led to near-disaster and we finally merged the company with another corporation.

Now let me digress here about the break-up of my first marriage very briefly. As I said, I have guilt feelings about it and find it hard to go over it again. I think the strain began to tell on my wife fairly early. I was working long hours and late in the earlier job as industrial relations assistant in that first plant. You see then I used to get about 450 grievances a week and this was a plant of about 6,000 people. I had secretaries on both shifts. I had six guys who investigated the grievances, but I personally wrote all the answers. That's also something I started in the first big corporation I went to—writing a grievance answer, which reviewed the case, the position of each of the parties and then came to a conclusion—all in a report. This was ultimately adopted in that big company. But it took time, and at that point I hadn't learned to delegate. One of the things this fellow who was plant manager for whom I worked taught me was how to delegate. It was painful but I eventually learned. He was single and at five o'clock every night he'd walk by my office on the way home and he'd say: "Aren't you going home?" and I'd say: "You got to be crazy—who's going to write up all these grievances?" He'd answer: "They're people out there"—he'd point to the department—"who are just dying to help you, if you'd let them." The way I'd respond was . . . you know I'd never really say it . . . but what I meant was: "Hey, look, this is my big chance. If I fail, it's because I can't do it, not because I gave it to somebody else who couldn't do it. I'm going to make it myself or fail on my own."

Well, finally, of course, I couldn't, and he was relentless. First, he'd chide me, and finally he'd say: "Where is this?" I'd say: "I didn't have the time," and he'd answer: "You know, Ken, we've got to get it done. I don't care whether you haven't the time. There'd been time if you'd delegate." So finally I learned the hard way. As I say, it was painful but it was a lot better than sitting down and explaining why I couldn't do it. He brought it home to me loud and clear. So it was during that period I'd come down at night and dictate and I was just never home. During that time we had two children a year apart, so that's when the strain began to show. Then we went down south for two years in that other plant and finally up to headquarters in New York, when she was in about her seventh month of pregnancy. We were in New York only a year and then I went to this other plant; there was no question about it, the work came first. I was subconsciously more than consciously determined to be a business success. Actually the thing that motivated me most of all was not a great desire for success but a fear of failure and the fear of the things that go with failure. It wasn't until I really did fail later on that I realized the fear was much worse than the reality. I suppose that comes from childhood, but security and acceptance have always been important to me.

I remember once when I was young and we used to go downtown in this town in Indiana on Saturday night and girl-watch and pick up dates, usually girls who worked in the five-and-ten. We were standing around on a corner where there were three banks across the street from each other and we got to talking about money, having lots of money, and I remember saying that if someone guaranteed me $5,000 a year (a respectable sum in those days) for the rest of my life, I'd take it and never ask for anything more. Yes, security and acceptance—that's what I've looked for. Conflict across the table with the union never bothers me —that's competition. But conflict with people I cared about has always bothered me. I'll compromise to the point where I'll get myself in more trouble by compromising than by facing the issues, and I did that with my wife. I knew I was wrong and I made promises that I just knew intuitively I couldn't keep.

So when I remarried after we were divorced, I married my secretary because I thought surely she understood all these things. Well, she didn't understand, and now she's gone too. . . . I still see my first wife from time to time. I saw her when my youngest daughter got married a year ago and I've seen her intermittently in the last several years. My second marriage didn't last as long. It was when I was with my present great corporation first in the midwest and then out here. When I decided to pick up from the midwest and move out here to headquarters—I wanted to be where the power and action was, where the decisions were made—my second wife stayed behind. Would I do it over again that way? I'd have to say yes. If marriage is a partnership and each one tries to treat the other as a person on an equal basis, then in my mind, given my tendencies and what I think the corporation demands in performance, there is no way my marriage could have lasted. Only if to the wife the most important thing in the world is her husband's career would marriage to a man like me be lasting. I knew a few women like that in this corporation and I envy the men who have this kind of wife. It's the only way I could stay married.

Because the truth is: a lot more is demanded of you as an executive. Business moves faster today. Major things happen much more quickly than they used to, and if you're confronted with a situation, you've got to stay with it if you want to carry it through. The alternative is to walk away from it and carry out your family responsibilities. People have no idea of the pressures you face. I may sit here and say: "Yeah, I ought to be with Cynthia." I understand the problem but what am I going to do? For example, this week—and it's nothing very big— our chairman is going to take up something before the board on Thursday. It involves my function, and our senior vice president, my boss, is going to make the presentation. Our senior vp has a daughter in the hospital, but he's in Honolulu at a Far Eastern regional meeting. I don't know where our chairman is but he isn't here, and somebody has to put together this material for the meeting on Thursday. I had planned to take a vacation this week. So something has to give. Well, I'll tell you, other than this afternoon with you, I've been working on that presentation continuously. Suppose I were married and I'd said to Cynthia: "Yes, we'll go some place this week." Then what do I do? Do I walk out on our chairman, on the senior vp, my boss? The senior vp is dedicated enough. He didn't even stay here while his youngest daughter is in the hospital— serious enough to keep her there for a couple of weeks. Those kinds of pressure are there all the time.

A year ago I took a month's vacation at one time, and that's unheard of around here. Nobody does that. My boss was planning something for March. I said: "I won't be here." He answered: "That's all right. We'll do it later." I said: "Like when?" So he gave me a date later in March. So I said: "I planned to be gone all month." He thought a bomb had exploded, because you just don't do that. That's my experience in corporations generally. Ours is not unique, although ours is a very fascinating company because the loyalty and commitment under our chairman is almost unbelievable in this day and age.

Let me go back and pick up my career with this little 75 million dollar, family-owned company where we'd had all the fun but we weren't making any money. Finally my friend, Jay Sterling, a very bright guy but again very indecisive, a guy who didn't like conflict, went and merged his family company with this other outfit. Now this outfit was run by a real tough-minded son of a bitch named Sam Thatcher. Sam came in and forced my friend and boss right out of the room. He was willing to face all the tough decisions that my boss had been walking away from and the first thing you know my boss was out of a job. I finally left the merged company because I couldn't agree with Sam Thatcher. I was a trustee of my old boss's family trust for his children which contained a lot of stock in this merged company and I said that we ought to get rid of that stock, sell out. I said: "One man can't run a 250 million dollar company by himself." Well, I got news for you. Sam Thatcher doubled and tripled the value of the stock, and he made every single major decision. Talk about single-mindedness, he had just one goal in life—to make money. He not only made his money but he installed his son as president at 39, and the company's been doing well.

He wrote everything off in 1959 and nobody thought anything of it because it was a bad time. From that point on, you will find ten years that the company made more money each successive year. I was president of my old boss's division for a year and I had to call in every month and tell what we made. Then they'd tell me what to report, and they'd put the rest of it aside to feed out whenever it was needed in the annual report. That's why I left. It would be harder to get away with that kind of thing now, but that man would do anything to make money.

I had been made head of that division with the title of president in order largely to keep my boss's old organization together because there were a lot of good people in there. I had originally recruited a lot of them and I knew them and they trusted me. The company was going along well and all it needed was a custodian. I wasn't threatening to any of the other guys because I wasn't a line operator. They could accept me, whereas if one of the strong incoming line guys was given the presidency, they might not accept him. Well that was great, except that two months after I took over the bottom dropped out of everything and, as it turned out, we were not as good as we had thought, and a tremendous overhauling of the whole organization was needed. Instead of being a contributor our division turned up with a loss.

I was down in Florida on vacation with my family—this was in December— when we got the November report, and it showed we'd lost money, the first time the company had lost money for years. I left immediately. My family spent Christmas and all their vacation all by themselves while I was trying to understand what this was all about, and meeting with my former boss and the new executives. Finally I was very successful in reorienting the division and turning it back into a profit-making operation, and this whetted my appetite for being a line manager and a chief executive officer. However, I couldn't keep it up. Everything was fine while I was single-minded and had only one goal in sight, but when things eased up and other possibilities for the future intervened, my drive faded and my efforts began to be scattered.

One of the experiences I had while I had been with that family firm, however, had a major impact on my future. My boss, Jay Sterling, had been appointed to the Wage Stabilization Board during the Korean War as in industry member—the board was made up of representatives of industry, labor and the public. This was in 1952 when Harry Truman was president and Adlai Stevenson was going to run against Dwight Eisenhower, and the Coal Case came up. The miners had negotiated a contract that had broken through the original stabilization guidelines. Then new guidelines had been set and now these were broken also—the coal thing went right through the roof.

My boss, Jay, felt strongly, representing industry, that our board should make this a test case, but the other industry members seemed not to want to go along. "Look," they said, "the deal's already been made. Truman's agreed to allow this increase in return for which Lewis will support Adlai Stevenson against Eisenhower, so what's the use our going through all the motions?" So Jay called me up and said: "I want your advice." I flew down and we talked about it. He told me how the industry people felt and said: "Tonight, we're going to dinner with the chairman of our board and I want you to listen to him and we'll talk about it afterward."

The chairman, a very bright guy, representing the public, spent the whole evening questioning us. We got back to the hotel and Jay said: "Has the chairman made up his mind or have we convinced him?" I replied: "Of course, he's made up his mind. He's part of the deal. All he was doing was pumping us to find out where the industry people stand so he can find ways to counter." So Jay said: "You're dead wrong—this man's an honest man. If we can make a case, I think he'll support us." I replied: "You're so naive, it's unbelievable." He added: "I'll tell you something else: you're going to stay here and you're going to prove that we have a case, if we have one."

So I stayed there. The first thing I found out was that all the people who worked for the industry members of the board were members of the CIO Office Workers Union, so everything we did went immediately to the union. We brought in two gals from the outside, hired two more and the Board gave me a researcher, and we put together the case for the industry. At first these industry guys didn't pay any attention to Jay and then we began to get the facts and they started to listen. Finally we decided that one of the key board members, a man named Gerston, was the man we had to convince to swing it. The thing about Gerston was his vanity, so if we could convince him he would make a national showing, and boy, we had it.

So we started to work on him and finally convinced him we had a case. He convinced two other industry members and, to make a long story short, Jay was dead right. We did make a case, and the board did turn down the coal miners. They went up to the level they'd granted others and turned down the rest of it. Truman overruled us, the board resigned and that was the end of the board.

After that experience, though, Gerston, a big wheel in industry, offered me a job at $100,000 a year. I was thirty-five. I didn't take it. I rationalized that I didn't think I was ready. The truth was I was scared. I figured that anybody who would pay that much would expect a performance and . . . well, you would either perform or you're gone. Again my need for security emerged, and I didn't have the guts to take the chance. But from that moment on, making $100,000 became important to me. I had been offered it and I had not faced up to it. Nevertheless, the whole thing had been a tremendous experience—putting that whole case together with its national implications.

One of the things it taught me was that if management would work at it, would put in the time to get the facts and build a good case, it can win. The union hadn't been doing anything, and one of the things I've found is that for the most part the union won't put in the work. I thought when I got to dealing with the UAW at the national level this wouldn't be true, but it was just as true there at that time. We sat across the table from Walter Reuther and he was a philosopher and brilliant and had the working man's interests at heart—no question about it—but he wasn't prepared; they hadn't done their homework.

After I left the company which survived after the merger, I joined another family-owned company as operating vice president. I'd been there about a year and had looked at our company carefully, and I said: "We've only got one significant physical facility, and that's where the profits of this company are coming from—and that's down in Florida. Here we are trying to run it from New York City, and there's no way we're going to make it. Well, talk about naive, I was naive if I thought I was going to move the president from New York to Florida. So I finally said: "OK, why don't the president and the board stay in New York and the treasurer if he wants to be in touch with Wall Street, but let's get the operating people down to Florida." Well, that got a lot better reception than the original idea. Then I also recommended we sell one plant and close a little plant we had in another state. Well, it finally ended that my ideas were just out of keeping with anything they wanted to do. As it turns out, they've done everything I suggested except move corporate headquarters to Florida, although the vp of manufacturing now operates from down there.

Now the executive vice president in those days was a man named Jake Zimmerman to whom I reported. Zimmerman was not part of the family, but he was a very bright guy, though not too well organized and not very predictable. He would, however, tolerate all kinds of discussion until he made up his mind. But when he'd made up his mind, I'd back him all the way. I respected him. So when I contemplated moving to the big famous corporation I'm with now, I told him I was talking with them. I said I don't know if anything will come of it, but I am talking to them. He urged me not to go. I thought it important that my boss know first. I guess this is all part of my grandfather, my mother's father's, heritage to me—this loyalty. He wasn't the major influence on my life—in many ways he was subordinate to my grandmother, but he was German, Bavarian, and one of the things I picked up from him is that you always respect your superiors. You don't quarrel with your superiors, so I have always been a very loyal subordinate.

So when the offer came in from my present corporation and I decided to take it, I told Zimmerman and finally the president. When the president learned about it, he invited me over to his apartment. I thought that Zimmerman would be there too, but he wasn't. He offered me the executive vice presidency, so I said: "What about Jake?" He replied: "We are coming to a parting of the ways anyway." I answered: "Gee, I can't do that! He's my boss, and he's never done anything to hurt me. I work with him and I just can't." One thing I lack is what I call a killer instinct. I don't have the ability, when the opportunity is there, to capitalize on it, if it means conflict with someone I respect or that I've worked with or am close to. I don't even have to like the man, because I didn't particularly like Zimmerman, but he'd been my boss and he'd been fair and the thought of having the president go in there and say: "You're through and Ken is going to be executive vice president," was too much for me. I can't do that sort of thing. I think again that to be a successful line guy particularly, you have to be able to do that. On the other hand, if not doing that is compassion, that's probably a good trait for an industrial relations guy.

Eventually I went over to this worldwide corporation I have spent most of my career with. I started out as a line manager. They had approached me through a very strong vice president named Hugh Scott, on the basis that I knew something about the machinery business from the kind of thing I had been doing in this family firm. When I got inside, however, I realized that I had been brought in on a losing proposition. This thing they wanted me to take over was a little operation in a business that our big corporation had no real interest in and shouldn't have bothered with. Some of the top people had already said: "Get out of this business. We don't belong it in," but Hugh Scott was determined to prove them wrong. They had already gone through two managers before me and when I got inside it didn't take me long to realize it was hopeless.

Then we merged another business into the same division and I ran both of them for awhile. We then had a change in vps running the division and I reported to a senior vp named Harper Connors. Harper and I didn't agree on how to run the business, so now I come to that dark moment, the first real fall in my career, the crisis that I guess comes to everyone sometime in life. It was a Friday. Harper called me into his office. He's a big, somewhat inarticulate man, and we both sat there a moment and I could feel the tension. Finally, he said to me: "Ken, I think I have to replace you." I sat silent. Then I said: "Harper, you're the boss. If you have to, you have to."

That was all there was to it. You know it's one of the very fascinating things about corporate life—the way these things are done. No reasons were given— nothing. I hear these few words and I'm removed as division vice president, my salary substantially cut and I'm in limbo. I'd heard reasons from other people, and I suppose it had something to do with our basic conflict over that business, but I never heard any reasons from Harper. I suppose it doesn't always happen that way but I believe it happens that way more often than not. There's a kind of creed at the executive level, you understand. You don't want to show your ignorance or embarrass your boss. Presumably I understood why Harper was relieving me, I was aware of the politics of the whole situation, and if Harper had wanted to explain it to me, he would have explained it to me. Now I know him well enough to know that he couldn't have told me. He had made an intuitive decision. The last thing I'd done just before he made his decision had been a presentation before our chairman in Harper's presence, saying that we were going to have to get out of that business. We've done so since, but at that time this was against Harper's judgment. Subsequently he put into my job a guy in whom he had great confidence and who had worked with Harper throughout his career up the corporate structure. This man did a very creditable job but it was hopeless. That business could not compete for the necessary corporate funds and, as I said, it was closed down.

Meanwhile, I was in limbo. Harper had offered me a job as his administrative manager but had left the door open for me to look around inside the corporation or out. Our chairman talked to me three times. He couldn't have been nicer. He offered me a job as manager of new businesses. I looked at that for awhile and finally declined it. I felt it was outside the kind of competence I had which lies in the organizational and marketing area. It seemed to me since our corporate core was manufacturing, the only kind of guy who could make good in that sort of job would be a man who understands the technical aspects of the products. The chairman didn't agree with me, but I guess one of the great feelings I have about our chairman is his largeness of spirit. I ran into a lot of guys who don't know you when you're down. One vice president I remember in particular just couldn't get rid of me fast enough. As far as he was concerned I was dead. There was nothing to be gained by being nice to me, and he showed his colors right there. I had thought I was particularly qualified to do corporate planning, because I'd had planning skills supplemented by line experience, but this man just couldn't have been less interested. He's not with the company any more.

But this was indeed my dark period. My wife had been left behind. That marriage was breaking up and I was here and there wasn't anybody. I was all by myself and was beginning to lose confidence in myself and in my aims. I stayed at work for two weeks after my fall, and I did this for two reasons—one I had some commitments and was trying to take care of them and two I didn't want to seem to be running away. I believed everyone was looking at me, thinking of me as a failure, and, of course, most people didn't really care. They didn't know much about it in a big company like ours. It's not a big deal to others. A lot of people you work with, unless their relationship to you is based on the power structure, treat you just as they always did before your fall. In fact, I believe—although this is an afterthought—a lot of people had seen me as pretty successful and my plunge made them feel: "Well, anyway he's human." But this was the lowest point, a very, very tough time for me. It got me where I lived.

So finally, after I'd looked around awhile, traveling at the company's expense and everything, I decided I'd take Harper up on his offer of the administrative manager's job, and it really worked out very well in many ways. Harper is a very conceptual guy with a lot of ideas and one of the skills I was able to bring to him was the ability to understand him. He is very inarticulate. By contrast I am relatively articulate, so I could express his views better than he could, and I understood what he was driving at sometimes when he himself didn't fully understand it. I have a great liking for him even under the circumstances. I worked for him for about a year. I really zeroed in on the job. I took over the management information system, the division controller's job and group communications and the planning for a number of plants scheduled to be built. There was a lot of accounting in my job and while I found Harper stimulating I didn't find the job all that stimulating, since it was mostly administrative and didn't give me the chance to contrive, devise, develop and to conceptualize things. Still I was not all that unhappy and I had decided by that time that I was going to make my career finally with this corporation. The outlook was good, the money was good even under the circumstances of the cut and I had come to have the highest regard for our chairman. I felt he was going to take the company and go places with it. As you know, he has. His timing on acquisitions and new facilities has been fantastic.

So after I'd been working in this area awhile, one day a senior vice president came to me and said: "Would you be interested in moving into employee relations?" I said: "Yes, under the right circumstances." The director of industrial relations had quit, and this senior vice president had decided to add a few areas such as salary administration, communications and so on to create a vice presidency. My background fitted what he was looking for, so finally I came into my own again, was promoted to vice president and moved into an area that I was most at home in, even though I had come into the corporation as a line manager.

This area has taken on new and increasing importance. In the old days, they used to staff employee relations slots with men who hadn't been able to make it on the line, and our present corporation, great as it is, is in terms of its business culture, some twenty years behind Detroit and New York, and so our chairman is just beginning to say to the organization: "Human resources are a major component and we see Ken as a professional human resources man."

So now I'm where I want to be. There're about a 100 top executives under our chairman and his senior vps who make the strategic policy decisions, and these top executives, our level, are what make the company go. A lot of conceptualizing is done by us. As a matter of fact, the chairman and his senior vps are all better reactors than they are originators, so they much prefer that you promote things with them. They like to shoot things down rather than originate. I find that very acceptable because basically I am a conceptualizer. So you find there is a great opportunity at our level for developing new things. I know this is true. Our chairman sees me as one of the main change agents in the company, the guy who has caused more change to happen than anyone else, and I'm very controversial for that reason.

So looking back I find that I've found my metier and I've concentrated my efforts in the human resources area, and in general I feel much more comfortable about everything that goes on around me. I'm much less of a perfectionist than I used to be—I don't know whether that's good or bad. I pass on things now up to senior management that ten years ago I just never would have done. I think I am a lot more open with people than I used to be. I've always had a good relationship with people who report to me, and I have a particularly interesting group of such associates now. One is a psychologist, doing human research, another a gal who's become the first corporate manager at that level and the only female manager of about 500 top managers across the country. She came into my group as a third level supervisor and I like to think I contributed to the corporation by stepping aside so that she could show what she could do. Another is a very interesting young fellow in his mid-thirties, who in my opinion is never going to make it in the corporation because he is a white knight on a white charger and the corporation isn't ready for that yet. But all of these people are very stimulating. One of the things we are trying to do—I guess one of my assets is an analytical mind—is to bring analytical techniques to bear on human resources. We are using the computer for some very interesting studies in human resources, and we are fortunate that our chairman understands the computer and sees how you can use information systems in this area.

As for my personal life, now that my second marriage has failed, there are, of course, the times of loneliness, but I would have to say that my work fulfills me, and, as our chairman once jokingly remarked, he didn't think I could afford any more marriages.

Now you've asked me whether I think the corporation and corporate life have changed much in the years I've been working and I must answer yes. My own experience seems to bear this out. I remember years ago I was offered a chance to go east on a job I didn't think was a good one or one that I wanted and I turned it down. People told me: "You might as well quit. Your career is over." Now this might be true in some companies still, but it isn't in ours. We now consider the needs and desires and wants and values of people in the organization to a much greater extent than formerly. We don't expect or demand the kind of blind obedience or loyalty that was characteristic of corporations twenty years ago. Also there's much more opportunity to find your own life style in the corporation. It's no longer considered so undignified or terrible to be different from others. In many companies the man with the gray flannel suit doesn't really exist anymore, and styles fit the region and the culture. We have a pretty open way of life out here in the southwest.

While life styles may be freer, the pressures on the executive, nevertheless, have grown even more because of the complexities of the modern enterprise. I no longer have to worry about a home life or a marriage. I don't have to worry about anything except business, so in that way I'm luckier than some. If I've a social engagement, it's because I made it—my wife didn't make it—or it's expected of me. So if I want just to work, I can do that. Nothing interferes with that. A lot of times that's all I do. I will just work and come home and eat and go to bed, and I find fulfillment in this.

To conclude, let me say again, yes, the corporation and business life styles have improved. Perhaps motivations and goals haven't changed much—the transforming of resources into wealth, and perhaps corporation executives still cling to old standards and norms that have been outmoded to some degree. For example, while the idea that "creeping socialism" as the ultimate in moral reprehensibleness may have waned, the epithets hurled at those with noneconomic aims who most threaten business seem now to be "liberal," "far-out" and "dreamer". We still say people don't understand business. That's why I say one of the men who works for me may not make it in the corporation. He's as bright as all get-out but he's a white knight in a noneconomic church. Still, the corporation offers enormous challenge and variety.

Finally, let me say about my own life, there've been enormous pressures in the executive world, and I've had to pay a price for my struggles in the corporation. Our world does require single-mindedness and strong motivation to succeed. What we call single-mindedness, will to give of oneself and sacrifice for our enterprise, others call ambition, love of power and ruthlessness. I wouldn't go along with that. If you want to succeed anywhere, you must pay a price, whether it's in the corporation or anywhere else. You have to decide yourself whether the price is worth it. I've loved the work. I gave up two marriages for it. I wish I hadn't had to, but that's the way it was. I still look forward every morning to my work in the corporation and to the years I'll be spending there. That work has given me most of what I want and need. I've enjoyed it. . . .

*   *   *   *

Pressure—yes, the pressures were heavy enough where Ken Burdett is, but there was something more. *"A lot of times . . . I will just work and come home and eat and go to bed. . . ."* My associate and I spent an evening talking about this man. We admired him. We found him interesting and human, and my associate, a warm, happily married woman, could not see how such a man could have given up a home, companionship and love even for the pleasures of work. A man can see this more readily, I had thought. Blessed is he who loves his work; his life is one long feast. But I too thought how high the price had been, and that old phrase from long ago returned to me again and again: "Loneliness goes with the territory. . . ."

We now move to another man under heavy pressure, a senior vp, who remembers the good old days. . . .

8

"I Was Lucky. It Was Hard Work but I Had a Lot of Freedom. . . ."

A senior vice president remembers his days in the field

Some people are lucky. They seem to be born golden boys, and Tom Lassiter is one. He's a good-looking man in his forties, a senior vice president of an extremely successful oil company. But Tom is fortunate in other ways also. He has an attractive personality, grew up in a warm, interesting, protective family and learned to work hard while young. What he seems to have enjoyed most and remember best, though, was his days in the field as an oil scout. . .

I look at my life and I see two things: a great deal of freedom and good relationships with people. And I see work. And the work is where the pleasure is.

I am one of those Midwesterners, born in Ohio, who grew up in both an academic and an industrial environment. Our city was the location of a well known university as well as a center of heavy industry. My father was a college professor. He was raised in Massachusetts, attended Columbia where he received a degree in accounting. Following graduation he joined a shipping company, working initially in England and later in Buenos Aires. He worked three years in Buenos Aires when the company went bankrupt and all he had left was a return ticket on a boat back to the U.S. On the ship he was befriended by a man who turned out to be the dean of commerce at this well known university in Ohio. It was the turning point of his life. My father was then 26. He went to the university city with this benefactor, saw the university and it was love at first sight. He stayed there 36 years, met and married my mother, had four children and in time became dean of the commerce school when his benefactor became president of the university.

My mother was an accomplished woman, an artist, and after graduation from the Art Institute of Chicago, became fashion editor of a large Chicago daily paper. When she and my father married, she was actually earning a higher salary than he. There were four of us in the family and we had a happy childhood. Although I grew up during the depression, we suffered few of its hardships. My father had a steady pay check and although we lived in a modest house, we even had a maid. Food was plentiful, the necessities of life were provided, but there were few luxuries. We didn't own an automobile until just before the war.

Life for children in that city was pleasant and comfortable. I remember when I was nine or ten, my older brother and I would usually go to a movie on Sunday afternoon. It cost a nickel to get in then and we'd use another nickel of our dime allowance for candy. Then we'd come back and walk into the house and the odor of a standing rib roast would emanate from the kitchen. We used to carp about this. "Roast beef, again!" In fact later on in life when we'd have a party and would have as the piece de resistance roast beef, if anyone in the family was there who remembered, he'd say: "Roast beef, again!"

My mother was the strong one in our family. My dad was somewhat of a pacifist. He was a commanding personality, though, six feet six, 230 pounds, white hair, a grand moustache and, his trademark, a white handkerchief flowing from his breast pocket. We used to kid him about having his handkerchief at "decision level." Beautiful clothes. He became very well known in the community, and later in the business world, as he expanded his interests beyond the educational field into consulting work. He was in demand as a lecturer and after dinner speaker, primarily on the subject of economics. He was known as "the Dean" and that's the way he was always referred to—"the Dean."

But it was my mother who was the disciplinarian. When we were disciplined for doing something we weren't supposed to, she was the one to give it to us and we knew we deserved it. She was a strong woman, a very strong woman, and I suppose I was her favorite, although later in life she and my older brother became very close and she relied on him a great deal. Our house was a reading house. There were always plenty of books and magazines around and both my mother and father were voracious readers. We were exposed to a myriad of periodicals from Harper's to Black Mask.

I know people who tell me their childhood was unhappy. Mine was quite the opposite. We had lots of friends and we had a good relationship with our parents. There was always plenty of activity. We learned to work early. We had summer jobs since there wasn't much money around, and if you wanted any you had to go out and earn it. Early in life I sold newspapers, worked in a root beer stand earning tips and later as a stock boy in a grocery store. In high school I worked in a sheet metal shop, on a construction gang, and often as a painter. One Christmas my older brother and I sold Christmas wreaths. We earned good money. It seems as though we were always working when we could. There was a strong inclination to work.

I recall high school as probably a period in my life when I had more fun than at any other time. I really enjoyed those years. As a kid, I had a lot of friends and we did a lot of things together, some good, some bad. From one viewpoint you have to look at it in the context of the times, because it was during the war—World War II—and despite all the problems, the casualties and the horrors of war, it was kind of a free-wheeling period in the United States . . . factories were working and people were employed—there was plenty of money. It was a boom time.

We were in a great high school too. It was an integrated high school, probably 10 to 12 percent black, and we got along pretty well with the Blacks, particularly in athletics where we got to know them on the basketball or baseball teams. I don't remember any overt discrimination, though there wasn't any social mingling that I remember. This was in the 1940's and, of course, you didn't have the social rapport between Whites and Blacks that you sometimes have today. But as for the school, it was great. Teachers took an interest in the students, and I often reflect on it because I received a tremendous education there. I look back on it as a period when I had a strong determination to be at the top. I recall being with the guidance counselor in the eighth or ninth grade and somehow indicating that I wanted to be an engineer. Well, math soon disabused me of that idea. I wasn't a whiz in math, but I did excel in the humanities. My electives were taken in English courses and later on literature, and I did very well in these. I wasn't the valedictorian of our class by any means, but I received good grades and worked hard. Also, I was active in athletics, particularly basketball and baseball. I was a starter in both sports during my junior and senior years. Despite the war it was a fun time for me. There was plenty of money in circulation and it was an interesting period.

In college the going got a little rougher. I was only 17 when I enrolled as a freshman in 1946. This was the first postwar year when a lot of veterans were pouring back from the service into college, men who had seen war and whose average age was 22. My closest friend during my freshman year was a guy 31 years old, and while I was only 17 we were good friends. These older men were highly motivated. They wanted an education and were anxious to get into the work force. A lot of them had lost up to four years in the service and they wanted to make them up quickly. As a result, there was real competition in the classroom. In high school I was an A student. In college I ended up with a high C average. As I had learned from childhood, I tried to do what I had to do with a smile; perhaps I wasn't as highly motivated or ambitious as were many others.

What did I learn in college? I was certainly influenced by certain professors, particularly an English teacher who taught rhetoric and composition. We had to produce an essay for him every class. His comments on our papers were terse, pungent and often scathing. It was such a fundamental course, yet I think probably the most rewarding because he taught us how to write. While my main courses were in business, economics, marketing, business law, accounting, finance, my electives and other courses included a good deal of philosophy as well as literature and associated English courses. In retrospect, what I really gained from college was the kind of basic foundation which helped to prepare me how to live. Following graduation I was eager to get a permanent job and I made a stab in two directions with ludicrous results. At one point I thought I'd do well in advertising. I went so far as to take a comprehensive test sponsored by the American Association of Advertising Agencies which was conducted in Chicago during the spring of my senior year. After all, I thought, I'd do well in marketing, promotion and that type of activity. I was a gregarious type, liked being with people, doing things with people. The test results were negative. The message was clear—stay out of advertising. I was also interested in retailing and arranged for an interview with one of the prestigious department stores in New York. During the interview it was determined that I was color blind and that ended that. Then the Korean war broke out and I—well, I was 1A in the draft.

Korea was not a popular spot and I wasn't eager to be sent there as an infantryman. On three different occasions I applied for a direct commission or sought entry into the Army or Navy cadets. Each time I was rejected either because of my color-blindness or having had no previous military experience. Finally, I was drafted. Due to an old foot injury, I was given a low physical profile classification which kept me out of the infantry and I ended up in a medical training battalion in Maryland. Eventually I was transferred to a base in Michigan where I operated a testing center. Another enlisted man and I administered a battery of tests to all new recruits who came into the reception center. It was a good job by Army standards.

I made some very close friends while in the service. One fellow I met there was an usher at my wedding and we have maintained our friendship for some twenty-five years. About four years ago, we ran into each other by accident, and then we lost touch for almost a year. He had been made a senior partner in one of the big investment houses and he finally decided there had to be more to life than fighting that situation. He was very successful, hard working, tenacious, extremely knowledgeable, but I think he just got tired of the rat race and took off for a year. Eventually, he returned to New York and joined one of the major hotel operating companies. As it turned out, our company became involved in a land development project which envisioned a resort hotel and we ended up negotiating a lease with this same hotel company that my friend had joined. We met again—small world.

But to get back, while I was in the Army I had a lot of time to think about what I was going to do. Somehow the thought of going to New York and the idea of being involved in that scene no longer appealed to me. Still, I had a compelling desire to get out into the business world. I felt I had lost two and a half years—half a year of deferment and those two years in the service. If I went back to school, law school or for a master's degree, I'd be twenty-six, twenty-seven when I graduated again—too late. I really wanted to get to work.

One of my uncles, my dad's youngest brother, was an executive with one of the major oil companies, and I wrote to him about career opportunities in the oil industry. He arranged an interview for me with one of the other major oil companies. As it turned out they had an opening for a land trainee in Wyoming. I had a notion that the real way to learn the business was from the ground up, get your hands dirty—that was really the way to do it. About the same time another oil company offered me a job as a roustabout in one of their district production offices in Texas, so I accepted that job. I felt this was the way to start. . . .

And this was how my career began. Let me say at the beginning that I was no stranger to work. I'd had summer jobs since I was a kid and when I got out of the army I came home and worked at an auto plant for six weeks. I was on a shift doing piece work, twelve men loading freight cars with unassembled auto parts. I liked the job, took home good money, paid off my debts, and now was ready to leave for Texas. I reflect on this sometimes. I wasn't compelled to leave home; I could have gotten a job nearby, but I guess I always knew that I would leave home eventually. At some point in life you have to be independent. You have to try to be your own man. So I bought a used car and started out to this first job down in the oil fields in Texas. It turned out to be the toughest year of my life.

A roustabout has a tough, unskilled, demanding, fairly unrewarding job. You're not on a rig. You're around the producing facilities—pipe line connections, tank batteries, the pumping wells. If a pump goes down, your crew gets out there and repairs the pump. You may be in some construction work but it's mostly maintenance, and that summer the weather was brutal. When I arrived, the area was in the midst of a drought and for thirty-five straight days the temperature was over 100 degrees. I rented a room in a private home, sharing it with another fellow also working in the oil fields. He was an Iranian student, getting his master's studying petroleum engineering. We shared this room and there was no air conditioning, and you can imagine how it seemed to a guy like me from a place that had greenery and trees, finding himself in a desert in the midst of a drought.

I had been assigned to a typical district production office where there were perhaps fifty people working—roustabouts, pumpers, gagers, maintenance men, foremen, petroleum engineers, a development geologist, draftsmen and office workers. This producing district could cover an area as large as a county, which in Texas could be pretty sizable. The company usually had compounds out in the fields, where they had built houses for people, since housing in some of those regions was not available, even in some of the towns or communities, simply because of the demand. There was a compound built by the company for the professional people, including the district superintendent, the geologist and the petroleum engineer. The rest of us lived wherever we could find a place. The company had a big overall operation in that division—covering two or three districts—and with some 500 people and out of that whole group there were not more than maybe ten or twelve scouts and landmen. The land group was a rare species, and there was a shortage of scouts and landmen, so it was a relatively small group, very close-knit. . . .

As I said, that year was tough. It wasn't so much the hard work—work, physical labor, never bothered me—it was the heat and the aridness of the area. This was a small town of some 12,000 or 13,000 people, no life of the mind at all, working with people I liked and enjoyed but who were not very stimulating. I realized after a while that there would be no future for me in the producing end of this business. It wasn't just that I was a laborer, a roustabout with no chance to go further; it was that in the producing end of the oil industry you really need a technical degree or an innate capability in either the scientific area or with machinery, and I had three strikes against me since I had none of these qualifications. So I got pretty discouraged. I tried to get transferred to one of the offshore rigs, which I felt had to be better than what I was going through there in West Texas. And then I got a break.

In order to survive, I had driven down to Dallas—a six-hour drive—to visit a friend of my dad's who had gotten into the oil business through a well-known oil man from Oklahoma City. My dad's friend, Sam Parker, and another, backed by the Oke City guy, got together a little money to buy leases. They ended up drilling 31 straight producing oil wells in a nearby county, right in the middle of one of country's largest oil fields—it was fabulous.

Well, Sam had made it big. My dad had written him a letter about me, so when I got to Dallas, I looked him up, and he and his wife, Irene, invited me over to their lovely home—swimming pool and all. Here I'd come from the grime and dust of a roustabout's life in the drought to this oasis, and it made all the difference in the world to me. I stayed at the Parkers' house several times on visits to Dallas and Sam became a confidant and friend. We talked often and I sought his advice. I knew I wanted to stay in the oil business—I liked the business and I like the people—but I knew also there'd be no future in the technical end, in the producing end—what could I do?

Well, Sam had mentioned the work of the landmen. I knew what a landman did, of course, but I was never actually exposed to their work of buying leases. Then I heard that one of the oil companies had a program to take a college graduate, if he were willing to go into the business end of the oil industry, and train him for a period of four or five months. He'd work a month as a roustabout, two months on a drilling rig followed by a stint with a geophysical crew and a civil engineering party. Finally, he would be assigned to the head office, where he would be exposed to exploration decisions being made every day. He would then be sent out to one of the district exploration offices as an oil scout, later to become a landman. It was an extensive and worthwhile training program.

Now, an oil scout is the first rung on the ladder to becoming a landman. The scout's job is to gather information covering all oil exploration activity conducted by competitor oil companies in a given geographical area. He will determine how many rigs are running, at what depths the wells are drilling, what companies are buying the leases, the prices paid, how many geophysical crews are operating. After all this information is gathered, it is evaluated in the regional offices by the explorationists working in that particular office. In many instances, oil is found along specific trends, and what occurs in one area may have a bearing on another area. So, information on an exploratory well could lead to the acquisition of leases several miles away which could eventually prove to be very valuable.

In the early days I was fortunate to meet and get to know an outstanding landman, a man I will call Jess Ross, truly a legendary figure. One of the great oil fields in Texas is named after him. The oil company I joined owned a lot of leases in that field. Oil and gas leases usually have a term—five, ten years, and our company had mostly ten-year leases there. The leases pay an annual rental, at that time, a dollar an acre. Usually, the oil companies prepare lease schedules each month for the purpose of reviewing each lease which has a rental due to determine whether they are going to continue to pay the rentals or whether they are just going to surrender and forfeit the lease.

Lease evaluations had been made over a period of months and sometimes years in the head office, and recommendations would be sent out to the district office. The district landman would review the recommendations, to pay or surrender, and then note his concurrence before returning the recommendations to the home office. In one particular county the recommendations went out from the home office to surrender the leases. Jess Ross ignored them. He just kept paying the rentals, thus perpetuating the leases. This accomplished two things: one, it put money in the pockets of the ranchers who had fallen on hard times during the drought. Those years the grass didn't grow any higher than a couple of inches, the cotton was stunted—those people were in real financial difficulties, and even though those checks were small, they helped. So they loved Jess Ross. And the second thing it did was to reward that oil company with one of the largest oil fields in the country. In fact, it still is a major producing oil field to this day.

"You see, you play these things by hunch—it's a gut feel." Jess said: "By God, there's got to be oil in the county." And the exploration manager, a vice president of the oil company, made the statement: "I'll eat my hat if they ever find a barrel of oil in that county." And when the big boom came in, somebody sent him a hat—deservedly.

So, I'd heard about Jess Ross, the legendary figure in this company, and I called him up one day and introduced myself, told him what I wanted to do and asked him if I could come over and talk to him.

He says: "Yeah, come on over." So one afternoon after work I drove the 30 to 40 miles to this small town where he ran the district office. It was a typical little West Texas town and I drove around and found the neat brick building where he had his quarters. I went to his secretary and she ushered me into a huge, well-furnished office—attractive paintings, beautiful guns, well decorated, a great mahogany desk—very, very, nice. In the room were two people. One was sitting behind the large desk. He had a big ten-gallon hat on, white hair, cowboy boots, legs propped on the desk. This was Jess Ross. The other lounged in front, also an older man. Jess Ross rose, a tall, slim man around six feet, typical Texan, weathered face, shrewd, kindly, knowledgeable. He introduced me to the other man—his brother-in-law, a doctor. We sat down. Jess never took his cowboy hat off. When I was seated, Jess said: "Well, Tom, where're you from?" I answered: "Mr. Ross, I'm from Ohio." "Ohio," he exclaims. "Ohio!" If there's one thing we really hate down here, it's you goddam Yankees!"

Am I going to slug this guy or am I going to get up and leave and say the hell with it and walk out? And then all of a sudden he and the doctor roared with laughter. And he said "Tom, I was born in Toledo, but if you tell anybody I'm going to kick your ass from here to Dallas. They don't know that. They all think I'm a native West Texan, and furthermore, I'm the president of the West Texas Chamber of Commerce."

This was about four o'clock in the afternoon. Later, after the doctor departed, I sat there with Jess Ross and we conversed for four hours. I'll remember that conversation the rest of my life. Here was a busy man, a man who had made his name in the world I wanted to enter, a man who had been responsible for discovering oil worth hundreds of millions of dollars, and he had time to sit down with a young guy who didn't even know what the hell he was doing, and for more than four hours try to give him some advice.

Jess Ross capsuled his life for me and he did it for a reason. He had little formal education—made 10th grade, became a cable tool driller in the midwest, kept migrating, ended up in Texas, went to work for one of the major oil companies, became district landman. In the old oil companies before they became so regimented, a district job, whether you were district superintendent, district landman, district geologist—these were the good jobs. You had a lot of freedom, a lot of independence to work within your district, within those geographical boundaries. You were king of your territory. Your job was highly respected—it meant something in the industry and in the community. You didn't have to be a vice president. You were a "district landman." So, here I was with one of the legendary district landmen and he was asking me plenty of penetrating questions. What are you really doing here? Are you kidding yourself? Why do you want to be in the business—come on, really be honest with me? Those were the kinds of questions. We had talked for four hours and when I left, he shook hands with me and he said: "I'm going to help you. I want you to stick it out. It may not be next week or next month, but you stick it out. I'm going to help you."

I had made one decision, after I learned more about the business in those first three months. That was I would give it a year—that was my cutoff—and if I couldn't dig myself out of the job I was in now as a pick and shovel man in the producing department, then I'd leave. I wasn't going to leave the oil business but my plan was to use my vacation period just knocking on doors trying to get a job as an oil scout. I'd hit Oklahoma City, Tulsa, Dallas, Fort Worth and Houston. . . . Here I am, a guy with a college degree, been in the army, have a year's experience in the oil business as a roustabout and I want to be an oil scout or a landman. . . .

One week before my time was up, the call came from the home office for an interview with a major oil company. The chief scout called me. He said: "We've set up an interview for you with the vice president in charge of exploration and the chief landman." I was thrilled. And so was the district superintendent, Walt Cory, who was also trying to get me a better job and wasn't making too much progress on it. Walt was tickled to death. So with his blessing I took a couple of days off and drove to Dallas and had an interview.

The interview lasted probably two hours—a lot of time for two busy executives; one, a vice president in charge of exploration, very bright, very aggressive, a fine geologist, and the other the chief landman. We sat around for some two hours, and believe it or not we never talked about the oil business. We talked about music, art, literature, and I found this very unusual. Later in life when I had to do some interviewing of my own, I realized that you learn more about a person by such informal discussion of key interests than by going over the character of the business itself. They knew why I was there and so did I, but this way we got to really know each other. At the end of the interview, I went to the chief scout's office and he said: "Nice to have you here. We'll let you know." I answered: "Please don't leave me out on a limb. Give me an answer as soon as possible."

I had not intended to wait for more than a week. Then I was prepared to start interviewing with other companies. I was staying at a hotel across the street and I went back over there to relax in my room. About four o'clock the phone rang. It was the chief scout. He said: "You've got the job." And that's how my career as an oil scout began.

I was going to be assigned to an exploration district in Louisiana, but first I went through a training program. I spent two months working on a rig as a roughneck, and if I had thought working as a roustabout was hard, wrestling all that iron on a drilling rig gave me some new ideas on physical labor. Then I spent a month with a geophysical crew and finally some time with a civil engineering party. This was a real learning experience—this training period—and I enjoyed it. I had begun to like West Texas, the people, the heat and the hard work and I'd made a number of good friends there, so it was something of a wrench when my tour of training was over.

The exploration district consisted of several professional people—geologists, geophysicists, landmen, as well as draftsmen, secretaries and an oil scout. The best place to see what a scout does is at the weekly oil scout check, as they call it—a meeting conducted once a week in which the scouts exchange information. In our division, the scouts would meet on a Wednesday, and they'd bring in all the drilling information on every well that was drilling in that division. Each scout would report on the geophysical crews in his district; he would have to collect samples from the various wells; they'd bring in information on leasing activity in their districts; what company was buying leases, where, how many acres, what kind of prices were being paid. Scouts also brought in information on farm-out deals, and joint venture deals under which two or more parties arranged to pool their respective leases and share well costs as well as proceeds from oil or gas on some mutually agreed basis. This kind of information was important because diverse ownership of leases forced the lease owners to pool leases in order to evaluate a geological prospect.

Now a scout has to be ingenious, because a good deal of this information was confidential, and companies didn't want it divulged for obvious reasons. There were cases when a scout might drive up to a rig, only to be confronted by a burly roughneck saying: "If you're not authorized, pal, take off. . ." So, many times, the scout had to use his ingenuity to gather information. You'd hear stories. An oil scout would go out in the woods, climb a tree and with a pair of binoculars he'd look through them and count the lengths of drill pipe stacked in the derrick. As the well was being drilled the drill bits had to be replaced, and in order to change bits the drill pipe had to be pulled and stacked. Once the drill pipe was out of the hole you could tell roughly how deep the well was being drilled. It was difficult to determine whether this kind of information would prove to be valuable to the geologists for evaluation of a prospect, but the scout was the eyes and ears of the oil business, out gathering essential information for his company, and many times drilling data you'd gone to great trouble to get could possibly lead to the acquisition of leases on potentially valuable prospects.

Now I was lucky. When I was transferred to Louisiana I moved into a special kind of oil territory, one that was booming. First of all, there was a lot of off-shore drilling as well as drilling in the marshes, which made access to the rigs difficult. Either you had to hire a boat or a helicopter to reach the rigs, which was costly and time consuming. As a result you had to rely much more on your contacts within the operating companies and on telephoned information. I remember one ingenious scout who bought himself a short wave radio and monitored at 6 or 7 in the morning the radio reports coming in from the offshore rigs. He was soon found out but he got a lot of information while it lasted. I made a host of contacts; I got to know people all over South Louisiana. It was stimulating. I called them "my bird dogs." They were people on the scene who could furnish information. This was the place to be. Everything was beginning to boom. The success ratio of drilling was fantastically high here. At that time the national average for wildcat wells was one well brought in for every nine drilled. Here in South Louisiana it was one for every five. It seemed as though significant oil and gas fields were being discovered every week both offshore and onshore. And I moved into one of the great cities of the world to live—New Orleans. I was lucky all along. I found an apartment even though housing was tight at that time. More importantly, though, I met the girl I eventually married. I met Anne through her father. Oddly enough he had been a student in my father's classes at the university and actually recalls the day I was born. As he relates it, my father entered one morning and said to the class: "Gentlemen, I wish to announce that the second heir to my mortgages has just arrived. . ."

I worked in this exploration district for about a year and a half, then was transferred to another district also in Louisiana. Again I was extremely fortunate because in the new district the district landman, to whom I reported, allowed me to take part in new activities which proved to be most rewarding, then as well as in years to come. There were only the three of us in the Land Department, the district landman, another landman and myself as the scout. When I arrived, the district landman gave me a typewriter and a draft book and said: "Come on, Tom, you're going out to buy us some leases." So I went to the field and started buying leases. The three of us did everything. I scouted mostly but I bought leases and settled damage claims also. Many times we'd go out to the drilling rigs at two in the morning or on weekends to get information. When a core was pulled or a log run the scout was on the scene. I loved it, although I didn't sleep a great deal. Meanwhile, Anne and I were married and one day a fellow I knew in New Orleans, an exploration manager, called me and asked me if I didn't want to go to work for his company as a landman. I accepted and we moved back to New Orleans.

It was a big break, because I had discovered that I would have to work for five years as a scout before becoming a landman. I made a decent salary but I couldn't wait. I look back on those days with great pleasure. These were the days when I learned the oil business. I learned my trade. In this new job, the company I joined drilled or participated in almost 50 wildcat wells in South Louisiana and operated about 40 of them. I never worked so hard in my life. I worked for that company for four years and I suspect I gained more experience doing everything in those four years than I would have in ten years with a major oil company. Morning, noon and night, I was on the go. . . .

So, that's how I got started, and the early years are the ones I look back on. Since then, it's been pretty much up all the way. Eventually, I joined one of the successful independent oil companies as a landman. In a few years I was promoted to manager of the land department, then became a vice president and was asked to manage a real estate division, and finally have reached, over the years, a senior vice presidency in charge of international operations. All of it has been good; all of it great but you look back on the times when you learned most, when you were most alive. . . .

Today the oil business is in the spotlight because of energy shortages compounded by Middle East pressures. The industry is under tremendous pressure from the government, pressure for information, for reports, for explanations. Our main job today is to find new oil to replace our dwindling reserves, whether the oil's here in this country or in other parts of the world. The big question is whether new oil is economic. In most oil fields you are fortunate to get 30 per cent of the oil out. Seventy per cent stays in the ground—there's no means of getting it out even with secondary recovery programs. A lot of research money is being spent and will continue to be spent on ways to improve the recovery of existing oil. If we could only find a way to recover 90 per cent of it, we'd be on easy street! Today the U.S. is dependent on the world market for oil and has been for the last ten years. We produce about 9 million barrels a day in this country, and that's our peak capacity, and we consume between 15 and 16 million barrels a day. We're importing about 40 per cent of our crude requirements from Venezuela, Canada, Indonesia, and the Arab countries. We are the largest energy consuming nation in the world with oil and gas now accounting for some 75 per cent of the energy requirements in this country. The balance comes from coal, nuclear, steam—those last two being very small percentages.

But look at our coal reserves. We have coal that could supply the current energy needs of this country for 400 years, most of it in the western states of Montana, Wyoming and Colorado. Montana alone has more coal in it than any other three states of the Union combined, but of course there's the headache of strip mining, getting it out, high sulfur content and transportation. Contrast this with our earlier hopes for nuclear energy to fill the increasing gap of dwindling oil reserves. Ten years ago projections indicated that nuclear energy would gradually supplant fossil fuels as the dominant energy source in this country. But there were bugs in the technology, delays and difficulties, environmental and social factors and so nuclear energy hasn't come on stream as predicted. We continue to rely on oil and gas to fulfill our energy requirements.

So today one of our big headaches in the oil business is capital. I suppose this is true in every high technology business, but it's especially severe in the oil industry. We are being blamed for higher oil and fuel prices but you just can't get the oil out of the ground, refine it and deliver it at the cheap energy prices we had in the old days. We are the villains today, but I think reason will prevail and there'll be a recognition that producing oil is an expensive business and that it has to be paid for somehow.

But to get back to my own life, I feel I was lucky in almost everything that's happened to me. I came along at a time when scouts and landmen had a great deal of freedom, when oil companies were not nearly so centralized. I remember all the good friends I made out there, my bosses who helped me along, the great life I had. That part of the oil business was not a bureaucracy; we had freedom to make decisions, to get our work done the best way we could. There was little or no politics that I recall. Now I believe things may be different in some of the bigger companies. What can I say? I was lucky then; it's tough now. The pressures are greater and it's not as much fun. I can only be thankful for those great times we had. . . .

9

"From the Platform I Could See the Old Man's Face and I Knew My Career Had Ended. . . ."

A rising corporate star takes the wrong road

Here again Will Warrant represents a "reconstruction" composed of two tapings and material which could not be released because the executive might be readily identified. Yet these experiences indicate some of the darker aspects not only of the corporate world but also of American life in this fast-moving, complex, high-pressure late twentieth century. I would not go so far as to say this is a representative corporate life, since I suspect these dangers occur in all our major subcultures in a civilization where drink and women are part of the rewards of achievement, and bribes are waiting for the powerful. Will is a handsome, magnetic, clean-cut looking man and before the scandal he was a highly respected, highly successful executive vice president of one of the country's largest general merchandizing corporations. He is six feet tall, wears beautifully tailored, stylish clothes, sports gold cufflinks and he moves fast. He has a warm personality and a flashing smile and he knew how to make deals and get things done. He was the inside track man, being groomed for the succession up to the afternoon he stood up on that platform and saw the Old Man's face and knew the show was over. . . .

The thing is they all do it. I'm not saying it's right but you have to live in this world and if you want to get things done, you've got to make the best deal you can. You've got to pay the price. Everything costs something and it's done in a lot of companies too.

Ours is one of the big merchandising corporations of the world. We sell everything from appliances to diamonds. Our customers lie in the upper middle class, and our job is to find out what they need and want for their life style and get it for them. In a way we're like Sears or Monkey Ward's, except we're a class

159

operation and under the domination of one man, a genius, but like many geniuses, killing the thing he loves. I was able to loosen the Old Man's grip a little on the company and help us decentralize, because he saw in me the son he never had. My downfall broke him. He looks about a hundred years old now and he's retiring at the end of the year. I'm sorry about that. I loved the Old Man with all his faults, and he truly was like a father to me. . . . I hope some day he hears this.

I suppose if I'd laid off the sauce, been a little more careful, taken it a little easy, it would have been all right; and if I'd never met Trevor's wife. . . . What I miss most now is the kids. Michelle will make out fine but my daughter, "Mickey," and the boy, Tommy—I miss them like hell.

When you're down, you're down and there's not one hell of a whole lot you can do about it. The friends I used to have—they're typical in the world I moved in—were fair-weather friends. Sure, I've borrowed a bit from 'em, but hell when I was up and the going was good, I did 'em many a favor. But that's the way the world is, Old Buddy, and I've known it from the start. . . .

I wish I could forget that afternoon of the convention. I wish I could forget a lot of things. Most of all, I guess, I wish I could forget the day I first dealt with Trevor and the evening I first saw Mrs. Trevor. But I can't and I never will. I don't blame it all on Trevor either. He did what he had to do. The chips fell and I got what was coming to me and that's all there is to it. I suppose in a way confession is good for the soul but I guess what I'm really doing is trying to tell the Old Man how it could have happened. I had everything and I blew it.

Well, let me get back a little bit. The problem here was basically too great centralization, not enough flexibility in an operation of this size. The area merchandise and store managers had to follow too rigid procedures, do too much paperwork, check back with headquarters too often. The Old Man had built his success on this kind of control but now the company had grown too big; there were too many stores and the six buyer areas and overseas divisions were much too large and complex for this type of centralized control. I helped plan and put through a reorganization that gave the people down the line a lot more control. The Old Man was very uneasy about it. He kind of hated the idea and anyhow he was 72 years old and it's hard to let go even a little at that age. But because of me he went along with it and the following year you could see everything start to bloom. Everything began to grow and leap up and we had the most profitable year in our history when everybody else in the industry was having a hard time. The boys down on the local level had a good feel as to what would sell in their areas and with more control and authority could expand, change or pull in their horns according as they diagnosed the situation. So our mix of products really hit the market and we came through with flying colors. The Old Man made me executive vp and I became his confidant and, I guess, his son, and he spoke to me about becoming his successor, if anything happened to him. So you may ask why or how could I have blown it?

I don't know. I'll never know. I'm usually a pretty easy-going guy. I'm not all that gung-ho ambitious. I've always sort of been at the top. Things have come easy to me. I guess I never had to struggle too hard. It was always take hold strongly, let go loosely. It was easy or not at all with me. I never really cared enough. Nobody had a handle on me. Was it because I was the idol of my family—my mother thought I was the greatest thing since the Second Coming; my father and I were very close and he was a high liver and I admired him extravagantly. We always had plenty of money. I went to the best schools, ending up at Exeter and Stanford and I usually near the top of my class without having to work too hard at it. I was in the best fraternities or societies and then in the best clubs and most of the social and other activities at school. I like to live well and I like people who live well. I won't bore you with my background—it reads like Big Man on the Campus and I developed a lot of connections. The job here came to me through one of my father's friends, Andy Soames, a vp in merchandising. He thought I'd like it because it was a big expense account kind of job and they could use my connections. They didn't know then—and nor did I—that I had a feel for this sort of thing and that I had a lot of organizing ability.

So things worked out almost from the start. I used some of my connections to get Pendleton's into some very hot premium items that turned out to fit beautifully into their merchandising image. I was negotiating with top people, suppliers like Trevor, who were millionaires already, even though some of 'em were rough diamonds. My name and connections opened a lot of doors for me, and these people fitted into the quality merchandising Old Man Pendleton's growing company was doing. They knew once we took 'em on, they'd have a tremendously enlarged market for their quality goods or products, and as long as their quality and value held up, they'd have a home here.

I don't know how to describe Mr. Pendleton. His public image was ferocious. He was a frail, silent, purse-mouthed man who didn't drink, didn't smoke and went to church regularly. He dressed in dark, old-fashioned suits with vests, took out a big old turnip watch to look at the time and wore a permanent scowl. He did not permit swearing or bawdy talk in his presence and any form of licentiousness was anathema to him. He would not condone the slightest business irregularity and his word was his bond. He never argued about anything. God had told him what he had to do. He had built the store and he was it. The fact that we were now a worldwide conglomerate, pandering to the effete tastes of the rich and near rich made no difference. Everything Pendleton's sold was first quality, first class and if through some fluke a product or piece of goods did not meet Pendleton's standards, no efforts were spared to make good on it to the customer. Whatever Pendleton's was to the public and its customers, to the Old Man it was still his store and around him the top quality standards and the Blue Laws were still in force. His simple cluttered old-fashioned office at the top of the Pendleton Building in Chicago was right out of the 19th century.

So why did he like me? Why did he choose me of all the able men around him? Was I the Prodigal Son? Was he going to save me from myself? Who knows? But I suppose of those around him, I was the only one who remained himself. I did not try to hide the fact that I liked good expensive things and that I lived well and considered that my due. I am not good at dissembling and I have never felt the need to. I am what I am. But the fact was the Old Man liked me and in the end we became very close. I could see beneath his frozen exterior that he was a kind man, a father, a man who cared.

Furthermore, the Old Man liked my wife and family. I married Michelle because she is elegant and I like elegant things. But she's something of a cold fish too. She married me, I suppose, because in a way I'm a premium product or used to be. I won't be coy about it. I'm good looking; I have personality and plenty of money and that's what a French girl with social connections and a practical head on her shoulders looks for. I needed an elegant wife in this career and Michelle—I have to admit it—was a great asset. Her elegance, her charm, her French accent, her ability to judge people and the fact you remember her once you see her—all these qualities fitted in with the scheme of my life. I suppose we never got to know each other too well. I don't know. We came from different worlds and her world had disappeared in the war. The man in Michelle's life had been her father, an aristocrat and something of an autocrat as well, I guess. I never met him, thank God. He died under mysterious circumstances during the German occupation, but—well, I can't say ours was exactly a love match. Michelle had been married before and it hadn't worked out. But from the moment I saw her, I wanted her, and I pursued her. I have always been willing to put every effort and all my resources into something I want badly. Michelle was different from the women I had been going around with. I like things with class, things that are different, and Michelle is it. Oh hell, I'm rambling. Here let me freshen that up for you.

Anyhow, Michelle was a straight shooter, a bit on the practical side maybe, but she kind of liked the life we led; she was socially gifted and she was interested in seeing me succeed. She was, I believe, proud of my potential and she liked winners. I don't blame her. I don't think she was so shocked at what I did—I had a less than edifying history with women—but she was outraged at my drinking and loss of control and indiscretion. A career came first with her and anyone who blew a career, the chance to reach the top, was not for her.

I must have been having a breakdown and not realized it. I suppose it all started about the time I began to care about making good. That's what gets you. You learn to care and then they've got you by the balls—pardon me, but that's it. In the old days I was free. I didn't care; I played it the way I wanted to; I called the shots as I saw 'em.

I don't know exactly when it was that I began to get an emotional investment in what I was doing. You try to think back and it doesn't seem to be any one thing; it's just you begin waking up in the morning thinking about your appointments for the day or about this region or that problem or about what could be done with certain merchandising techniques or about one or another of the men who report to you or even about the Old Man, and suddenly you begin to like what you're doing, to care.

Hell, yes, I remember how it started. It was the summer we took in Cadmum's down in Atlanta, and we got a bargain on it. The Old Man calls me up to Chicago and gets me up to his big old office and he sits there, purse-mouthed, silent, the way he always does, scaring hell out of people. People can't stand silence and the Old Man always gets to them that way, sitting there, purse-mouthed and still, until you can almost hear the stillness and it gets to be unbearable. Well, I wasn't going to be pushed around. I didn't care. I'd heard about it. I'd been introduced to the Old Man at one of the big regional meetings and he seemed to have paid no attention to me and I'd thought: "Screw him." I'd been doing one hell of a job for them in that region, so I wasn't putting up with any of the Old Man's terror tactics. I didn't need the money; I didn't need the job. So I sat there across from him in the big cluttered old-fashioned office, he in his black suit and stiff collar and me in my good looking, expensive, made-to-measure clothes, and I just sat there, saying nothing, silent and at ease waiting the old bastard out. Finally out of the stillness, this old voice croaked:

"Pretty good arrangement with Cadmum—how'd you get on to it?"

"Goldstein," I said. Goldstein was the area manager, in Atlanta then, now a vp. "Goldstein's been trying to get us to make a deal with Cadmum's for two years now. Nobody'd listen to him. Headquarters kept turning him down. I took it on myself."

"Hmmm," the Old Man said. "That's what I called you up here for. I don't want any deals even of that small size made without headquarters being behind it. May have to kill it."

"In that case," I said, "I quit. The trouble with Pendleton's is it's still operating like a little two-bit country store. We've got a lot of good men all over the country tied hand and foot by headquarters. There're a hundred opportunities like that going to waste because good men have to run like a bunch of morons to Daddy and then get shafted for their pains. Pendleton's is on the skids. It could have been big time but it's going down shit creek and headquarters is going with it."

"I don't like swearing or obscene language," the Old Man said.

"It's your store and my language," I said and stood up.

"Sit down," he said. "Why is it that young untried men still wet behind the ears suddenly think they know it all? I've been in this business more than forty years and I've seen your kind come and go, smart alecks, who think they have all the answers."

"Mr. Pendleton," I said, "I have nothing to lose and I couldn't care less but I know what I know and I'm telling you the way it is. You've already lost three great opportunities to expand into major areas that Pendleton's could serve with distinction because you wouldn't listen to some of your good men. You're an old man and you don't know how to listen any more, and pretty soon Pendleton's won't be the organization it could be; it won't have the elite markets it could have, and then in a few more years it'll be in financial trouble; it'll go down and you and headquarters will go down with it," and I got up again.

"Sit down," he said once more. We sat there opposite one another again in total silence. I was sure I had pulled the plug, and, oddly enough, I felt good about it—I was glad to get out from under. The Old Man's squeaky croak finally broke the silence.

"Prepare me a report on the three opportunities we've missed," he said. "Good day."

Yes, that's when I began to care. Those days before Cadmum's come back to me now again and again. I see myself as I was then, free, without all this hassle, living the kind of life I wanted to live and I see myself now. . . . Well, what's the use talking about it.

The Old Man had apparently been looking for someone like me, someone who talked to him as I had talked to him and he had been looking for a son too, the son he'd never had, and I guess I filled both parts. My report on the missed opportunities was couched in the terms anyone could read because, while I didn't think he would accept it, I wanted to leave it as a legacy to those who came after me in case anyone could make out of this overgrown store the beautiful multinational merchandising organization inherent in its markets.

"Rotten report," the Old man said. "Full of these ambitious expansions that have no sound financial underpinnings. Anybody can make proposals like these. How you goin' to pay for 'em? What if we hit a bad year? What about cash flow? How we goin' to finance expansion into these markets? Who knows anything about these areas? We'll end up like all these big-talking overambitious organizations—bankrupt. I can't do everything myself. . . . Still, we'll give your Pacific Coast plan a try and see how far we get with that. . . ."

Yes, those were the days. Everything I touched turned to gold. At the big convention in Houston the next year, it was clear I was the new messiah. I still didn't care that much. I still had some sense of humor, but it was all getting to me. I was one of those honored by being seated on the platform and given a few minutes to, as they put it, "make some remarks about the coming year. . . ."

The Old Man never sat on the dais. He sat always a little off center in the second row of the crowded auditorium, a form of snobbery that made him stand out like a light. He never said anything at these conventions either and always retired early so as not to dampen the festivities. Yet he was nevertheless as conspicuous by his nonparticipation as if he had run the whole show. He was the spectre at the feast, and if he said good morning to someone there, that man was made. He did something unprecedented at that Houston convention: he put his bony hand on my shoulder. "We'll try the European plan next," he had croaked in a low voice. No one had heard what he said to me, but they saw that gesture and suddenly I had become Mr. Big.

Still there was a lot of business done at these big conventions and a lot of reassessments and reshuffling of power, who would be up, who down in the year ahead. The tensions were great and there was the inevitable letting off of steam after hours, not as bad as at the regional meetings for the salesmen and buyers but pretty bad even with the top brass. Only the Old Man stood apart and in an odd way gave the whole a sense of structure by being conspicuous by his silence and making himself scarce at the end of the day's session so he couldn't possibly see what might be going on. That was the first convention of my rise and I guess I thoroughly enjoyed it in spite of myself.

I don't want to go into the years since that first convention. Our reorganization took three years to complete and they were great years. But from that first convention the effects of the new approach began to show and more and more the men began to come to me with their plans and proposals and more and more the Old Man began to delegate authority to me until by the third year I was virtually in command.

This is not to say that the Old Man let go entirely. He was still the top boss, the man, and in the beginning he did not delegate easily. He had the infuriating habit of second-guessing, changing his mind, countermanding orders, and twice it got to the point that I offered my resignation. The second occasion seemed crucial; I actually had left the office and remained out that week, but we had become too close by then and I realized he did not want to take up the burden of the reins again when I received his short note. I knew then I had won—he needed me. Don't misunderstand me. The Old Man was still in charge, and I paid attention to his wishes, but on the important issues of the welfare of the organization and our new program, I had won and we began to make the right moves and to burgeon. The Old Man knew what he was doing and I believe in a way he was proud of me. There was no meanness about him and his absolute integrity had a strong hold on us all.

It's odd that he cared for me, though. I can't understand it. I was everything he was not. I was a hedonist, a pleasure-lover; he was a Calvinist, a worshipper of the hard way. I was a drinker—not out of hand, though, at that time; he was a teetotaler. I suppose I could be called a womanizer; he was a celibate and an ascetic, who was overly courteous and ill at ease with women. I have a very ambivalent feeling about religion; he was a hard shell Baptist who never missed Sunday services. From the Old Man's viewpoint, I suppose, if ever there was a Prodigal Son, I was he, and yet he found my company pleasant and relaxing, my careless outspokenness amusing and refreshing and my brilliance such as it was a source of pride. So I began by mocking and disagreeing with him and ended by loving and admiring him. We became each bound in a strange way to the other. That's why I'm telling you this. I would like him to know how I felt about him. . . .

So let's turn now to last summer—that terrible summer when it happened. There've been a lot of versions of what took place. I'll tell you mine. The two previous seasons had been the most demanding and difficult of the organization's entire history and the most hectic of my life. A lot of our area and regional men were suddenly sensing changes and with their new authority were taking steps to adjust to them. After three tremendous years, it seemed to them we might be entering a recession. There was not much to go on except a very minor softening and their instincts, their feel for the way the wind was blowing in their communities and neighborhoods and the way people were talking. All intangible hints suggested a possible downturn and most of them decided to follow their hunches. I was under a great deal of tension particularly since what they were doing made no sense to me. I am a fighter and I never run scared. I was harassed and impatient. But the way we were set up under my reorganization, I had to sit still while they did what they wanted in this area; I had to hold while they cut back on their inventories, reduced their call for items made in our plants and generally played havoc with what had been an upward trend.

Also I had to travel a great deal, twice to Frankfurt, once to Mexico City, several times to South American cities and of course to our various regional headquarters throughout the country. I suppose my drinking had now become a problem. I was not getting enough sleep and it almost seemed as if my life were being lived in air terminals. I had always been able to hold my liquor well, but I was beginning to need it now. I was also growing short tempered and twice I remember I became abusive. From one who is in power as I was this can be devastating to people who had to deal with me and some of my relationships were beginning to suffer. I seemed to know something was wrong with me but I was beginning to move in a fog of fatigue and I couldn't seem to do anything about it. Michelle was no longer accompanying me on these trips largely on the grounds the children needed her but actually because these business trips had become extremely hurried and fatiguing, and, I realize now, my intermittent drinking was giving her concern.

So on some of these trips I began to find temporary relaxation in what you might call feminine entertainment, women I had known from previous business conferences and contacts, a somewhat stupid habit for a man in my situation, but I must admit I had grown accustomed to the more ephemeral type of female relationship. The pressures were increasing. Our suppliers were beginning to complain about our erratic orders, diminished in certain big selling items, increased in others. It made no sense to them, and some of the big ones were coming to me. This was where I made my mistake with Trevor.

Trevor was my baby—one of our largest and most valuable suppliers and my connections had brought him in. He was a great success. On two of his products, the market had expanded so fast his company could not keep up with the orders. These were quality items too, expensive to fabricate and not something any old supplier could handle. So for two years now, we had been urging him to expand. Expanding meant rather heavy financing and Trevor was a tough, cautious man. Finally, he came to us, that is, he came to me, and suggested that our organization help him expand by investing in his company at least to the extent that would get him started in the expansion.

I remember that afternoon of our first talk on the subject of our investing. We had had lunch at one of my clubs and again I had been impressed with the man. He was short, pudgy, rather soft-looking, middle-aged type with a quiet matter-of-fact voice—deceptively ordinary until you looked at his eyes. They were cold as death, killer eyes. He was a man, it seemed to me, who could be deadly. Otherwise, he was a very quiet appearing man, usually expensively dressed in gray. I knew he was very well off—we had investigated him. In fact, he was a millionaire, but I could see how he was not one to take any risks with his own money. I told him I would see what the company could do.

For reasons which escape me still, the Old Man turned me down flat. He did not like Trevor—no reason. Trevor was a very reputable man and his products were superb. But the Old Man was adamant.

I was angry. I was completely taken aback. I wanted that expansion and I wanted it badly and Trevor was my man. It also seemed to me a great investment and Pendleton's had done this sort of thing very profitably with other suppliers before. I brooded about it. However, in this instance the Old Man was backed by some of our vps—their reasons being that a recession seemed to be shaping up and this was no time to go into financing a fairly big supplier for expansion.

I called Trevor for a meeting. I had to give him the bad news. He asked me if I wouldn't stop over at his place for a drink that evening. We could talk there. He would send the car for me. I agreed. He lived in what could only be called a mansion in one of our loveliest suburbs near our top country club. When the chauffeur drove up the beautiful curved drive under the portico, my irrational feeling of bitterness toward the Old Man for turning us down welled up once more.

Trevor stood at the entrance. He shook my hand and taking my elbow escorted me into the large cool, high-ceilinged living room—a truly beautiful 18th century salon. This was the beginning of my downfall. This is where I first saw Mrs. Trevor. Standing near a low coffee table beside one of the sofas was one of the most striking women—girls rather—I had ever seen. She turned slowly like part of the decor of that lovely salon. She had long beautiful red hair, a pale translucent skin, full lips and cool, mysterious green eyes. She must have been accustomed to the shock she produced in men, for the half smile she turned on me was both shy and knowing. So must Trevor have been accustomed to the sensation his wife created, but his voice was as usual low and matter of fact. "This is my wife, Caroline," he said.

I remember smiling at her and thinking: what a ridiculous thing for a pudgy, gray little man like Trevor to have a wife like this. But I am not completely stupid and I remembered Trevor's eyes and the quality of the things his firm makes and the beauty of these surroundings and I realized how idiotic my reaction had been. I visualized his appearing at one or another of these conventions with that wife on his arm and the sensation among the young studs, the big time salesmen and managers, and I could imagine them in their own physical glory thinking: My God, look at Trevor's wife—that's for me. How did an old fart like him even with all his money buy something like that; and none of them realizing that Trevor, that gray, pudgy little nonentity, was twice the man they would ever be.

"My husband speaks about you often," the girl was saying in her soft and to me mysterious voice. "I'll leave you two to talk business."

"Would you have Joe bring us some drinks?" Trevor asked. So though I had heard of her—one of the vps had mentioned that Trevor had a stunning wife— that was the first time I'd seen her.

I told Trevor the company couldn't invest during this period. Then—and I don't know why I said this; it came to me out of the blue—I added: "Would you be willing to let me help you get some outside financing?"

The gray, pudgy man leaned over and touched my knee. "I appreciate your interest, Will," he said. "I regard you as a friend. If together with your help we can work out some outside financing, would you be willing to accept a fee?"

"I couldn't do that, Phil," I answered, "but I'll see what I can come up with. I have some connections."

When I left about seven—I had a dinner to attend—on an impulse I stopped at an outside phone booth, asked the operator for Trevor's home number and when a feminine voice answered said: "May I speak to Mrs. Trevor?"

When her voice came on, I said, "This is Warrant. Would you meet me privately tomorrow at 3:30 in the afternoon at Larue's? I'll wait in the lounge. I want to ask you something about your husband."

There was a long pause. Then her voice came again, cold, excited, breathy, "Of course not," she said. "You must be insane." That was how it began.

It's odd how difficult it is to trace which were the steps that led irrevocably into the quicksand. Every move one makes when you're having a breakdown as

I seemed to be—even the most moronic—appears natural and inevitable to yourself, whatever it might seem to an objective observer. It was not the drinking either, for on that day and during most of these meetings I had not been drinking.

"I don't know why I'm here," Mrs. Trevor had said at that first rendezvous. We were standing in the lounge, her luminous beauty soft in the glow of the high-ceilinged entrance to the cocktail area. I remember there was a scattering of businessmen and couples at the tables and the murmur of their voices underlay our conversation. "I don't know why I'm here," she repeated. "What is it you wanted to say to me?"

"I'm not sure."

"This is insane. I have to go now."

"No, stay a minute. Let's sit down and talk. I do have something to ask you."

"What is it? What do you want to talk about?"

"I'll get to it. Can we sit a minute?"

I am trying to give you snatches of those meetings. They made no sense. I had no plan, no real intention. Everything was impulse, instinct, a desire so complete and compulsive that I had not even formulated any goal for it or articulated to myself where I really intended to go. It was just that at this period I had to see this girl and the why of it would come to me later. All this was in the midst of one of the most hectic periods of my life with the storm clouds gathering and I was inundated with all kinds of cutback and reassessment problems.

So was it the first time or the third I finally asked her the crucial question? Was it then or from the moment I saw her that I decided I would help Trevor get that financing and if he had to have some commitment from me on it, he would have it.

"What does your husband really think of me, Caroline?" I had asked. "I have to know this. It's important if I'm to help him. . . ." I remember she had bridled at the intimacy of my tones, for from the moment I had seen her I felt I had known her all my life and whether she knew it or not or would ever know it or not, I felt she belonged to me in some essential way. She must have sensed something of this herself.

"He admires you," she answered slowly. "He speaks of you often. He regards you as a friend, not only an important major customer. He feels you have brought him lots of problems but you've put him where he wants to be. That's why I'm here," she added quickly as if she had just thought of it. "I want you to know that. I'm here because of my husband, not because of you. Now I have to go. . . ."

"All right. I'll meet you here again next week. Same time, same place. We have more things to discuss. . . ."

"No," she answered. "No," she repeated.

I turned and walked away. I think it was at the next week's meeting she said to me: "You know this isn't going to get you anywhere. This is the last time. I'm not available for an affair. I've never been unfaithful to my husband and I never will be. He's twice the man you are."

"I didn't ask you," I said. "And I know that, Caroline. I'll see you next week. Same time."

"No, never again," she repeated.

I believe she did miss a week before the pressure of whatever it was between us became too great. I am vague about this because I had begun drinking again, but I believe on one occasion I sat alone in that lounge waiting for her for quite a while before I realized she was not coming.

By this time I had worked out leads to outside financing for Trevor. The kicker, though, was that I had to make a commitment on the part of Pendleton's for a certain number of orders, something I could not take a chance on in this uncertain economy, or I would have to make some kind of personal commitment as an investor in Trevor's company. I realized I was taking a big chance on this; I would have to think it over carefully. Meanwhile I had appointments in New Orleans and New York. I was away three weeks. When I returned I hadn't yet made up my mind. I had spent a couple of bad nights on that trip, one with a woman friend in New Orleans, but the image of that girl—the red hair, the green eyes, the delicate lilac skin, the soft voice, the willowy body—kept coming between me and my friend, and for the first time I found myself impotent with someone I liked. It was a harrowing experience. My friend realized, however, I was under tremendous pressure and was not put out. She felt I was suffering from fatigue. In New York, however, with a girl I had always enjoyed tremendously—young, smart, very high quality—it happened again. I was appalled and for the first time began to feel something terrible was happening to me.

I suppose, as one of my women friends has told me, I don't really know what love is or I have no capacity for it. Another had said to me: "You know, Will, I feel sorry for you. You don't have the ability to give of yourself. You're nothing but a taker." Perhaps they were both right, but when I got back from this three-week trip, I felt confused and driven, and I knew I had to see Trevor's wife again. I also had to come to some decision about the financing, whether to commit myself or back out before it was too late.

"It's very important we talk again," I said to her over the phone. I was calling from a company suite in one of the swank hotels in town the morning after I had arrived back.

"You know I can't make it," she answered. Her voice was soft, agitated. "You know I can't do it." But I knew she'd be there.

Let me digress a moment. I don't want to think of what happened. I'd like to hold off on that fatal afternoon at the convention for a moment. You've asked about corporate life and its stultifying effect and about what a lot of people call the growing threat of the multinationals to the world. I suppose I'm not the man to ask about these popular idiocies. I've never felt any stultifying effect working in the corporate structure.

We live in a society where we're part of a lot of groups—the family, the community, the town, the state, the law firm, the store, the repair shop or whatever, and some of these groups we need to belong to—like the family and the nation state—and some we voluntarily belong to for economic and other purposes. I've found the corporate setup one of the more useful and productive in the world. It depends what your own goals and needs are, of course, and a lot on your temperament. Corporate life isn't for everybody but it can be one hell of a good life, more varied, more interesting, more supportive than most others in this chaotic world. It tends to magnify your strengths and to cover most of your weaknesses. As somebody said: It enables common people to accomplish uncommon things.

I don't really know what you mean by the corporate life style either. Corporate life styles vary all over the lot. As for the threat of the corporation to the world, it's about the only economic form that seems to be able to allocate resources where they'll produce the most wealth and to bring together people of all races, colors, creeds and degrees of opinion for productive not ideological ends. Oh hell, I'm no good at this kind of speculation. My instinct tells me that while there's a lot wrong with us, while the better organized ideologies— socialism, state government, authoritarianism, or if you prefer, tyranny—have all had their chance to show what they can do, we're the only ones with our pluralistic, market-oriented multiplicity of corporations who have even made a dent in alleviating the poverty and misery of the world. We're being lambasted for being too rich and using too many of the world's resources. We also produce most of the world's wealth and it seems to me as far as the human condition is concerned, rich is better.

In or out of the corporation you still have to deal with people, their desires, their hatreds, their lusts, and it's people with their needs and wants and terrors that cause the problems of the world, not organizations. But, of course, there're pressures in corporate life, terrible pressures if you're up high enough, and they get worse as you go higher. Certainly I'm the man who can tell you about that.

Pendleton's had been kind of a one-man show until I came along, if you can call any operation as big as that a one-man show. Now with the reorganization we were tapping the knowledge and experience and talent of a lot of our people and it had become a different ball-game. But for me things were closing down and coming apart, and I don't know why. I suppose it could have been the pressures. I suppose it was fatigue and my drinking or maybe it was just me. Anyhow my insane feeling about Trevor's wife seemed to be getting worse.

Now it's the morning of the big annual convention, a clear, hot beautiful Texas day—the day my career was to come to an end. By evening it would all be gone, everything—my reputation, my power, my status, my scale of life, everything I'd worked so hard for. Power is the name of the game in this world and mine had brought me to the heights and given me almost everything I had wanted; soon the cataclysm. Unfortunately I had started drinking the night before, and while I don't think I had behaved any worse than many of them, I believe I had played a very dangerous game by going off with one of the women—fortunately not somebody's wife—who had been brought by one of the merchandise vps as an assistant. It was stupid with the Old Man having arrived, even though as usual he had immediately retired. It was even more stupid in that I got back to the hotel at about two in the morning, and, though I tried to get up for breakfast, I was still a little drunk by as late as ten when the telephone call came.

I was down in the bar when they paged me. I went to the phone. It was her voice, agitated, soft and trembling. "I told him," she said softly. "I'm sorry, Will. I had to do it. I couldn't go on. I told Phil of our meetings. I'm sorry. . . ."

I put down the receiver and went back to the bar. I had two or three more drinks, trying not to think about it. But the stupidity of it kept whirling through my mind, what could she have told him, I thought. We hadn't done anything. I hadn't touched her. We had just talked. Then I thought: how could she have done such a thing?"

But it was all closing in on me. I knew it and my mind kept veering off. Trevor would be at this meeting, I knew. All the big suppliers, the top executives, the board of directors, everybody of the brass would be here, but especially and most of all the Old Man. But what would it matter, I kept saying to myself. What could Trevor do about it anyhow? Nothing. Absolutely nothing, and so my mind kept going around and around. I ordered another drink. Someone must have come down to get me because the next thing I remember I was in my room and it was three-thirty and I was fumbling around with some notes. Mine was to be the main presentation, as usual, the wrap-up on the year's achievements. Now it was almost time and I could barely see straight. I'm drunk, I thought. I'm really drunk.

When I reached the carpeted area at the entrance to the huge auditorium, I could see the crowd was already going back after the break. I would be on in twenty minutes. I thought vaguely I'd better wash up first, see what I look like, pull myself together. And yet somehow underneath it all, underneath the confusion, the terror, the disorganization, the drunkenness, I didn't really care. I had a feeling it was all going to be over and I would be glad of it. I'd had enough of it. I'd had it too long. I'd been carrying it, whatever it was, responsibility, fatigue, complications much too long. This wasn't me. I wanted out. I'd had it.

I pushed into the men's room and stood there a moment in the white glare in front of the mirrors. It was quiet. Everyone had gone back into the meeting. I stood along the row of sinks. My vision in the mirrors seemed blurred. I stood there a moment trying to pull myself together. The sweep of the mirrors above the white washstands gave me back only this blurred shape. Then it happened.

"Warrant." The voice was soft. I turned. There he stood—the pudgy, little, soft-looking man in gray, facing me near the washstand—Trevor. He was looking at me with a cold, deadly stare. His voice was almost gentle.

"You didn't think I'd sell my wife for a little financing, did you, Warrant?" he said. I stood there. His eyes were cold and deadly. He surveyed me for a long moment. "You're through, Warrant," he said softly. "I've spoken with Mr. Pendleton about your investing in my company. I've also told him I'm bowing out as a supplier." He remained motionless, surveying me. I could see the contempt. "I feel sorry for you, Warrant," he ended softly. "You're nothing. Underneath, you're really nothing." When I looked up, he was gone.

"Are you all right, Mr. Warrant?" It was a younger voice, one of the younger executives. I couldn't think of his name. "They're waiting for you, sir," he said.

"Be right along," I answered or I think I answered, because now things begin to get very indistinct. The next thing I remember I was standing there at the lecturne, looking out over the crowd. Or I seemed to be, and then I saw him.

He was there, this frail black form, seated in his usual place in the second row, and for an instant my vision seemed to clear. Then I saw his face. His lips were pressed together, his face dead white and he looked a hundred years old. It seemed to me we must have stared at each other in that vast crowded ballroom for minutes on end. Then very slowly and tremblingly, the Old Man rose, and while the crowd watched in stricken silence, he made his way slowly and doggedly along the row to the aisle. Someone took his arm and helped him as he walked tremblingly the long walk up the aisle through the hushed crowd to the double doors in the dim background. Someone opened one of the doors for him and the Old Man walked slowly through and disappeared from our view.

From the platform I had been able to see the Old Man's face and I knew my career had ended.

Gradually all the eyes were now turning back to me. That's truly about all I remember of that afternoon. I must have given a ranting, rambling, incoherent summary, because I remember hearing someone's voice—Old Aspery, I believe, behind me—saying: "Someone get that man off the platform!" Then I could feel hands on my arms and myself being led down the side steps near the curtain and off the platform and that's literally all I remember. That was how the crackup came. It was like climbing to the high board, surveying the multitude far below and then diving into oblivion. . . .

The thing I regret most is the children. I'll always miss them. But I guess I haven't really changed much. I am what I am. The thing I hate worst, thinking back on it is—not so much that I blew it, not that I lost my wife, not that I made a fool of myself, not that I threw a career away and fell from the heights—but that I didn't get what I wanted, I never got Mrs. Trevor. . . .

*   *   *   *

That, of course, is not the way it ended. It is my interpretation of the character of one of our subjects, and, while most of what happened to him verges
closely on reality, that is not the way he told it nor the way he felt about himself and what happened to him.

We had returned from a taping out west and I was sitting in my apartment in
town working out some chess moves and mulling over this problem of disguising
a man like this. I realized I didn't really know how it had been with him or if it
had happened as he had told it or as I imagined it. But this executive had one
thing in common with two others we taped: the strains of his situation had
proved too much for him. . . .

It was late at night and I sat there a long time thinking about this and about
how a valid picture of this might be presented. I could not bring myself not to
use most of this material, even reconstructed, for this seemed to me so representative of what can happen when the pressures become too great and when a
man at the highest levels has a serious character defect. . . .

So here is a man, a subject, not as he was but as I reconstructed him, an
executive who almost made it to the top—almost. . . .

PART IV

Here is one who reached it. . . .

Uncertain beginnings, struggles, getting there, strains and pressures—all of this —and at last we reach the top. . . . The heights glitter and we wonder at the rare, the chosen, the incomprehensible, who make it to the stratosphere. We ask ourselves: how did he do it? What combination of superior talent, great ambition, powerful character and fantastic luck brought this man to the summit out of all those who fought and struggled and worked and climbed just as hard and as resourcefully? What makes the Arthur Mitchells of this world. For as he himself has said: "I was not the brightest. . . ."

Yet when you look at his biography it looks so easy—it looked so easy I hesitated approaching him for the taping—the steady progress, the step by step ascent, the inexorable rise through the great corporate hierarchy—engineer, assistant plant manager, plant manager, merchandise manager, administrative manager, assistant vice president, vice president-merchandising, executive vice president, president, chairman of the board and chief executive officer. . . . Then one thinks of other darlings of destiny, the great Duke of Wellington's mother looking over at her fifteen-year-old son about to enter the army and saying: "I vow to God I don't know what I shall do with my awkward son, Arthur. I fear he is food for powder and nothing more. . . ."

No, it is not easy and there is no known formula revealed to us by Providence or God. It was difficult to disguise this man who dominated an industry for ten years and sits on dozens of boards and government business committees and whose name is much in the press. A lot has been lost in the taping and disguising, but we did our best and here are his words on how it was with him on the way up. It is no explanation but, as in every story eventually, we have come at last to a happy ending. . . .

10

"Would I Do It Over Again? I Would Have to Say, Considering Everything and With One Reservation, I Would. . . ."

The Chairman of the Board looks over his life in the corporate world

If ever a man looked like a chairman of the board, Arthur M. Mitchell does. A tall, ruggedly handsome man in his sixties, he has dominated his field, served as chief executive officer of one of the world's largest corporations for many years and in every respect ranks at the top of the corporate hierarchy. He sits on a number of boards of major companies; his name is known in the business world and beyond, and he has long been in the public eye as an adviser and captain of industry.

He has an easy, gracious manner, a pleasant, reasonable and sincere personality, is deeply interested in a wide range of subjects and concerned with world problems. He has a slow, warm voice and gives the impression that he has all the time in the world. No one in his presence for very long can fail to be impressed.

That evening I got home and I was standing in the bedroom when it happened. Something in me snapped, and suddenly I knew I was in over my head; I knew I'd come to the end of the line. I needed help badly. . . .

It had been building for a long time. I suppose the pattern had been set in my childhood. I had to succeed. I had to do everything as if my life depended on it. I had to give whatever I was assigned to everything I had, and I'd come to something that was too much for me. Now I knew I had to have some kind of lifeline or I'd go under. . . .

I think probably people looking at a chairman of the board's official biography expect to see someone, who, if you will, is born to success, in the sense that his progression went on up and he took each step in stride and grew in stature and

177

self-confidence and became the very natural choice at each step of the way; going from vice president to executive vice president, to president and ending up as chairman of the board and living happily ever after. But I suspect if we had the stories of say twenty-five chairmen of the board . . . I'd be very surprised if at least half of them didn't have . . . say some moments, some episodes in their lives very different from this story-book production. I think in my own case, had it not been for what happened to me that Friday evening and thereafter, I'm not sure what would have been the story of my life from then on, but I know I would have been a very different kind of person, good or bad, better or worse, but at any rate not the same.

What happened was this. . . . But to understand it, I suppose, as I grew to understand it, you have to go back to—I know this sounds antediluvian—the situation of my family way back when my father—a spoiled, cocky young man— was riding high on his father's reputation in one of the prairie states. In a sense, as you'll see, I was an unwanted child.

My father was the youngest son of a successful contractor working out through these prairie states at a time when at least one of them was still a territory. My mother was one of six children of a poor but self-reliant southern farmer. She was visiting friends in this little town where my father at the age of twenty was working. He had dropped out of college to take over the family business since his older brother had died suddenly. So here you are—age twenty —thrown into a thriving construction business, driving the only Packard in town or in the state when this southern belle comes to town for a visit. Sparks flew and out of that came a marriage and ten months after the marriage came me.

Well, this business of putting in electric light systems, water systems, and sewer systems through all the new towns throughout this great region kept us hopping, and I suspect that before the marriage was a year old, both parties felt that it was probably a mistake. Their values were different; their backgrounds were different, their ideas of the future and, I think, of homelife were different. My father was an adventurer. He liked excitement. He wanted to do things. He wanted to travel, to see things. He was a driven man also—he wanted to excel in everything, but mostly he wanted to be where the action was, where there was excitement. So we were uprooted time and again.

I am convinced my father, age twenty-two, after a year of marriage and birth of a child, felt that a child was a piece of baggage and in the way. I really do. I guess I can understand it now. I couldn't at age one. Nor could I understand it at age ten, when finally they got divorced.

Divorce in those days in the Bible Belt was something you didn't do. My mother was trying to hang onto the marriage, but it was very unsatisfactory. My mother's been reluctant to talk about it over the years except for casual references, but it is very clear there was no closeness at all in that marriage. I remember incidents where it was very obvious that I was too much bother, where I was in the way. No question about it. Well, my mother and I stayed behind in the South with my mother's family when my father volunteered and went over as an officer and stayed all through World War I, plus another couple of years participating in the reconstruction of France.

So finally my parents were divorced when I was age ten. But during this, as you might guess, some of the dependence on relatives and the money bind rubbed off on me but good. Because of pride my mother felt she had no one else to talk to, and she talked to me almost as if I were an adult. So it became evident to me very early that, first, you had to cope with life—the cherries weren't out on the trees just for the picking—that you had to save in order to have money to pay bills with. It was also important to earn people's respect when your mother was the only divorcee in a Bible Belt town. You had to be especially circumspect. I was reminded many times: "Son, people will expect you as the son of a divorcee to do crazy, screwball things. However, you must not do them. We're alone here in town and everything will reflect on me." Yes, yes, it's true. I wasn't aware at the time that this might now be considered a grave deprivation. Nonetheless, it was a fact. Some of my buddies would do crazy, wild things and would be reprimanded for them, but I just could not take any risks at all.

In a sense I tried harder than I ordinarily might have. I don't think I was the brightest guy in school. Nonetheless, I ended up graduating with honors from high school. I attribute this to the fact I just had to do it. I had one break by having some musical talent, and I began to take a few lessons. This helped financially, for when I was in high school and in college I was able to play in a dance orchestra to make most of my expenses.

Anyhow I graduated from high school and went to the college of engineering at the state university. I suppose I picked engineering because that was the fashionable profession. It was an age where technological changes such as radio and airplanes and other developments taken so for granted today—and perhaps outstripped by even more fantastic and mind-expanding scientific developments —had made a deep impression on boys of my age. So going into engineering seemed natural to me.

When I was in high school, my father and I began carrying on a formal correspondence once a month. He was back from Europe and had gone into a construction company. Later he went to work as general manager in a plant making gas from coal in upstate New York and ended up as president of that company.

In college I worked hard at my subjects—technical subjects, engineering mostly. In fact, I was a "grind," had virtually no social life, and graduated with honors. My father then offered me one year at an Ivy League graduate business school and it was here my eyes were opened to some of the larger aspects of life. I took courses in the humanities, and began to read a lot, and I suddenly began to see the world in its larger sense. I guess I had what you might call an awakening. Here I was a small-town boy from a provincial part of the world and now I was reading, I was coming into contact with great minds, and I was seeing how narrow the corner was in which I'd been living.

But now it was the depression and times were hard, and there were not many job openings. One of the big corporations, however, sent in recruiters to the college, and I was lucky enough to go to try for their executive recruiting program. I suppose my marks, the combination of engineering and business school, plus the fact that I had become fairly articulate as a member of the debating team, and had obviously been highly motivated resulted in my being one of the few selected in that year.

I was sent out as a production engineer to a plant in a bleak area where there was little to do but work long hours during those Depression years. One of the first bosses I had at the plant was a big burly Irishman with a very short fuse. He was known and feared, and when I was assigned to him, I knew I'd have to learn to live with this character. He had the habit of blowing up on the slightest provocation. He would go out on the line and he'd invariably see something amiss, or an order delayed, or something not just as he thought it should be, then he would, without finding out why or listening to any reason, immediately call in his chief assistant—me—and start yelling about it. It would do no good to try to tell him the reason, even if it were a very simple reason or a very good sensible reason. He would shout right through the attempted explanation.

Fortunately, I developed a method of coping with this man and he grew to like me and trust me. My method was very simple. When he would call me in and start on his tirade, I would sit down and pull out a notebook and pencil and I would take down what he was saying or take notes about the difficulty. I wouldn't say anything. I'd just listen, and pretty soon he would have blown off the steam and he'd settle down. Then I'd say: "I'll go out and find out what happened, and I'll come back and report to you."

Then I'd see what it was, have it fixed up or get the explanation. Later, I'd tell him, and he'd usually have forgotten about it or he'd say: "Well, that's all right." or "As long as it's fixed up," or "Forget it—it wasn't important." The thing was he needed someone to listen to him when he got excited. Pressures got to him easily and he blew up when anything seemed to him to be going wrong. I learned a valuable lesson from him. I learned how important it was to understand the person as well as what he's saying. My pulling out my pad and taking notes and listening to him were what calmed him down. If I'd tried to argue with him or point out to him any unreasonableness in his response, I'd have gotten nowhere—except perhaps the gate. So I learned to live with him and he took a liking to me. Later he was transferred. With his temperament he had gotten as far as he was going, but he recommended me for his job as he moved on.

A second major lesson was not long in being presented to me. It was what you might call a major crisis in my life and it came about this way. Production people in plants build up certain habits and rituals, which they then begin to take for granted. In one of our big plants, I had noticed while I was there that the production men would knock off about 4:30 in the afternoon to start washing up for the 5:00 o'clock quitting whistle. This somehow stuck in my craw. As an overly conscientious individual accustomed to working long hours I found it hard to swallow this kind of laxity. So I decided I'd try to do something about it. At least I'd make these people know that their knocking off so early was not going unnoticed. So I got the habit of taking a walk through part of the plant around 4:30–4:45 each evening.

Well, this went on for awhile. Then one morning, the plant manager, a big fatherly old-timer, called me into his office and shut the door. He walked over to me and put his arm around my shoulders, and he said: "Art, you're a good young fellow and a fine engineer and a hard worker, but I have something to tell you that I'm afraid's going to be a shock to you. Did you know that the men out in this plant have been signing a petition asking that you be removed from your job?" I stood there for a minute stunned, and then my legs gave way and I had to sit down.

"Now, Art," the old man went on in his fatherly voice, "I know this is hard on you and it's a bad situation. There're two things we can do. One, I can have you transferred to another plant. Or secondly you can stay and see what you can do about it. It's up to you."

Well, I sat there so shaken I couldn't trust myself to say anything for a minute or two. I just sat there in shock. But at last, I pulled myself together and said: "Harry, I've never run from a situation in my life and I'm not going to start now. I'll stay and see what I can do about this."

That night I went home and I couldn't sleep. I knew I'd made a bad mistake and I had to think how I could work it out, how I could remedy it. I decided upon a plan which I hoped would work. In the next few months I went into that plant almost every day and began calling the men by their names and stopping to talk. Gradually I built up my friendships with these production men and we developed a good warm relationship of mutual respect and understanding. It was a tough lesson to learn but I learned it for good—that healthy relationships with people are essential in any team effort, in any management effort.

After a few years as division production manager, I was switched over to marketing—a major shift where success meant a promising future. I succeeded, so I then moved up to assistant to the general manager, and finally to vice president and general manager of one of the company's biggest, most important divisions. I had been in that position for about 16 months, when the whole accumulation of responsibility, the risks, and the nature of my own driven character overwhelmed me and I stood there on that Friday evening and felt that I could not go on, felt that I'd come to the end of the line.

To understand this fully, though, you must understand the magnitude of what I had been given. First of all, I was now right under the gimlet eyes of those at the top. This unit was the biggest earner in the corporation and it involved having tens of millions of dollars of inventory on hand in a volatile commodity situation, where there was a constant risk of losing millions. Secondly, I was reporting to a man who was relatively new in his position and was determined to make good, and to show that he was very much better than his predecessor. While his treatment of me was in actual fact absolutely correct and considerate, I had the subconscious concern and fear that any misstep on my part would be disastrous to the whole enterprise. I suppose that this constant worry and the constant living with this tremendous responsibility was what brought me to that moment of complete exhaustion, that moment of the major crisis, the midnight of my life. . . .

Now you must understand also, it wasn't overwork. I would say that I've worked throughout my career an average of 65 to 70 hours a week and it's never hurt me. I can't do my paperwork at the office; too many people to see, too many plants to visit, too many meetings, too many people to counsel with. That briefcase was usually stuffed full every evening and every night I'd spend a couple of hours working and often a lot of time on weekends, and it never hurt me. No, you could see this as an example of the theory that work never killed anyone, but worry has. I think that's true. The hard work, the hours—I don't think they had much to do with it, but the pressure, the nagging concern that doesn't let you sleep nights, that doesn't give you the carefree moments I think everyone needs—I think that gradually these can wear you down, until one day—bang. . . .

Then that load that I carried from my childhood, that feeling that I couldn't afford one false step, not because of the neighbors or because of the company, but because of that thing inside me from the past. If I owed ten dollars, that would worry me very much. If a report was due next Thursday and it was not finished by Monday, I worried until it was done, and then worried about whether it was good enough. I suppose I never let up on myself, and so the time came with the accumulation of all these other things that I went home one night and the world fell apart for me. . . . I cracked under the strain. . . .

So I knew I needed help. I knew what I had to do. I asked my wife to call the office Monday morning and give some excuse—because this was absolute torture. I felt my career was at an end and I had to resort to prevarication. I asked her to call and say that I had been hospitalized with what seemed to be the flu or walking pneumonia or whatever, and I went into the hospital. The company doctor, a fine man, I'm sure knew what the score was, and he came to see me. I was not in the hospital very long—about three weeks. Then I stayed home for a couple of weeks, after which I started coming back to work half-time. But because of this very understanding doctor, the word in the company and to my superiors was: Not only would this man recover, but he will be a stronger man when he recovers. I suspect he indicated something like "this fellow has overworked and needs to get a little better perspective on things and needs most of all a rest."

But meanwhile, something very significant happened to me. I'd gone to my doctor and I'd just had a good physical examination not long before, so he recognized the pressure for what it was. Following his advice, I started seeing one of the top psychiatrists in New York, one of the finest men I've ever met. He was a kind, warm, folksy type of man, a homey type—and we got on a first-name basis after an hour or two. He was the friendly sort rather than the "lie down on the couch and tell me about your life" type. Really, I think what I did was, in effect, to consider this man almost as a father figure, and I think actually here was the understanding, supportive father figure that I hadn't had and had needed in my life.

But you must remember this was a hard thing to do in those days. It was not an era where psychiatry was widely accepted. It had to be concealed or it would have been the kiss of death in the corporate world—or at least I feared this was the case. So I had these terrible fears and I had to try to keep up this sort of pretense, and frankly it was of deep concern. When the number two man in the company would meet with me, I of course talked very confidently—even casually. But I was always concerned about how our president felt about what had happened to me. I had always been, supposedly, the strong figure that was carrying all the burdens and now I was reverting—I suppose I was reverting—to the fact that I needed someone to take care of me. Looking back on it, I believe these men understood. I now believe in spite of everything they were probably aware of what had happened and their insight and sensitivity and understanding of people came to my rescue and somehow I survived. I cannot believe from my own experience that corporations are cold, cruel or inhuman organizations and that the men who run them are without regard for human values. I was soon back in the swing of things again. I spent about two years with this father figure, this psychiatrist, and I became a different man. I grew to understand myself better. I became stronger. I came to terms with this inner tension, this driven feeling. As I said, for better or worse, this experience, this dark night of my life changed me and I believe I became a stronger person. At any rate, I was not the same.

Before I go into the third major crisis of my career and try to answer the question you have asked: "Would I do it over again?" let me try to tell you what I think I've learned and say something about what I've found in a career in organizations.

Especially in recent years corporations have not been popular, and many evils have been ascribed to them. In this decade they are mistrusted and it is said that, especially in the case of multinational corporations like our own, they are wielding more and more power over the country's and the world's economy. I can't say that after more than forty years in corporate life that I have found that true. Looked at objectively, corporations have owned a steady 28 percent of America's wealth for the last half century, and the U.S. with 6 percent of the world's population still owns a third of the world's wealth, obviously a disproportionate part of the world economy that perhaps should not and probably cannot continue indefinitely.

But while it may be offensively trite to say corporations are people, this is the only way we who have lived in the corporate world have experienced them. One of the matters often brought up is: what happens to brilliant or original people in corporations? Are they stifled? Are they lost? I would have to say yes, sometimes, but often not.

I am not as bright or as smart as many of the people who work for me, but I would be foolish indeed if I did not admire and appreciate their superior talents and find the roles where those talents can be used. In an organization, sometimes such brilliant men can have their own talents and goals fulfilled, sometimes not, but there must be a willingness also to put up with the necessities of organizational life. For instance, we had a brilliant fellow as head of marketing in one of our divisions, and there was no question that the fellow was a creative genius. But he was impossible to work for. He was unpredictable. Schedules meant nothing to him. Paperwork was a nuisance. Deadlines meant nothing. It was hard to find where we could put this guy so as to use his brilliance, so that we could get something done and everything would not just end in a shambles.

There are people who are entrepreneurs and who can initiate things but they can't stand the constraints and compromises of corporate life. They're not effective in corporations, they're unhappy in organizations and they need to get out on their own and run their own shows. So obviously organization life is not for everybody, and it's very difficult to survive in a corporation if these constraints overwhelm you.

An organization is a little world of its own—true. But it has to be responsive to the great world in which it finds itself or it can't survive and prosper. It tends to follow the fashions of its economy and the values of its society. Back in the 1930s, for example, we ran into forces—the Great Depression—we couldn't control and we were pretty much controlled by them. Then in the 1940s, there was World War II and here again corporations had to respond to the needs of the nation and most of them did respond. Our corporation did also, though I guess you could say that as a consumer company we tried to take advantage of whatever consumer market opportunities were permitted to us even with shortage of supplies and the need to meet the demands of the war.

Then in the 1950s and 60s, I would characterize the values and demands to be growth, expansion, meeting the great variety and intensity of the consumer demands of those eras. We were also in the era where go-go companies were the thing and there was tremendous emphasis on recruiting of certain types, Harvard and Columbia MBAs, for example. Most large companies were after young men and women who were extremely aggressive and would help us find any wedge or segment of the market where we could leapfrog over our rivals to interest and intrigue the American public. This was the period of mergers and the rise of conglomerates and the emphasis was on performance, on earnings. I'm not saying that that was entirely wrong—it was a pattern. In our own company we did our best like everyone else to be as all out gung-ho as possible to meet the demands of expansion and growth. It was soon obvious other values were being neglected.

Well, it's so easy now to say we were wrong as a society, for example, to get into every conceivable convenience regardless of what it did—let's say—in the using up of resources, and energy. Now in the 70s, a lot of our extravagance, all of our extravagances are, of course, coming home to roost.

Before I turn to the last crisis of my own career and try to answer your key question, let me just draw two more observations from my experiences as the chief executive of one major corporation and as a member of the board of directors of a number of other major corporations in a number of other fields.

First of all, we obviously have overspent ourselves, we obviously have been extravagant and reckless—not just corporations but all of us, and we're going to have to live in a world where the cost in use of resources must be counted. A few years ago, it would have been very difficult for any of us to achieve a balanced approach to leadership of a company, when the watchword was growth. It would have been a pretty unpopular position for an executive to sit around and be a devil's advocate and say: "Just a minute. Just a minute. Does this really make sense? Look at the resources we're using." Or to say: "Wait a minute. Are we putting too great a burden on the environment? Are the values we're offering worth the use of our air and water or coal or oil or gas or forests?"

The truth is society as a whole, not just a group of us sitting in some board room or on a policy committee or in operating meetings, sets the values by which we must guide our performance. Not too many years ago, you may remember, one of the big automobile companies tried to sell a car that stressed a logical design, less chrome and new safety devices, and the company tried to plug it for its economy and safety. But power was the watchword that year and nobody would buy. People wanted big powerful cars that would get off the mark fast, and in those years big powerful cars sold like hotcakes. So that company had to turn around and try to scramble onto the bandwagon and get back into the race.

Today, of course, we see this company was ahead of its time. Our values, our needs have changed. So what I am saying is yes, corporations are going to have to meet the values of our society. We are going to have to take responsibilities we were never incorporated to take, because society tells us we have to, that these things—environmental impact, social considerations and so on—are important to us all and to the world, and we as corporations after all are only instruments of our societies, of our countries and of the human values of our civilization, and we are going to have to serve them, and develop executives who can serve them in the ways and under the rules that they have prescribed for us, if we are to survive and prosper.

Secondly, we who manage big corporations like this one are going to have to take a broader view, a global view of our practices. We are going to have to look not just at our own country's resources but at the world's resources and tastes and needs also. We have operated perhaps on too parochial a base. I know today there is an outcry over multinational companies, a question as to their loyalties, their responsibilities and to their awareness of all the values, needs and desires of all the peoples they serve. There is a question about their power and their responsiveness. But the economy of the world, as we realize in this era, is not infinite. Those who use resources must now begin to consider them on a global basis, and already we are seeing in several crises how interdependent we and the rest of the nations of the world are on each other. These are observations, it seems to me, that are inescapable to any executive who aspires to lead a great corporation.

I could say more, much more on these matters, but let me turn back to my own career now and relate the third major crisis in my business life, a crisis, I think you will agree, of a magnitude and of an agonizing nature not easily surpassed in the whole of our world. As chairman of the board and chief executive officer, I had to fire the president of our company, the man I had chosen to be my successor.

Before I go into this, let me detail briefly the remainder of my own rise in this corporation. After that second crisis of my life, my progress in the corporation continued and I was a stronger and, I believe, better executive. The big unit of the company for which I was responsible prospered and after three years I was made an executive vice president and a director of the corporation. You have asked about the nature of selection of individuals for positions of responsibility, whether much politics is involved and whether there is much in-fighting, as dramatized in many of the stories in the press and in books. I am sure that there is, though not on the scale and with the frequency indicated in the press and in the mind of the public. I think I have had the benefit of living the corporate life in two companies over the last forty-three years and I have seen very little of the bad politicking or in-fighting during that time. It is very difficult to determine whether situations of competition, which are inevitable, are basically politicking or not. On the medium levels, where men in competition must vie for visibility to be assessed by higher management, it is quite possible for an able man who is quiet and cannot push himself to have some of his abilities overlooked. This is something very difficult to know. Mostly, though, it's a matter of the judgment of the top executives and of the needs of the company. Of course, as you go toward the top, the competition becomes very intense.

In my own case, I was aware as I went up that I was in competition with others. At one time there were two of us who were made executive vice presidents at the same time, and without deliberately sitting down and pondering over it, I was aware that I was in competition with the other man for the next step, which was the presidency. We were all within six years of the chief executive's retirement. The man with whom I could be said to be in competition had come up a different way from me. I had come up as an operating man, and he had come up as a staff man in charge of finance, law and other staff functions. We never really overlapped very much. We couldn't really compare performances, so it simply had to be a matter of judgment of those above us, in terms of how they saw our development potential and in terms of the needs of the company.

As it happened, within three years, some changes were made and I was named president, and it is fair to say that the man with whom I was in competition did not necessarily agree with the choice. We went along together for a couple of years, however, and then it became clear we could not work well together and he left for another assignment. In decisions of this sort, of course, it is the chief executive officer who has a very very great deal to say about the choice of his successor. An outside board of directors can hardly spend the time, live from day to day, with the matters of succession, so they rely heavily on the judgment of the chief executive.

Now we come to the very agonizing period in my own career, where matters of succession were a central consideration in selecting a man for the presidency. Under my administration during the first few years after I succeeded to the chairmanship and became chief executive officer, the corporation had grown and prospered. We had tried also to set up organizational patterns which developed strong managers and the additional leadership we knew we would need for the goals we had set up. Incidentally, in the matter of planning, I had felt that plans that go much beyond three years are not very practical, at least in the areas in which our organization operated, although, of course, we could set general directions. But beyond two or three years, it was sort of pie in the sky since events and trends changed so rapidly and had been changing so rapidly during the last two or three decades.

Now I selected a very able man for the presidency with the expectation that he would succeed me. I had hoped that I might retire a little earlier than the usual retirement age, since I had been leading this corporation for quite a number of years, and I felt that that was long enough and it was time for a change.

Now how do you choose a successor? On what do you base your assessment of a man's potential? Of course, you base it greatly on previous performance. But additionally you must go by instinct, because there is no way you can tell how a man will perform under the conditions or power and authority of the top position. My associate was—and is—a very strong personality and I believed that his aggressive, gung-ho qualities were the kind our company needed in the years of expansion ahead. His performance at a lower level had, of course, been very good, but you just don't know how some people are going to react to greater and greater responsibility and power. First there is the fantastically increased load that comes on the individual. What's that going to do to him? Then there is the greater leeway in authority and ability to have his way than he has had. What's that going to do for him? Is he going to fit or is he going to overreact or what?

In the case of the man who was my heir-apparent, it developed that his aggressiveness and desire to expand the company as rapidly as possible led to actions which turned out to be very costly. New fields of endeavor were entered without proper caution and expansion of the company's commitments in such new areas was undertaken before we had learned these new fields and before we had developed expertise to manage them wisely. Perhaps even more important, he demonstrated a strong tendency to make decisions without having encouraged full participation by his top associates. His strong personality was such that it discouraged questioning or dissent. It became increasingly obvious that this was not the man to become the future chief executive of the company and that a major change was indicated. Unfortunately, in situations such as this there is no way to turn back, so that the only feasible solution was to work out an agreement to part company.

After individual consultations with the members of the board of directors, I had the painful chore of informing him of the change that had to be made. While not agreeing with some of the conclusions, he understood my position and made the episode less difficult than I had anticipated. I must say, however, that this was one of the most agonizing episodes in my life. A good part of my discomfort properly stemmed from a feeling of guilt on my part that I had made a bad error in judgment involving the most critical job in the entire company.

This happened a few years ago. I had to return to full direction of the corporation and we had some good years. Now we have another man—a very good man, I believe, a man who has been tested for three or four years and who will be able to take over when I retire a year or two from now. For I have about come to the end of my career. So let me turn now to the key, the crucial question you've asked me and try to answer it as honestly as I can: Would you do it over again?

I suppose we all at sometime particularly toward the end of our careers ask ourselves, consciously or subsconsciously, this kind of question. We try to assess our life. We try to look at it, as I've done here, and see what it all means and what kind of pattern we've made in the world. In my case, I feel in many ways mine was a most fortunate life, but I think a much more sensible, a much more meaningful answer could be given, had conditions allowed more leeway of choice. Today the options are far greater than they were when I was young. In many ways this places an even greater burden on young people today, since I don't think that many teenagers are qualified to decide what they want to do.

But the choices I had were narrower and looking at them I would have to say I was lucky. Take engineering, for example. I was intrigued with engineering for reasons I don't really understand today. Radio was in its infancy then and we were all wrapping wires over oatmeal boxes and making crystal sets and that sort of thing. Experts were saying that this is the field of the future and so forth, so obviously I had to take engineering. I chose it. My mother was delighted and I do think that if I had to do it all over again I would probably have done that. Regardless of what you may meet in life, there are certain kinds of discipline or disciplines that are excellent. Engineering is one; law is another. They are good disciplines for the mind. If I had the opportunity to go to business school again for a year—I would certainly have done that. I wish that I could have gone two years, because after four years of engineering, I knew very little about anything else. I am particularly glad I had the chance to take some of the humanities and I would have liked to take more, if I were to do it over again.

In my day, at that time, the choices of work were very, very limited, and the fact that I was hired by one of the major corporations in the country, the chance to work for that kind of corporation—that is something I would certainly do again. I would think that the years I spent with that first major corporation, the kind of difficult training, the hard work, the long hours I gave myself—I think about all of these things and that I was very, very fortunate.

Now looking at another aspect of this, however, I have one major reservation. Whether I would have devoted as many hours or worked as hard as I did at the expense of my family, I am not so sure. I was tremendously fortunate in my wife and children, but they were asked to take more perhaps than they should have in allowances for my career. I don't believe my daughter suffered so much, being so young at this time, but my son did. I failed to develop a relationship with my son and he dropped out of college and took some years to find himself. If I hadn't disciplined myself so severely and given my family so little time, I think actually I could have made about the same progress and not have pursued this career as assiduously as I did. I feel my son was short-changed by my compulsion and it took us about fifteen years to more or less bridge that gap in our relationship later on. Fortunately he found himself and has established himself in the field in which he finds fulfillment and is happily married. I am very proud of him and we are close friends.

But mine was a compulsion hard to live with. I had to succeed, as I've pointed out. I had subconsciously subscribed to the old saying: There's no substitute for winning and no cure for losing. This is a hard way to live. In the course of my life, I had to succeed; I could not fail. I think that's an enormous pressure for someone to be under. I believe I would have had a more pleasant and let's say a warmer life, if the pressures on me, external and self-imposed, would not have been so great. So I would have to say I have this major reservation.

On the other hand, I do not know what impact on my abilities a less driven attitude would have had. I'm glad I learned the hard way a lot of things about self-discipline and that you must succeed or at least you must not fail. But I think you pay quite a price for it and in this I believe I would have second thoughts.

Now in terms of what I've done at the first major company I worked in—moving from engineering into production—and taking on early supervisory responsibilities, I believe this was excellent training and really paved the way for a future in general management. I would not want to miss any of the things I learned in my progress here. Then as I moved into general management, I had to grow and learn, and I had to keep reaching higher and higher. I moved from production to marketing, sales and advertising, and gained a much wider knowledge of our own business and of the business world in general.

Well, I had the good fortune to end up, according to the medical reports, in good health, so that actually I feel I can cope with the rest of life, can lead it pleasantly and in a less hectic and driven fashion. I was able to provide for my family and relatives also. I was able to see that my mother lives comfortably. The various trust funds for my children will help protect them from financial worries and I was able to help those close to me. So that it all kind of seems worthwhile, and I didn't, as some people have to, work my tail off finally. . . to end up with a gold watch.

In the later phases, it was pretty rewarding along the way. I got to know more and more sophisticated and outstanding people and to become involved in major efforts outside. I traveled extensively and was exposed to different points of view, different ways of thinking, so that I saw things through foreign eyes, and some of my provincialism was washed away. We had business interests in Western Europe and in the Orient and you could not be exposed to these interests without ending up with a broader point of view.

Then I also served on government advisory committees and saw the problems and difficulties of great undertakings in those areas, and I have served in civic areas and on national boards and am serving on the boards of other great corporations. I have been given the opportunities that these positions offer for meeting all my ego needs, honors and so on, which serve largely to feed the ego and sometimes are quite undeserved. But mostly it is the way you grow, when you sit down to lunch, for instance, and there is the Prime Minister of Singapore or a sheik from some country in the Middle East and you get a chance to meet interesting people and to see the world through other eyes. These are tremendous rewards, rewards to keep a person growing, and these, of course, I cannot be thankful enough to have received.

Our problems are very great in the world and the world is changing fast, though I think it will be for the better. But you have asked: Would I do it over again? I would have to say, considering everything and with that one reservation we discussed, I would be glad to do it over again. . . .

EPILOGUE

What, Then, Do These Executives Seem to Be Saying about the Corporate World?

And so we concluded our odyssey.

Now at the end it is time to sum up, to try to find what it is these lives have to say about this particular subculture of our civilization. For our society has been called a business civilization and it has been said that business is the United States' principal national contribution, "the aggregator and articulator of our interests," someone has termed it, "the broker of our hopes and the builder of our road to riches, both tangible and spiritual." Whether this is so or not, I do not know, but the study of the life styles of those who direct the most powerful agent of our business culture, the corporation, surely should have something to say to us. Since I had been part of it, I too at last must turn, and, as we had done with the others, look at that part of my life that briefly had flowered within the corporate world and see what meaning all of our lives had. So I go first to something I had written twenty years ago.

> All I want, he had once told himself, is to get my money and get home to dinner. Now it was too late. The Empire had bought and paid for him, and he would have to keep going up. . . .

So ends a novel on the corporate world as it seemed to me then. For I had been a corporation man and I was leaving such a world forever. The novel was a picture of corporate pressures on the lives of four men and it was greeted with outrage mingled with some enthusiasm. One man was an executive whose promising career was ruined by love, another by drink, another whose driving ruthless ambition finally defeated him and the fourth, a young man who came, not to stay, only to observe, but was finally caught by the world in which he found himself.

How does this world, I asked myself, as one man, an outsider, saw it, compare with the realities as our actual executives seem to find them twenty years later? How do these executives themselves compare with those in this fictional world?

Strangely enough, I found they compared in a number of important respects quite closely. The pressures and the fun are there, also the wide variety of life styles within and the variety of personalities accommodated. But, most of all, it is the sense of the corporation's dominance of the lives of so many of its executives that holds. One of the characters in the novel notes that behind and beyond everything they do lies the shadow of the Empire, a living presence dominating their actions. Of our executives, whose voices you have just heard, Ken Burdett, our vice president, who gave up two wives to the job, most directly expresses this sense: "The corporation, the job," he says, "has dominated my whole life. Everything else has been secondary. . . ."

One has to ask what it is that makes this intangible presence, the corporation itself, beyond any of its characteristics—the pay, the friends made, the status gained—so powerful as to have caught at least for a time an outsider like myself whose aims and orientation were so alien, even inimical to organization life? What is it that puzzles those who gaze at this life from afar and see the tremendous hold the organization has on dynamic, intelligent, often gifted men and women, a hold that expresses itself in the term "loyalty" and often takes precedence over home, family and even country? Finally, what is it that sociologists and others who study the organization sense beyond the forms and behavior patterns of organizational life?

Perhaps there is no one all-encompassing answer, but it seems to have to do with two major aspects of human life: personal identity and power. Those who work for an organization come to identify themselves strongly with it as they would with their family, community and country, but because its objectives and ambiance are so clearly defined and focused, their identity with it is stronger and more specific than those of other forms of community life. This identification satisfies or partially satisfies one of the deepest, most intense hungers of the mature individual—the hunger to give himself or herself to something large and worthwhile, to something that will outlast him or her and that will make a difference in the world. It is a hunger that in most people is deeper even than the need for personal glory, wealth or honor.

So he or she identifies with the corporation even with all its idiocies and defects, and, if one is torn away from it through retirement or termination, one is torn away from an essential part of oneself. If a man, one tends to feel emasculated, if a woman executive, to lose her significance, her reason for being, like the wife and mother whose children grow up and leave home and who finds she has long lost her husband to his career. All of these feelings, of course, are intensified by the sense of the corporation's presence in their lives eight hours a day, five days a week over the years.

The second tremendous hold in addition to identity is the hold of status and power. In a sense, the corporation extends and magnifies the power of ordinary men a thousandfold. It clearly defines and legitimizes status and authority. It shows the way up and thus it provides immediate and compelling goals to those within it.   It also provides a pattern of criteria for excellence or progress in a chaotic and confusing world.   Not least, of course, it provides security and a comfortable way of making a living.

But to return to the status aspect of corporate life, this explains so much that seems puzzling or insane about the corporate world.   Here status is clearly marked to those who know.   One of the men we taped told how outraged he was, when he began his career, that he could not have a second bookcase for his office to house his many books.   Unfortunately for him he found in that corporation a bookcase was a status symbol.   So only a person a level above him could have two bookcases.   Rank and order, of course, appear everywhere in the world where human beings gather together, but in the corporation they are more clearly defined than, say, in a community or a neighborhood, and they play an extremely important role in the functioning of a large and complex enterprise: they legitimize function and authority.   While each person must eventually prove himself and find his level in the human order as is the case with all gregarious species, a big enterprise could not be undertaken, if each member had to start out from scratch to establish his level and authority.   Too much time would be wasted, and to get the great enterprises accomplished that are the reasons for being of most large corporations, an order of authority and function must be quickly established.   So we have these physical evidences, some subtle, some blatant, of authority—the large office, the rug on the floor, the large desk, drapes, the silver decanter—and the customs and traditions who can have lunch with whom, who comes to whose office, who precedes or follows in entering a room or an elevator.

This kind of thing is laughed at and looked down upon on the surface, but underneath, all organization people respect it and follow its precepts, and when one does not, disaster usually follows.   Many companies of late years have tried, in the interests of democracy and the myth that all are born equal, to eradicate these signs of status, usually with bad results.   They have attempted to do away with private offices, to cut down on what they term the frills.   Sometimes the chief executive, who sees himself as a plain, down-to-earth, shirtsleeve type, decides to sit out with the peons or places himself in a small, mean office, while his executives are situated in larger, more elaborate quarters.   This, of course, is a form of reverse snobbery, and his executives may well eventually come to equate status with smaller, plainer offices and vie with each other in plain down-to-earthness.   But generally the attempt to eradicate status strikes at the heart of human self-esteem and is doomed to fail.

> Take but degree away, untune that string
> And hark what discord follows. . . .

So to the man or woman who by great effort has earned his or her status within the corporation, the corporate shadow, the corporate presence is very real indeed; it is the guarantor of the status and thus of the worth of all that effort and struggle. Even outside the organization, the corporate or organizational presence is very real and important. To be from IBM, Xerox, Kodak, General Electric, General Motors, Bankers Trust or Price Waterhouse means something. It means something in the world and it means something to the man or woman in his or her neighborhood. The organization stands over him, placing him and magnifying him in his community. Thus we are not talking here of trivial matters. Not every man is an Einstein or a Leonardo da Vinci. Most of us are ordinary people with ordinary abilities and we do our best. But we must create our identities and find our status where we can, and the corporation provides these essential ingredients of human life for the millions who commit themselves to it.

Yet it is not all that simple. The winds of life blow through the corporate halls also, the disasters and the terrors. Some of them seem not only incongruous but to be magnified in the structured environment of the corporation. Most of us who have lived the corporate life have witnessed one or another of these disasters. I remember during a bad time after World War II, a friend had an affair with the office *femme fatale*, a secretary. On Christmas Eve, having left his wife and children for her, when she failed to show up he jumped out of a hotel window and killed himself. I too have watched a good man who worked for me go down the boozy path to the end. I too saw the wrong man's career shattered by political conniving and have seen the bullying and the fear. These are part of the human condition and not, I believe, unique to corporate life, but the corporate structure and the fact that a person's livelihood and status are at stake render the victim particularly helpless.

Equally important, however, is the exhilaration of the work, the pleasures of achievement. Some of our subjects laughed at this, but everywhere we went and with almost everyone we interviewed, this exhilaration and pleasure in the work—at least at times in the subject's life—showed through. The variety of executive work was enormous—almost all of it beginning with some specialty and then moving into areas of planning and organizing projects, trying to get people to carry out parts of the whole, coaching and persuading, or, as they called it, administering, and reviewing. . . .

Sometimes it seemed to me that one could identify a certain rhythm to a corporate life, a corporate career. It appeared to be composed of initially a sort of drifting into the corporation, almost by accident, in order to make a living. Then comes the gradually increasing interest in the work itself, the accelerating learning process, the longer hours as the nature of the job and the responsibilities grew more complex and heavier, the increasing identification with the company and its life styles and objectives, the intermittent periods of frustration and triumph, the hardening and quickening of ambition, and a sense of the self, an increasing sense of one's importance in the scheme of things. Then as one goes up in the hierarchy, the struggle for power begins, usually muted or hidden, along with the awareness of potentiality. One day there comes a period when all seems to rise to a crescendo and hangs there in the balance. Either you break through now into higher management or you face the dilemma of leaving.

You, the executive, begin to look at the outside world again, to test yourself in the market place. What are they paying people like me, you ask yourself. What are engineers or financial men or systems men or industrial relations or marketing men getting these days at auction? What contacts do I have? What am I really worth? Am I a hot product or does my kind of expertise come a dime a dozen? You're in your forties now and you have suddenly begun to feel this is your last chance. You're either going to make it here, crash through here or in the market place or you're going to have to settle for a home in the company and the long pull.

You feel geared to the crisis. You look around. You intimate your ambitions to your superiors. You look at the office politics and the general needs of the corporation and how you might fit in. You make discreet inquiries of your contacts and talk once more to the officer of one of your company's big competitors who asked you to drop up sometime. Nothing special seems to happen—certainly nothing as clearly or as cleanly as you visualized it. It's not yes, not no. It's half-promises, hints, and time slipping away. Then abruptly you get that half promotion, except that the superior you are transferred to is a fair-haired boy ten years younger than you and occupying the vice presidential seat you had hoped for. Maybe he'll move up soon, you tell yourself, because obviously they're grooming him for the top. Then one morning, the fair-haired boy, yesterday's hero, is gone—he made the jump over to a competitor in a higher slot, and now you're in your fifties and the great moment has arrived.

Except for some reason it doesn't seem so great. It's good, it's all right, but if they'd given it to you ten years ago it would have been great, a beautiful shining thing. There's another factor here also. Even though you have finally reached the spot you wanted to be in, it turns out to be a job just like any other job and somehow it's been toned down to your abilities. There's been a slight reorganization and the broadened responsibilities the press release says you've assumed turn out to be not so broadened after all. They seem to have been tailored somehow to what they think you can do, not what your predecessor was doing. Suddenly you realize you've made it, you're there! You're in the big time. You're in the position of power and authority you've dreamed of, but it's not quite what you thought it might be. It's ok; it's nice but it isn't great, and your power isn't quite as great as you thought it would be. The company's grown and there're now two levels above you, though the chairman still puts his arm around your shoulder and calls you Charlie. You are a vice president.

Now you find you are becoming like many of those you used to wonder about. You remember your days in the field as the great times and you look around at the younger fellows and you see they don't really know what it is. You find yourself trying to tell them, and they listen attentively and politely but they don't seem really to be hearing you too well. Still you're a big shot and a vp and you have the big office, and at least they listen to you in committee meetings. But things seem to be moving too fast nowadays and that family feeling the company used to have seems to be fading. It's all rush, rush, all push and shove and scramble, all these young guys trying to climb over each other; not the way it was when you were younger.

Camus has said: "Every achievement is an enslavement," and this seems to be borne out as you've moved up. You look around more carefully and you begin to notice things, and then one evening as you're sitting there—it's autumn and it's been a very upset, indeterminate day. . . . That evening sitting in the big office—you're in your early sixties now—there comes this chilling moment. That morning the personnel vp had asked you very casually about your plans for retirement, and the company has this dumb rule that forces everybody to retire at sixty-five at the height of their ability and experience, and suddenly you remember reading somewhere in some dumb book this passage:

> Now it confronted each of them: the terrible dispensability of them all. It was more than just here today and gone tomorrow. It was that really, basically, you were of no consequence to the firm as an individual. They might pretend otherwise, but the Empire had seen a thousand like you, and it would see other thousands like you in the future. You were nothing here— nothing. And if you went out tomorrow, the waters would close over you immediately; there would be no remembrance, no recourse, no sign. A saying returned to him from Emerson, one he had learned long ago and with which he had once comforted himself: Every man is wanted but not much. Well, here they weren't really wanted at all.

You know it isn't true, but for a moment, as you sit there this autumn evening, you find you can almost believe it. . . .

These are some of the elements, it seems to me, of one of the more typical life styles as I found them during our tapings of corporate lives. Whether these elements are unique to the corporation I do not know, but I doubt it. Old teachers, old professionals, old politicians, old soldiers never die; they just fade away. But the corporate world can only use men and women a comparatively short time, and then they must go out, shorn of their power and identity from that place they have loved, and make a new life in a somewhat alien world. Or so it may seem.

Finally, it must be said: Every corporation has its own personality and what is true in one is not necessarily true in another. As can be seen from these tapings, there are a number of representative life styles in this world. Someone has said: "There is no wealth but of men," and my experience with these tapings and in this study leads me to believe it.

For a moment we might ask ourselves what each of these "lives" we have taped seems to be saying about the world of the corporation and its inhabitants. The interpretations given here are, of course, my own and have no objective validity.   Others might well have viewed these executives differently, had they seen and talked to them as I and my associate did. Here, then, are some thoughts about the tapings themselves:

Bob Blake, it seemed to me, was a comer in the corporation with very little insight, struggling blindly upward to a level which would be somewhere near the upper part of middle management, perhaps in marketing. The corporation, it seemed to me, would find a use for him, harness his energy and accommodate him in his increasing rambunctiousness until he reached his own goal, that of most corporation men, not necessarily the top but near enough for the comfortable life and a little of the power.

Jane Killian impressed me deeply not just because she was attractive but because she seemed to have the driving, almost ruthless ambition of the potential chief executive. When I asked her if, despite her attractiveness, the reason she had not built up a deep relationship might be because she had married the company, this worried her a great deal. During the many times we met after I had asked this question, she brought it up again and asked: "Am I really married to the company? I don't like that. I don't want to be!" She has the ability, however, to look at herself in a detached manner and this too may stand her in good stead as she goes up.

My conglomerate executive, Howard Carver, who subsumed the characteristics and experiences of three men who decided not to release their transcript and interviews singly, would have been happier had he—or they—had the guts to get out before their vested interest in the life and economic stability of the corporation had become too great. Yet one of these men was highly intelligent, in fact brilliant, and the others were above average men with substantial ability. They did not really belong in corporate life; the life style was bad for them.

Anthony Rossi, our fourth executive, on the other hand, though an entrepreneur, a type not usually happy in organization life, nevertheless seemed to me a winner, who had found his niche, running the show in a small company. He seemed to me cheerful, uncomplicated, ambitious, independent and unafraid. He had no great insight but I found him refreshing—a self-made man who was glad he had made himself the way he is.

Of all our executives, Joseph Hardy, a black executive in a white world, exhibits the most contradictory traits. Obviously a rough diamond to begin with, he managed to stampede through against heavy cultural odds. He is driven to make good in a world that for him is full of social and emotional booby traps that he must reconnoitre almost as he had to do as an officer in Vietnam under enemy fire. Today he is a hot premium product, a Black in a business world that values him for his rarity and needs him to display for our culture's sake. He is tall, handsome and tortured both by his ambition, his need to win and by the strain and uncertainty of his position and his future. He could become president of a white company and he could break under the strain.

Our fifth executive, David Danbury, presents no such problem. He is the quintessential corporate man. He is contented where he is. Quiet, matter of fact and somewhat unemotional, he has a good analytic mind and an ability to negotiate, looking only at the facts and to carry out orders. Despite the strains of a job with a great deal of travel involved, he managed to have a fortunate home life, a wife who understood the problems of his position and children who flourished. He was a man who felt that his life was better than those of his parents and that his children's lives would be better than his in terms of opportunity, education and wealth or comfort, and he derived great satisfaction from this perspective. He also, it seemed to me, harbored a certain concealed enjoyment out of the things that happened to him. He was a good soldier in the corporate world and he knew himself, both his strengths and his weaknesses.

To me, certainly one of the most interesting men we met was our sixth executive, Ken Burdett, and he seemed to me one of the most revealing in terms of corporate life. Here was a man who literally gave up two wives and a home life for his job and yet struck me as a sensitive, humane person, highly intelligent and with real insight into his situation and himself. The pleasure he took in his work seemed to me very real and intense and I believe he had weighed the price of giving so much of himself to the job and decided it was worth paying. I remember a fine line in an ad some years back which went: "Loneliness goes with territory. . ." I think of it when I think of Ken Burdett, but I realize, as he said, if he had it to do over again he would still pay that price for it.

I don't know what to say of Tom Lassiter. Tall, good-looking, of a cultivated family, living in a fine house in a beautiful city with an attractive wife and daughters, he seemed to me not to have lived as fully as some of the others we met, and yet I am aware this superficial impression may well arise from my own inability to be engaged deeply by the premium products of good fortune. Golden boys, like happy families and young lovers, I find difficult to turn my attention to, perhaps because my own good fortune has made me, through some atavistic need, more interested in the darker aspects, the chaos and the turmoil of life. At any rate, here was a man whose attractiveness and friendliness have carried him high into a rich and fortunate corporate world.

It is to men like Will Warrant that my interest and attention constantly turn— the darker aspects of life and weaknesses that could easily have been my own, and yet I realize how little representative he must be both because of his brilliance and because of his weaknesses. The drinking problem, the woman problem, the conflicts of interest where the rewards are great are all part of the human condition. They manifest themselves in the corporate world, usually highly muted by the protective power of the corporation, which tends to muffle the weaknesses of its minions and support their strengths. Where the man is extremely brilliant and rises too high, the protective cordon is sometimes pierced, as here, and the man's weaknesses burst forth like a flash fire, to be muffled and put out as quickly and with as little disturbance as possible. The public's recent interest in public morality both in business and in politics has intensified reaction against such weaknesses.

Our chairman of the board and chief executive officer, Arthur M. Mitchell, to a great degree embodies and symbolizes the creme de la creme of the corporate world. He is just the kind of man, it seems to me, on whom responsible corporate world leadership will have to depend and he represents with his broad view, his sense of responsibility and his human qualities the truly committed, the truly serious man for all seasons. He is not without flaws. He came a long way. He was subjected to heavy pressures. He made some bad mistakes, but he never let the side down. He took everything he had to take with courage and resourcefulness. He did what he had to do. He is a man of character, a man who can be trusted and I came to admire him. His rising to the top seemed to me to show that the world knows quality when it sees it.

Finally to round out this very personal view, let me add one or two memories of the corporate world, seen by that vain and self-absorbed younger man that I once was; some brief fragrance, some subtle ambiance of how it was then.

There was the delicious quietness of the Wall Street area in the very early morning, when I would come down—the outsider, the alien in the busy organization man's cosmos—to do my surrepticious writing before the white collar day began. I would take the subway from my uptown apartment while it was still dark, and, cocooned in the rumbling horrors of the Lexington Avenue Express, hurtle down toward the Wall. Swaying with me in the cars were that small special group, distinctive like night people, mostly construction workers, nurses, cleaning people—the true early morning coterie, so different from day people, who know nothing of the city as it turns from dark to early dawn, quiet and mint-fresh.

I would get out into the fresh morning and go to a little all-night coffee joint nearby for a quick breakfast of egg, English muffin and coffee. Then into the immense, silent, shadowy A.T.&T. Building with its massive marble pillars where I had a little office on the 16th floor in my disguise as a minor supervisor. There I would sit, a lovely view from the windows before me of the great downtown world now awash in the sea of dawn, and struggle with that world that for the first time I was beginning to care about and to look at. Self-absorbed and arrogant all my life, I was only now, a man in the fullness of his time, beginning to care about anything but himself. A son, a brother, a lover, a husband, a father, I am now ready at last to turn from my own stifling self-absorption to the lives of others, and, as the morning begins, as my fellow workers started to arrive, as the clock hand drew toward nine, I would put away my scribbling, dig myself out of myself and the dream world that seemed more real to me than my own life and, without too much of a wrench, for I enjoyed my job, put on my sensible office face for the warm routines of our busy day. . . .

Another moment: It is dusk of an autumn evening and I have stayed late and am leaving with a briefcase packed with work. I have just come back from a business trip halfway across the continent. I am tired. I know I have done a good job and that I will probably be promoted, and while I was doing it I had given it all of myself. But now, as I stand there in the dusk on the corner, the shadows of the downtown buildings beginning to merge into each other, I look up and I see the great building I have emerged from rising, rising into the dusk, and I know suddenly this is not for me and however high I might climb in that world, however great the pleasures of the work, the joys of that kind of power, I can never be fulfilled by them, I can never be of them, I will always be an outsider. . . . Somewhere Jorge Luis Borges has written: "Any destiny at all, however long and complicated, consists of a single moment, the moment in which a man once and for all knows who he is." That moment came to me on that beautiful autumn evening.

And finally, a third moment only a few years later. I am in the spacious office of the president, a big, warm, powerful man. My dark novel on corporate life has just burst on the horizon and this big man sits there, his heavy features still suffused with outrage, his voice shaking: "How could you give up a promising career for this—for this!" For the work has incensed him, the stir it has made in the world increased his fury and I am about to be fired, though with the admonition that I say nothing about it, remain a month or so longer and slip away so that there will be no new flare-up of publicity on my work. . . And this is how on a spendid Friday morning in summer, one who was told, perhaps only to make what he supposedly has lost the more bitter-sweet, that he might have reached a high position, he might have gone far in the company, at last leaves the corporate life forever. . . .

With these tentative personal views, we must conclude our study as we began. This is raw material for future sociologists and historians. Our thoughts and in-terpretations here may prove misleading or quite wrong, and we do not even know yet how these corporate life styles compare with those of other life styles in our society—how the motivations of executives, ways of seeing them-selves, loyalties and commitments differ or are similar to those who have entered and are an influence in the other worlds of education, politics, the professions, science, the arts and the underground. We hope to move on and explore these other lives for whatever experiences and insights those who have committed themselves to these worlds can give us.

All of us naturally attempt to find meaning in the chaos of life and the author is no exception. Even in our raw materials, by cutting repetitions, pulling out as titles the phrase that seemed to me most significant in each transcript, and setting the often rambling revelations of each subject in sequential order by

time of event and period in each subject's life, I may have unconsciously empha-
sized certain aspects of the subjects' lives that do not play the role they seem to
me and to the subject himself to play. My own experiences in the corporate
world, though generally enjoyable and felicitous, may also have somehow biased
my objectivity rather than have increased my ability to judge our subjects'
values. On the other hand, after studying the approaches of sociologists and
historians in collecting and evaluating this kind of material and considering the
oral history transcripts beginning to become a significant factor in modern
historical research, it has seemed to me that our approach—this version of that
developed by the late Oscar Lewis in his works *The Children of Sanchez* and
La Vida in which he was exploring the subculture of poverty by taping the lives
of two poor families—is the best approach for probing deeply into the lives of
our subjects, even though the time each subject was able to give us in the press
and complexity of their careers was relatively brief. Oscar Lewis took six years
in taping the lives in his Mexican family; we were able to take only a day or two
out of the lives of each of our subjects for this probing. Most of our transcripts,
however, were two or three times the length of these published versions. I
eliminated the questions we asked and gave only the subjects' answers. I took
out duplicate scenes where the subject told of an incident at two different times
or in two different ways, either selecting one version or melding the detail of
the two.

None of this was done arbitrarily and in every case the subject went over my
editing carefully to check its validity and made changes where he or she felt
his or her identity might be glimpsed or where the edited version distorted what
was meant. So from my own and the subject's viewpoint, this is the way it was,
as we perceived it and as told in the subject's own words.

Did any of our subjects deceive us or try to deceive us? The answer is yes, but
oddly enough when we got the transcripts of our tapes, it became very clear
when a subject was either attempting to conceal something or distorting what
happened. These are transcripts we did not use at all, because the subjects, either
consciously or unconsciously, were not revealing themselves. They were building
a false persona for reasons of fear, prestige or the desire to seem something they
were not. We have one transcript of an executive that is a classic of double talk.
We have transcripts of glib speakers, who did not have the insight or for psycho-
logical reasons could not get into themselves or their lives except on a very
superficial plane. I used none of these. On the other side of the coin, many of
these transcripts reveal experiences the subject had never revealed to anyone in
the world before, neither wife, husband or lover, and insights he or she had
never believed himself or herself capable of.

This was the most typical and prevailing experience. It was as if the three of
us, the subject, my associate and I, were exploring the subject's life together and
together stumbling upon experiences and truths we had never noticed or that had

never been revealed before. When such revelations came, they were profoundly exciting and fulfilling experiences. I hope our edited and disguised transcripts have been able to capture some of this.

It would be interesting to know what sociologists and historians make of these tapings. If they show even in a minor degree something of what it was like to live in the corporate world in the America of the late twentieth century, then we shall have achieved our purpose, and the labor, the care, and the intensity of this work will have been—even beyond the pleasure it gave us—worthwhile.